Multi-Modal User Interactions in Controlled Environments

MULTIMEDIA SYSTEMS AND APPLICATIONS SERIES

Consulting Editor

Borko Furht
Florida Atlantic University

For a complete list of titles in this series, please visit our website:
www.springer.com/series/6298

Chaabane Djeraba • Adel Lablack
Yassine Benabbas

Multi-Modal User Interactions in Controlled Environments

Foreword by Anne Bajart

 Springer

Prof. Chaabane Djeraba
Laboratoire d'Informatique
Fondamentale de Lille
University Lille 1
59655 Villeneuve d'Ascq
Cité scientifique
France
Chabane.Djeraba@lifl.fr

Yassine Benabbas
Laboratoire d'Informatique
Fondamentale de Lille
University Lille 1
59655 Villeneuve d'Ascq
Cité scientifique
France
yassine.benabbas@lifl.fr

Adel Lablack
Laboratoire d'Informatique
Fondamentale de Lille
University Lille 1
59655 Villeneuve d'Ascq
Cité scientifique
France
adel.lablack@lifl.fr

ISBN 978-1-4614-2631-8   ISBN 978-1-4419-0316-7 (eBook)
DOI 10.1007/978-1-4419-0316-7
Springer New York Dordrecht Heidelberg London

Springer is part of Springer Science+Business Media (www.springer.com)

This book is dedicated to all researchers, professionals, policy makers and social actors interested in the research, development and deep impact of technology on video information extraction.

Foreword

The MIAUCE project was funded by the Sixth EU Framework Programme for Research and Technological Development (FP6). FP6 marked a decisive step towards the integration and coordination of research in Europe. It strengthened Europe's long-term economic base and contributed to the creation of the European Research Area (ERA), with a budget of 17.5 billion euros for 2002-2006. MIAUCE was selected under the Call 2.5.7 "Multimodal Interfaces", with the goal to develop natural and easy-to-use interfaces that communicate intelligently via several modalities. It began on 1st September 2006 and received funding of 2.4 million euros over three years. It is part of a 100-strong portfolio of projects covering areas including scene recognition, behaviour modeling, planning and reasoning or learning and adaptation. MIAUCE was a challenging project which attempted to merge technical, societal and industrial aspects of the multimodal behavior of users (emotion, eye gaze, body move) within the context of real-life applications (security, customized marketing and interactive TV). This book provides an in-depth discussion of the project's main research work and highlights its contribution to fields such as the multimodal interaction analysis of user behaviour, the detection of events and the context capture of situations or the tracking of head pose and visual gaze.

MIAUCE has achieved valuable and recognized scientific results - as illustrated by this book - but MIAUCE has also provided a unique opportunity to develop a multi-disciplinary approach towards the "multimodal observation society", as mentioned by the project itself. The efficient and fruitful collaboration between all the project partners on this topic is reflected in Appendix A "Societal recommendations" of this book. As the EU project officer for MIAUCE, I had the chance to follow its development and its findings closely. I now hope that this book will stimulate in its readers the same interest and curiosity about the work carried out.

Luxembourg   *Anne Bajart*
5th March 2010   Project Officer, European Commission
DG Information Society and Media
Cognitive Systems, Interaction, Robotics

Preface

This book presents a vision of the future in which computation will be human-centred and totally disseminated in a real environment. Computers will capture and analyze our multimodal behavior within our real environments, and hence they will be able to understand and predict our behavior: whatever, whenever, and however we need, and wherever we might be. Computers will enter the human world, tackling our goals, fulfilling our needs and helping us to achieve more while doing less. We will not have to explain these needs to computers; they will deduce them on the basis of behavior analysis. Such systems will boost our productivity and increase our wellbeing. They will help us to automate repetitive human tasks, optimize our gestures, find the information we need (when we need it, without forcing our eyes to examine thousands of items), and enable us to work together with other people through space and time. The development of such *ambient intelligent* systems, which could be seen as a *Big Brother*, needs to meet a certain number of criteria (legal, social, and ethical) in order to make them socially acceptable and to conform to what we might call *Human Dignity*. As a result, any such development and deployment must be done with proper investigation of the relevant legal, social and ethical issues.

The purpose of this book is to investigate the capture and analysis of user's multimodal behavior (abnormal event detection, gaze and flow estimation) within a real environment in order to adapt the response of the computer/environment to the user. Such data is captured using non-intrusive sensors (cameras) installed in the environment. This multimodal behavioral data will be analyzed to infer user intention and will be used to assist the user in his/her day-to-day tasks by seamlessly adapting the system's (computer/environment) response to his/her requirement. We aim to investigate how captured multimodal behavior is transformed into information that aids the user in dealing with his/her environment. The book considers both real-time and off-line return of information. The information is returned on classical output devices (display screens, media screens) installed in the environment. Thus, there is communication between the user and his environment and they form a loop: user (human)-environment. Communication happens in two ways: from the user to the environment (capture of multimodal user behavior) and from the environment to the user (output information as a response to the multimodal behavior) that will influence the multimodal user behavior.

This book is composed of chapters that describe different modalities: abnormal event, gaze and flow estimation. Each chapter describes the technical challenges, state-of-the-art techniques and proposed methods and applications. To illustrate the technical developments, we have examined two applications in security and marketing.

The intended audience is researchers (university teachers, PhD and Master students) and engineers in research and development areas.

Villeneuve d'Ascq   *Chaabane Djeraba*
5th March 2010   *Adel Lablack*
                                                               Yassine Benabbas

Acknowledgements

This book is the culmination of the specifically targeted research project *Miauce*, which was in operation between 2006 and 2009. *Miauce* was supported by the European community within the Sixth Framework Programme (FP6) for Research and Development. Miauce addresses the area of cognitive systems, with particular emphasis on the topic of Information Society Technologies, as stipulated under grant agreement IST-2005-5-033715.

The authors of the book are especially thankful to all project partners who made the book a huge success as well as a great learning experience for all involved. The book would not have been possible without the hard work and dedication of the European project research team composed of several young researchers and professionals: Nacim Ihaddadene (CNRS, France), Nicu Sebe (University of Trento, Italy), Roberto Valenti (University of Amsterdam, Netherlands), Jose Joemon (University of Glasgow, United Kingdom), Hideo Joho (University of Tsukuba, Japan), Yves Poulet (University of Namur, Belgium), Claire Lobet (University of Namur, Belgium), Antoinette Rouvroy (University of Namur, Belgium), Denis Darquennes (University of Namur, Belgium), Philippe Gougeon (University of Namur, Belgium), Francisco Gomez-Molinero (Visual-Tools Company, Spain), Cristina Sandoval Alonso (Visual-Tools Company, Spain), Ainars Blaudums (Tilde Company, Latvia), Aivars Berzins (Tilde Company, Latvia).

Contents

Chapter 1
Introduction

1.1 Introduction

Human-computer interaction is the study of the interaction between people (users) and computers. It is often considered as the intersection of the computer and behavioral sciences. Interaction between users and computers occurs at the user interface (or simply interface), which includes input and output data. For example, video documents (output data) are displayed on a personal computer, as the basis for a search method. The search method's input data is received from users. The input data are composed of emotion expressed facially (happy, not happy, etc.) with other user interactions (feedbacks) of the answers of previous queries. The video documents are displayed, taking into account the user's profile (elderly, young, etc.), and adapted to the user's context (mobile, outdoors, domestic environment, professional environment, etc.). Surveillance is another example of human-computer interaction. To illustrate, a camera is installed in an airport to monitor the situation of escalator exits. The main objective of the surveillance system is to observe some locations continuously to protect them from intrusions, thefts and collisions. The video streams are analysed in real-time, and as soon as a dangerous event (e.g. people collapsing) is detected by the computer, an alert is triggered to notify the security team, who need to take prompt actions in this critical situation (e.g. stopping the escalator). This form of interaction takes the context into consideration to give a better understanding of the situation, supported by the analysis of this interaction. This involves the contextualised configuration of the system settings, the presentation of the system settings for various camera locations and the visualisation of the analysis in a system-user interface. By optimising the system configuration to the environment of installed cameras, the same underlying detection algorithms can be applied to different locations.

With the advance of computer vision technologies, human-computer interaction will attain a new stage of advancement, where the human is positioned in the loop of interactions and where the machine is pervasive. In recent years, human-computer interaction has evolved into human-machine communication. The objec-

C. Djeraba et al., *Multi-Modal User Interactions in Controlled Environments,*
DOI 10.1007/978-1-4419-0316-7_1, © Springer Science+Business Media, LLC 2010

tive of human-machine communication is to transform the communication between humans and machines into something approaching human-to-human communication. Moreover, the machine can support human-to-human communication (e.g. an interface for the disabled people). For this reason, various aspects of human communication have been considered in human-machine communication. The human-machine communication interface includes different types of input data, such as natural language, gestures, facial expression, gaze and handwritten characters, etc. Because human-computer interaction studies both the human and the computer, it draws on supporting knowledge on both the machine and the human side. On the machine side, techniques in computer vision are relevant. On the human side, social sciences and human factors are relevant. Due to the multidisciplinary nature of human machine interaction, people with different backgrounds (e.g. technical and societal) contribute to its success. Human-computer interaction is sometimes referred to as man-machine interaction or computer-human interaction or simply as multimodal interaction. Multimodality in human-computer interaction is the concept that allows users to move seamlessly between different modes of interaction, from visual to vocal to tactile to motion-sensitive, according to changes in context or user preference. The advantage of multiple input modalities is improved usability. The weaknesses of one modality are offset by the strengths of another. For example, in a crowded environment observed by cameras, it is difficult for security personnel to continuously observe the entire scene for a whole day. However, it is easier to observe the same location when automatic image and sound analysis is provided. These 2 modalities are useful in effectively detecting dangerous situations (e.g. collapsing). Consider also how one would access and search through digital media collections from devices or set-top boxes that operate using voice and text search. Finally, tools for patients with disabilities in a healthcare environment could use eye gaze or verbal commands, with no need for physical movement.

1.2 Objective

This book aims to study techniques that contribute to understand and predict user behavior in real-life and controlled environments (e.g. personal environment, airport, mall, etc.). To achieve this objective, we analyse multimodal interaction to infer user intentions, something which could be used to assist them in their day-to-day tasks by adapting the system's response to their needs. Another objective is to capture and analyze human multi-modal behavior within a real environment, and hence be able to understand and predict human behavior. The system output is a human-centred system, totally disseminated in the real environment. On the basis of human behavior analysis, such a system helps boost human productivity, increases wellbeing, and optimizes human behavior and cooperation. More precisely, we assess the feasibility of capturing and analyzing the multimodal interactions of users (abnormal event, flow, eye gaze), while taking into account the context and profiling capture. The study has proven useful in several application domains, such as detecting collapsed situations in escalator exits of an airport and estimating the flow of people in front of a shop or the hot areas inside the shop. Capturing and analyzing multimodal interactions of the user could be seen as a further step towards a society dominated by *Big Brother*. In response to this, the relevant societal issues have been examined to meet a certain number of criteria (legal, social, and ethical) in order to make the technical developments socially acceptable. These developments conform to what we might call *Human Dignity*.

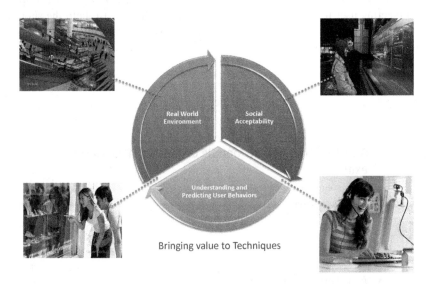

Fig. 1.1 Objective of the book

1.3 Practical Applications

The technical achievements have been applied to 2 application domains: security and marketing. The technical achievements have been balanced by a discussion of the social issues and the results are recommendations addressed to public authorities.

1. In security applications, we developed a system for detecting collapsing events in the escalator exits of an airport. The system is reliable (less than one false alarm per hour) and works in real time. The application has the potential to help security personnel to detect abnormal behavior from video streams. The basic idea

is to analyze video streams with the purpose of detecting potentially dangerous behavior so that the security operators can be warned to pay attention to the important events taking place in an area under surveillance. The approach proposed is now being tested under real-world conditions in an international airport.

2. In marketing, we developed the following set of applications: a system that estimates the flow of people walking in front of a shop over a given period of time, heat maps inside a shop and recommendation algorithms. The potential use and impact is to simplify the everyday activities of the user, in relation to the acquisition of his/her everyday or contextual needs (e.g. food, hygiene products). The analysis of user behavior in front of the shelves will have a great impact on meeting user needs and service personalization. It will also help the shop to optimize its merchandizing practices and to increase the visibility of its products for improved sales and profits.

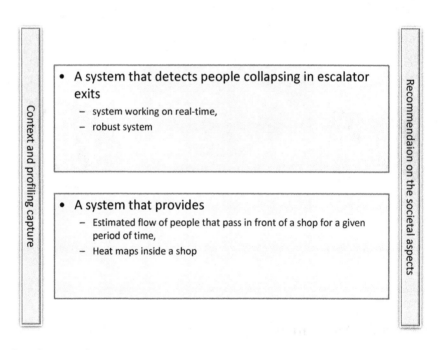

Fig. 1.2 Applications

1.4 Research Challenges

1.4.1 Event Detection

Several studies have been dedicated to crowd scene analysis. They generally analyze crowd density and distribution with the intention of deriving statistics from the crowd for traffic planning. However, few of them address the topic of detecting complex events (e.g. collapsing people, one objective of this book) from video streams in a crowded environment. Some works deal with specific scenarios, such as analyzing crowd emergency scenarios. Other works detect flow instabilities from video streams, characterized by very high crowd density (e.g. marathon). In the reference literature, we also have methods that are, in principle, less dedicated to specific complex events, without concrete proof of their reliability. Many approaches include the investigation of video features/descriptors (e.g. blobs, motions) on one hand, and inference methods (learning, classification, adaptive and incremental processes) on the other. The inference methods, and particularly learning/classification methods, are widely used. The most reliable methods are those dedicated to specific events. Furthermore, extracting high quality features/descriptors and representation models on which methods (e.g. learning) operate is still a very challenging problem. We focus our approach on suitable video features, and an extensible framework that could potentially be reused to deal with other abnormal events (e.g. collapsing people, panic, opposite flows). The central idea of our approach is to use local motion features (e.g. sudden motion variation), instead of tracking people one by one, which does not achieve good results because it is too complex to track individuals in a crowded environment.

1.4.2 Flow Estimation

One of the most important challenges for crowd analysis is flow estimation or people counting, a method for estimating the number of people present in an area of interest. Many approaches addressing the issue can be found in literature in the area. Approaches are divided into two classes: the first includes works using sensors other than a camera (for example, infrared, ultrasound, light ray sensors and others), while the second covers works using camera sensors. We will focus on the latter in this paper. The main parameters for consideration are areas of interest, camera location and the number of cameras used. An area of interest is defined here as the area of the scene from which flow estimation is calculated. It is used to specify precise counting locations (such as a shop entrance) and to reduce computation complexity. The area can range from a single virtual line to include the whole scene. Approaches using a line of interest count people who cross that line, whilst approaches covering an entire area count the persons inside that particular area. An implicit advantage of using virtual lines is being able to determine people's direction ("left" or "right", "entering" or "leaving" etc.). Most approaches deal with a single camera location which is either positioned at an angle of less than 45 degrees or vertically-mounted at the top of the scene. The first location is harder to handle than the second one since there are more occlusions and people's shapes change depending on their distance from the camera. Certain approaches require a pre-configuration step in which the parameters (for example, spatial coordinates, focal length) of the camera are inputted manually into the system so that it functions properly. The number of cameras is also important as stereoscopic appraoches yield better results than single camera approaches. The drawback, however, is the considerable increase in computation time and the need for a delicate calibration step. In this book, we lay out a flow estimation approach that uses a virtual line and a single camera, and supports different camera locations. This combination produces an efficient system that does not require manual parametrization since the camera parameters are inferred via machine learning. The approach is ready to be deployed in a real-world people counting system.

1.4.3 Gaze Estimation

The possibility of taking advantage of information conveyed in gaze/fixation has attracted many researchers in human-computer interaction. Most of the work in this area so far is grouped in 4 interrelated categories: gaze/fixation as a pointing mechanism in direct manipulation interfaces, eye gaze/fixation as a disambiguation channel in speech or multimodal input, eye gaze/fixation as a facilitator in computer supported human-human communication and collaboration, and finally eye gaze/fixation as a diagnostic approach to physical phenomena. Our method belongs to the last category. These state-of-the-art approaches deal well with eye gaze/fixation capture in personal environments where manual calibration and a limited number of cameras are used. However, these approaches are not suitable for dealing with multi-user environment, in which we track eye gaze and eye fixation in dynamic situations where the head and the body are moving freely. This state-of-the-art method lacks any understanding of the semantics associated with eye gaze/fixation communication between a human and his/her environment. So, the specific aim of our book is to deal with these parameters and to provide a real-time interface that can use the specific context to improve the performance in a specific application scenario.

1.4.4 Role of the Context

The main purpose of context and user profiling is to find and present information to the user in response to his/her multimodal interaction. The information presented here will be adapted to current context and user needs. In addition to this, the contextual data will be used to assist in the analysis of multimodal behavior, such as eye gaze and body motion analysis. Furthermore, contextual data and user profiles will be enriched and updated based on the results of multimodal analysis. Thus, we captured the contextual changes and the changes in the user interests (as reflected in the user profiles) as they evolve. Such updates will be based mainly on implicit feedback obtained from user interaction data. However, capturing such contextual data and user profiles is difficult. To begin with, there is no consensus on defining context. It is currently agreed that the context is an important factor that needs to be captured. Research in this area, however, is in its infancy. Serious investigation is needed to capture and represent the context and the controlled environment makes it possible to achieve this. It is possible to study the role of context mainly because all the user interactions deal with one or more dimensions of context. For example, the multimodal analysis and the multimodal interfaces provide rich contextual data related to user interaction. Such data is complementary and can be used for the development of behavioral analysis techniques. In addition, they can be used to interpret multimodal interaction data in situations where sufficient information is not available (e.g. in situations where eye blink detection is not possible, we can use eye gaze or body motion detection).

1.4.5 Societal Issues

Analyzing user's multimodal behavior does not deal exclusively with technical challenges, but also with the legal, sociological and ethical challenges that are involved in the use of multiple sensors in the user environment. All these issues have been investigated in the appendix of the book. The approaches investigated in the book raise issues that are not exclusively technological. They also relate to the serious risk of breaching privacy by unsolicited observation of individual's gestures and habits (hence the idea of *Big Brother*). So they may influence the decisions or at least limit the possibilities of choice. Our investigations will also be devoted to the limits imposed by privacy legislation and the principle of self-determination. We are convinced that these issues must be considered very seriously in the design of technologies and infrastructure, in order to ensure the social acceptability of these technologies before they can be used.

1.5 Technical Contribution

The research problem of analyzing multimodal interactions of user behavior in a controlled environment is relevant for achieving the general objective of multimodal interface. The multimodal interactions are implicitly and automatically captured from the human environment through camera sensors. In a multimodal interface, the communication between the user and his environment forms a loop: user - environment (see Figure 1.3). The book focuses only on the communication from the user to the environment. We have considered 2 forms of interactions, associated with personal and non-personal environments, respectively. Abnormal event detection and estimation of the flow of people are situated in a non-personal environment (e.g. airport, shop), where the subject is further away from the camera sensor. Eye gaze has been studied in both environments.

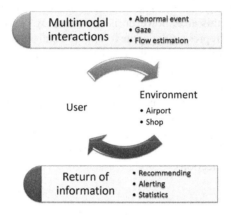

Fig. 1.3 Interaction loop user-environment.

Several significant results are outlined and these contribute to scientific progress and methodology in the area of multimodal interface. These results concern the research into gaze, abnormal event detection and flow estimation. They are reinforced by context capture.

The gaze modality was analyzed in personal and non-personal environments (in front of a shop shelf). We determined the subject gaze on the basis of the head pose estimation (by tracking a cylindrical model). A complementary approach for head pose estimation and visual field estimation was formulated by using a static detection of pose, based on template matching, where several low level descriptors have been studied. To summarize, significant progress has been reported, especially in a personal environment, but eye gaze estimation in an unconstrained environment remains difficult.

The event detection modality was used for automatic detection of abnormal behavior in real time. It has been validated on collapsing event detection on escalator exits in an airport environment. One important contribution is the development of a framework that makes the method potentially adaptable to other applications related to abnormal behavior detection. The framework is composed of 3 level features: low-level (e.g. points of interests, optical flow, blobs), intermediate-level (e.g. density, histogram directions) and high level (e.g. entropy). We enhanced the framework with a direction model constructed of a mixture of Von Mises distributions applied to the orientation of the optical flow vectors. Major flows were then detected by retrieving the most important orientations from the mixture. Several crowd-related events have also been detected using a probabilistic model applied to the mean motion magnitude of the optical flow vectors on each frame of the scene. In addition, spatio-temporal relationship analysis of the crowd, using the direction model and directional statistics, has been used according to the category of the event. The flow estimation was based on spatio-temporal optical flow analysis. Using a single vertical overhead or oblique mounted camera, our technique counts the number of people crossing a virtual line, by using an online blob detector and a linear classifier. In addition to the counting information, this technique identified the speed of observed blobs: fast, slow and stationary. It also identifies the nature of the blob: one person, 2 people or a group of people. The suggested technique was validated by several realistic experiments. We showed the real-time performance and the high counting accuracy of this technique on indoor and outdoor realistic dataset.

Considering the notion of context and profile capturing, we carried out the following steps: firstly, we performed the contextual analysis on the technical outputs, related to the security application (abnormal event detection on escalator exists). The results show that the contextual analysis can suggest a system configuration which improved the performance of the baseline *context-free* system. For example, we examined 6 contextual factors (day, season, month, morning, afternoon, night, illumination, person presence). The analysis, using machine learning tools, suggested that certain contextual factors can improve the context-free detector. For example, the morning context can increase its performance by 9%. This means that knowing the time of day can help predict abnormal scenes. The strongest context factor was the presence (or absence) of illumination: A 0.13 improvement in precision can be expected with the absence of shadows and the presence of uniform illumination within the scene. These results strengthen our argument that it is important to consider the contextual factors in the design and implementation of multimodal interaction applications, and they demonstrated its feasibility.

1.6 How the Book is Organized

The book's technical ideas are presented in Chapter 2 (Abnormal Event Detection), Chapter 3 (Flow Estimation), Chapter 4 (Gaze Detection and Tracking), and Chapter 5 (Visual Field Detection). The social issues are discussed in the appendix. The appendix integrates the social, legal and ethical requirements into the design of the technology according to a *value-sensitive* design process. The privacy issues are necessary for the successful development and deployment of the proposed techniques. The societal aspects are investigated in smart interactions with technical aspects and by setting up an academic observatory that has interacted. Resulting from this inter-disciplinary approach (technical and societal issues) are the legal, social and ethical recommendations addressed to public authorities and policy makers. These recommendations include societal recommendations (public awareness, public policy on research and development, democratic requirement for Observation System Technology), legal recommendations (data protection) and privacy recommendations (beyond data protection, consumer protection). They have had an important impact on the deployments of techniques presented in the book and, more generally, they may have an impact on future techniques related to multimodal interaction analysis. To insure coherence of scientific and operational co-ordination between the different chapters, we consider 2 application scenarios, related to security and marketing. In the framework of these 2 scenarios, we paid considerable attention to cohesion between the technical issues (chapters 2, 3, 4 and 5). The multimodal interactions have been captured using non-intrusive sensors (cameras) installed in the controlled environment.

Applications	Chapter2	Chapter3	Chapter4	Chapter5
Security	✖	✖		
Marketing		✖	✖	✖

Fig. 1.4 Methodology.

We end the book by discussing way forward in our conclusion (Chapter 6).

Chapter 2
Abnormal Event Detection

Abstract This chapter presents a system that detects abnormal events extracted from videos in a crowded environment. At this stage, our intention is to stick to simple methods so as to enhance the real-time requirements of the processing. The efforts made and results achieved will lay the groundwork and serve as a benchmark for future work. The selected approach consists of extracting some portions of videos coinciding with sudden changes and abnormal motion variations in the points of interest. It performs calculations on information such as the density, direction and velocity of motion, and classifies the content as normal or abnormal. This approach will help to index abnormal events and will offer users the opportunity of making queries about content. Our approach has been tested on various videos in real-world conditions, namely incidents in airport escalator exits.

2.1 Introduction

Over the last few years, following the need from security staff to access informative data, the importance of intelligent tools identifying abnormal (suspect) behaviour in real time from video surveillance has increased. This is even truer given the boom in video surveillance systems for various environments, ranging from airports and malls to subway stations. The objective, then, is to develop a system which can detect abnormal events from video surveillance data in real time in order to improve security.

To give an example, this could be applied to security staff asking for video segments in which a particular event occurs during a week (e.g. collapsing) or searching for information on the following: determining the average frequency of abnormal events in one day considering all the video streams; establishing the link between crowd density and abnormal events; isolating the videos that are the most similar to the segmented one; etc.

The framework of this approach is based on three levels of features:

C. Djeraba et al., *Multi-Modal User Interactions in Controlled Environments*,
DOI 10.1007/978-1-4419-0316-7_2, © Springer Science+Business Media, LLC 2010

- **Low level:** This describes features directly extracted from motion (points of interest, blobs). Gaussian mixtures are used to detect the foregrounds in low-crowded areas (low density), while optical flows on points of interest reflect high-crowded areas (high density).

-**Intermediate level:** This describes features with more semantics than those at the low level. They are directly computed from low-level features such as crowd density, trajectory, velocity, direction, acceleration, energy. The density, for instance, is the ratio of blobs in the scene. Intermediate-level features are computed based on low-level features (blobs, points of interest) then stored in basic structures.

- **High level:** This describes features with more semantics than those at the intermediate level. They are numerous enough on which to base decisions. Both normal and abnormal events are present at this level.

The first level of features is generic but not domain-dependent. However, it is too weak from a semantic point of view. The second level does not depend on the application domain and contains more semantics than the first level. The third level completely depends on the application domain, with a high level of semantics necessary to make contextual decisions. With regard to the latter, the high level of features applies to the normal or abnormal dimension of the event in the video. This approach extracts abnormal events (those exhibiting a high level of features) based on intermediate-level features, which are themselves based on low-level features. If we consider the example of abnormal event detection, the high-level features are determined by the normality or abnormality of the event in the video. Our approach extracts abnormal events (high level features) on the basis of the intermediate level features. More precisely, considering the same example, the approach firstly calculates the motion heat map (intermediate level of features) over a period of time to extract the main regions of motion activity, based on blobs (low level of features). Using the heat map image improves the quality of the results and reduces the space for processing. Secondly, points of interest (low level of features) are extracted in the *hot* regions of the scene. Thirdly, optical flow (low level of features) is computed on these points of interest (low level of features), delimited by the hot areas of the scene. Fourthly, variations of motion (intermediate level of features) are estimated to pinpoint potential abnormal events (high level of features). We consider the scenario to be a crowded environment with no restriction on the number of people.

To be more precise, the approach firstly calculates the heat map of motion over a certain period of time, and proceeds by extracting the main regions of motion activity. Heat map images improve the accuracy of the results and reduce processing time. Secondly, points of interest are extracted within the hot regions of the scene. Thirdly, the optical flow is computed based on these points of interest, which are delimited by the hot areas. Fourthly, the variations in motion are estimated so as to pinpoint potential abnormal events. We have examined a crowded environment here, with no restriction regarding the number of people.

Section 2.2 of this chapter presents the related work. Sections 2.3 to 2.5 discuss the proposed approach. Sections 2.5.5 and 2.6.4 cover the experimental results. Finally, Section 2.7 outlines the conclusions, discussions and future work.

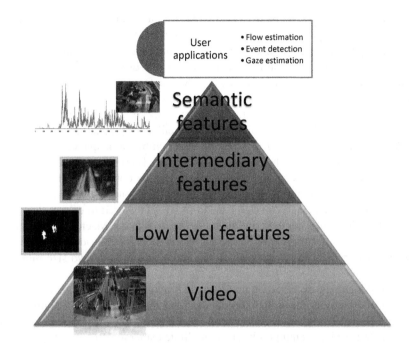

Fig. 2.1 Feature levels

2.2 Related Work

Complying with state-of-the-art approaches, various features have been proposed depending on the abnormal event in question. In addition, learning, adaptive and incremental processes have been studied and can, in general, be applied to categories of abnormal events. These are not solutions in dealing with abnormal events. Two types of approaches can be identified. The first one is related to crowd-flow analysis and the second, to abnormal event detection in crowd flows.

Studies belonging to the first category calculate density [79, 86, 110]. [92] describes a new technique for automatic estimation of crowd density - which is part of the automatic crowd monitoring problem - using texture information blazed in grey-scale transition probabilities on digitized images. Crowd density feature vectors are extracted from such images and used by a self-organizing neural network responsible for estimating crowd density. The technique proposed by [90] to estimate crowd density is based on Minkowski fractal dimension. Fractal dimension has been widely used to describe data texture in a large number of physical and biological sciences. Finally, [91] elaborates a technique to estimate crowd density in real time, based on the texture of crowd images. With this technique, the current image from a sequence of input images is classified into a crowd density class. The classification is then corrected by a low-pass filter based on the crowd density classification of the last n images of the input sequence.

[116] addresses the problem of evaluating people-counting systems. The relation between the real people number and the output of the people-counting system is used to motivate the computation of the maximum number of people as a scenario and geometry specific quantity which supports the evaluation of the system output. Based on the camera, field-of-view authors determine the maximum number of detectable people using a basic people model. The maximum number of people is computed for an overhead camera and for an arbitrary oblique camera orientation, which is the typical geometry of standard surveillance applications.

[79] goes one step further in estimating the number of people in crowded scenes in a complex background by using a single image. Therefore, information which is considered more valuable than crowd density can be obtained. There are two major steps in this system: recognition of the head-like contour and estimation of the crowd size. Firstly, Haar Wavelet Transform (HWT) is used to extract the featured area of the head-like contour, and then the Support Vector Machine (SVM) is used to identify whether this featured area is the contour of a head or not. Then, the perspective-transforming technique is used to estimate the crowd size more accurately.

These methods are based on textures and motion area ratio, as well as on developed static analysis for crowd surveillance, but they do not detect abnormal situations. There are also optical flow-based techniques [17], [30] to detect stationary crowds or tracking techniques by using multiple cameras [29].

The second category detects abnormal events in crowd flows. The general approach consists of modeling normal behavior, and then estimating the deviations between the normal behavior model and observed behavior patterns. These deviations are designated *abnormal*. The principle of these approaches is to exploit the fact that data on normal behavior is generally available, and data on abnormal behavior is generally less available. That is why the deviations from examples of normal behavior are used to characterize abnormality. In this category, [4] combines HMM and spectral clustering with the principal component for detecting crowd emergency scenarios. This method was tested in simulated data. [2] uses Lagrangian Particle Dynamics for the detection of flow instabilities; this method is efficient in the segmentation of high density crowd flows (marathons, political events, etc.).

In the same category, but for low-crowded scenes, authors in [123] propose a visual monitoring system that passively observes moving objects in a site and learns pattern activity from those observations, but also detects unusual events in the site that do not have common patterns using a hierarchical classification.

In addition, authors in [18] address the problem of detecting irregularities in visual data as a process of constructing a puzzle: the occurrence of regions in the observed data which can be composed using large contiguous chunks of data from the database is considered very likely, whereas the occurrence of regions in the observed data which cannot be composed from the database (unless using small fragmented pieces) is regarded as unlikely or suspicious. The spatial and spatio-temporal appearance-based patch descriptors are generated for each query and for each database patch. The inference problem is posed as an inference process in a probabilistic graphical model. Other work is related to the same area of detecting abnormal events by incremental approaches [31], [146], [59].

The state-of-the-art approach regarding the indexing of abnormal events is relatively weak [148], compared with the work on abnormal event detection or crowd flow analysis, as presented in the previous paragraphs. [148] proposes a semantic-based retrieval framework to track video sequences. In order to estimate the low-level motion data, a cluster tracking algorithm has been developed. A hierarchical self-organizing map is applied to learn the activity patterns. By using activity pattern analysis and semantic concept assignment, a set of activity models (representing the general and abnormal behaviour of vehicles) is generated, which serves as the indexing key for accessing video clips and individual vehicles at the semantic level. The proposed retrieval framework supports various types of queries, including by keywords, by sketch, and multiple object queries. Another work, such as [139], develops a framework of human motion tracking and event detection, meant for indexing. However, no direct contribution to indexing has been made.

Several state-of-the-art approaches outline specific event detections from a video. There is no perfect means of dealing with targeted specific events. As a result, an approach dealing with a specific event remains a challenge in itself. TRECVID uses the term *challenges*, instead of abnormal events or specific events detection from a video. Therefore, according to TRECVID's terminology, our application is a *challenge*. Generally, the state-of-the-art approaches deal with specific events and any adaptation to other applications (specific event detection) requires that the approach be completely redesigned.

Our methodology in designing a framework composed of three levels of features makes our approach more general and adaptable to various situations, mainly at the first and second level of features. At the second level (intermediate), a number of features are computed to cover the large range of applications. This in no way means that our approach is generic and application-independent; far from it. However, the organization of the features within this framework will certainly contribute to it being able to handle several abnormal events. We emphasize here that the results from our approach have been promising.

2.3 Proposed Approach

Our hypothesis is that abnormal events can be detected in a crowded context from video surveillance data. The method used requires us to concede that the detection of persons and tracking are difficult in crowded situations. For that reason, there is no need to represent the person tracking in the intermediate level of features; instead, we consider metrics deduced automatically from low-level features. The main idea is to study the general motion aspect, and more particularly sudden motion variations, instead of tracking subjects one by one. Tracking techniques in crowded scenes do not yield good results, not to mention the fact that most of the methods do not take factors like density, direction and velocity into account.

The approach proposed consists of several steps:

- Step 1: the motion heat map is created. The heat map represents the motion intensity: hot areas correspond to high motion intensity, cold areas to low motion intensity, etc.
- Step 2: Harris points of interest are observed in the hot regions of the scene. In the simplest case, applied in well limited areas, we would observe a binary heat map, white (movement), and black (no movement). In this case, the points of interest are applied to white regions.
- Step 3: Blobs are extracted, using Gaussian mixtures.
- Step 4: Optical flow is computed based on the points of interest.
- Step 5: Several factors are computed, including density, velocity, direction, etc.
- Step 6: In this step, we propose a high-level feature, called entropy, that classifies events as abnormal/normal, on the basis of intermediate-level features computed in the previous step.

The steps 1, 2, 3 and 4 do not depend on a specific application domain. They involve the extraction of low and intermediate levels of features. The sixth step is dependent on the application domain. It deals with the challenge of detecting abnormal events from a video. The majority of features are extracted in each frame.

2.3.1 Low-Level Features

2.3.1.1 Motion Heat Map

A heat map is a graphical representation of data where the values taken by a variable in a two-dimensional map are represented as colours. A motion heat map is a 2D histogram indicating the main regions of motion activity. This histogram is constructed using the accumulation of binary blobs representing moving objects, which were extracted following the background subtraction method. Assume that symbols H and I indicate heat map and intensity, respectively.

H is defined as:

$$H_n(i,j) = \begin{cases} H_{n-1}(i,j) + I_n(i,j), & if\ n \geq 1 \\ I_0(i,j), & if\ n = 0 \end{cases} \qquad (2.1)$$

where n is the frame number, and i and j are the coordinates (line and column) of the frame pixel (i,j).

The map created in this process is used as a mask to define the Region of Interest (RoI) for the next step of the method. The use of heat maps improves the quality of the results and reduces the processing time, which are important factors for real-time applications.

Figure 2.2 shows an example of the resulting heat map depicting motion in an escalator exit. The results are more significant when the video duration is long. In practice, even for the same place, the properties of abnormal events may vary depending on the context (day/night, indoor/outdoor, normal/peak time, etc.). We created a motion heat map for each set of conditions. When we consider that abnormal events happen when crowd density is high, there is no need to analyze the whole scene, in particular the scene in which there is little motion intensity, or no motion whatsoever. So, the approach focuses on specific regions where motion density is high. The threshold related to density elevation is contextual information.

Our approach can be seen as an extension of of [4]'s pre-processing step, in which optical flows are limited to the foreground. However, our approach takes into account sensitivity to motion intensity. In addition, the use of heat maps makes our approach more efficient in real-time processing.

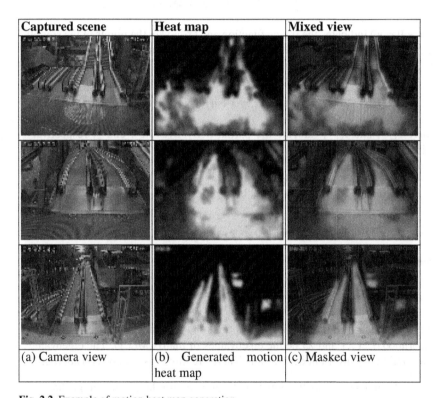

Captured scene	Heat map	Mixed view
(a) Camera view	(b) Generated motion heat map	(c) Masked view

Fig. 2.2 Example of motion heat map generation

2.3.1.2 Points of Interest

In this step, we start by extracting the foregrounds, using Gaussian mixtures. We then proceed by extracting a set of points of interest from each input frame. A mask is used to define the regions of interest, from which we extract points of interest.

This mask is determined using the heat map. In our approach, we consider Harris corner to be a point of interest [49]. The Harris corner detector is a famous point of interest detector due to its strong invariance in rotation, scale, illumination variation, and image noise [117]. It uses the local auto-correlation function of a signal, where the local auto-correlation function measures the local changes of the signal with patches shifted by a small amount in different directions. A discrete predecessor of the Harris detector was outlined by Moravec [98]; where the discreteness refers to the shifting of the patches.

Assume a point (x, y) and a shift $(\Delta x, \Delta y)$, and then the local auto-correlation function is defined as:

$$c(x,y) = \sum_{w} [I(x_i, y_i) - I(x_i + \Delta x, y_i + \Delta y)]^2 \tag{2.2}$$

where $I(x_i, y_i)$ indicates the image function and (x_i, y_i) are the points in the smooth circular window W centred on (x, y). The shifted image is approximated by a Taylor expansion truncated to the first order terms as:

$$I(x_i + \Delta x, y_i + \Delta y) \approx I(x_i, y_i) + [I_x(x_i y_i) I_y(x_i y_i)] \begin{bmatrix} \Delta x \\ \Delta y \end{bmatrix} \tag{2.3}$$

where $I_{x(.,.)}$ and $I_{y(.,.)}$ indicate the partial derivatives in x and y, respectively. Substituting the right hand site of Eq.2 into Eq. 1 yields:

$$c(x,y) = \sum_{w} ([I(x_i, y_i) I_y(x_i y_i)] \begin{bmatrix} \Delta x \\ \Delta y \end{bmatrix})^2 \tag{2.4}$$

$$= [\Delta x, \Delta y] M(x,y) \begin{bmatrix} \Delta x \\ \Delta y \end{bmatrix} \tag{2.5}$$

where:

$$M(x,y) = \begin{pmatrix} \sum_w [I_x(x_i, y_i)]^2 & \sum_w I_x(x_i y_i) I - y(x_i y_i) \\ \sum_w I_x(x_i y_i) I - y(x_i y_i) & \sum_w [I_y(x_i, y_i)]^2 \end{pmatrix} \tag{2.6}$$

The 2×2 symmetric matrix $M(x,y)$ captures the intensity structure of the local neighborhood. Let λ_1 and λ_2 be the eigenvalues of matrix $M(x,y)$. The eigenvalues form a rotationally invariant description. There are three cases to be considered:

1. If both λ_1 and λ_2 are small, so that the local auto-correlation function is flat, i.e., little change in c(x, y) in any direction, then the windowed image region is of approximately constant intensity.
2. If one eigenvalue is high and the other low so that the local auto-correlation function is rigidly shaped, then only shifts along the ridge (i.e., along the edge) cause little change in c(x, y) and there is a significant change in the orthogonal direction. This case indicates an *edge*.
3. If both λ_1 and λ_2 are high so that the local auto-correlation function is sharply peaked, then shifts in any direction will result in a significant increase in c(x, y). This case indicates a *corner*.

Fig. 2.3 An example of Harris corner detector

Figure 2.3 shows an example of a Harris corner detector. We believe that in video surveillance scenes, camera positions and lighting conditions enable us to capture and track a large number of corner features.

2.3.1.3 Tracking Points of Interest

Once we have defined the points of interest, we track these points over the next frames using optical flow techniques. For this, we use a Kanade-Lucas-Tomasi feature tracker [84]. The Shi-Tomasi algorithm [119] uses the smallest eigenvalues of an image block as the criterion for ensuring that the features which can be tracked reliably by Lucas-Kanade tracking algorithm are selected.

After matching the features between the frames, the result is a set of vectors:

$$V = \{V_1...V_n | V_i = (X_i, Y_i, M_i, \theta_i)\} \tag{2.7}$$

Where:

X_i: X coordinate of feature i,

Y_i : Y coordinate of feature i,

M_i: distance between feature i in frame t and its matched feature in frame t+1,

θ_i: motion direction of the feature i.

The video of images in Figure 2.4 was provided by a video surveillance company. They show the set of vectors obtained by optical flow feature tracking in two different situations. Image 2.4(a) of the figure shows an organized vector flow. Image 2.4(b) of the figure shows a cluttered vector flow due to the collapsing situation.

(a) Organized vector flow.   (b) Cluttered vector flow.

Fig. 2.4 Tracking points of interest on two sample frames

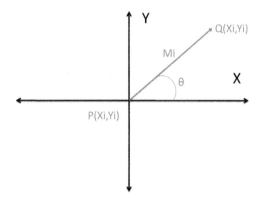

Fig. 2.5 Motion direction of feature

2.3.1.4 Mi and θ_i

Figure 2.5 illustrates feature i in frame t with its coordinate $P(Xi, Yi)$ and its matched feature in frame $t+1$ with coordinate $Q(Xi, Yi)$. We can easily calculate the Euclidean distance of these two points using the Euclidean metric as:

$$M_i = \sqrt{(Qx_i - Px_i)^2 + (Qy_i - Py_i)^2} \qquad (2.8)$$

The motion direction (θm) of feature i can be calculated using the following trigonometric function:

$$\theta_m = atan(\frac{y_i}{x_i}) \qquad (2.9)$$

where $x_i = Qx_iPx_i$ and $y_i = Qy_iPy_i$. But there are several potential problems if we wish to calculate motion direction using Equation 2.8; for example:

1. Equation 2.9 does not work for a complete range of angles from $0°$ to $360°$. Only angles between $-90°$ and $+90°$ will be returned, other angles will be out of phase. For instance, let us consider two defined points $(x_1 = 1, y_{1i} = 1)$ and $(x_2 = -1, y_2 = -1)$. Using Equation 2.9, point $(x_2 = -1, y_2 = -1)$ will produce the same angle as $(x_1 = 1, y_1 = 1)$ but these are not in the same quadrant.

2. Points on the vertical axis have $x_i = 0$, as a result, if we wish to calculate $\left(\frac{y_i}{x_i}\right)$ we will get ∞ which will generate an exception when calculated on the computer.

In order to avoid these problems, we use an $atan2(y_i, x_i)$ function which takes both x_i and y_i as arguments. Henceforth, the accurate direction of motion (θi) of feature i can be calculated as:

$$\theta_m = atan(y_i, x_i) = \begin{cases} \emptyset \sin(y_i) & if\ x_i > 0,\ y_i \neq 0 \\ 0 & if\, x_i > 0,\ y_i = 0 \\ \frac{\pi}{2} \sin(y_i) & if\, x_i = 0,\ y_i \neq 0 \\ undefined & if\ x_i = 0,\ y_i = 0 \\ (\pi - \theta) \sin(y_i) & if\ x_i < 0,\ y_i \neq 0 \\ \pi & if\ x_i < 0,\ y_i = 0 \end{cases} \tag{2.10}$$

where Φ is the angle in $[0, \pi/2]$ such that $\Phi = atan\left(\frac{y_i}{x_i}\right)$. The sign function $\sin(y_i)$ can be defined as:

$$\sin(y_i) = \begin{cases} -1; & y_i < 0 \\ 0; & y_i = 0 \\ 1; & y_i > 0 \end{cases} \tag{2.11}$$

Thus, function **atan2(y, x)** gracefully handles infinite slope, and places the angle in the correct quadrant [e.g. $atan2(1, 1) = \pi/4$ and $atan2(-1, -1) = -3\pi/4$].

2.3.2 Intermediate-Level Features

In this step, we define the intermediate-level features that will be necessary to induce the abnormal event.

2.3.2.1 Motion Area Ratio

This calculates the ratio between the number of blocks containing motion and the total number of blocks. We consider the frame to be divided into small blocks of equal size. In the crowded scenes, the area covered with moving blobs is bigger than that in non-crowded scenes. This measure is a form of density estimation. We divide each frame into the equal number of $N \times M$ blocks. For each block (i, j) we define:

$$blockmoving(i,j) = \begin{cases} 1 \, if \; movement \\ 0 \, otherwise \end{cases} \tag{2.12}$$

If there are several movements in one block, the cell is counted as one movement. We count the total number of moving cells divided by the number of blocks. The Motion Area Ratio (MR) is defined as:

$$M_R = \frac{\sum\limits_{i=1}^{N}\sum\limits_{j=1}^{M} blockmoving(i,\, j)}{N * M} \tag{2.13}$$

2.3.2.2 Direction Variance

After calculating the mean angle θ of the optical flow vectors in the current frame, we calculate the angle variance of these vectors as:

$$V_\emptyset = \frac{1}{n} \sum_{i-1}^{n} (\emptyset i - \emptyset)^2 \tag{2.14}$$

where $V_\emptyset$ is the variance of the angle for the current frame and n is the cardinality of the optical flows in the frame.

2.3.2.3 Motion Magnitude Variance

Observation shows that this variance increases in abnormal situations. When one person or many people walk evenly in different directions, they tend to have the same speed; which results in the motion magnitude variance having a small value. This is not the case in abnormal situations (e.g. collapsing situations, panic.), that is, behavior that often engenders a high value for the motion magnitude variance (V_m). If $\overline{M}$ is the mean of the motion magnitude, then (V_m) can be defined as:

$$V_M = \frac{1}{n} \sum_{i-1}^{n} (Mi - \overline{M})^2 \tag{2.15}$$

where n is the number of optical flows in the frame.

2.3.2.4 Direction Histogram

Direction Histogram DH indicates the direction tendencies, and PC_α indicates the number of the peaks. In the histogram, each column indicates the number of vectors in a given angle. DH is associated to the frame that can be defined as:

$$DH = DH(\theta_i), i = 1..s \tag{2.16}$$

$$DH(\theta i) = \frac{\int_{i=1}^{n} (angle(i))}{s} \qquad (2.17)$$

$$angle(i) = \begin{cases} 1, & if\ angle\,(i) = \ \theta i \\ 0, & if\ not \end{cases} \qquad (2.18)$$

where $DH(\theta i)$ is the normalized frequency of optical flows that have the same angle θi. DH is a vector of size s where s is the total number of angles considered: $[-\pi, +\pi]$. Finally, the maximum number of peaks is:

$$PC_\alpha = \max_{\alpha} DH \qquad (2.19)$$

where α is a constant that indicates the range of peak intervals.

2.3.2.5 Direction Map

Our current approach also takes into account the Direction Map which indicates the mean motion for each block of the video.

$$DM = \left\{ MMV_p^{\vec{h}}(i,\ j);;\ i = 1..\ N;;j = 1..M \right\} \qquad (2.20)$$

The direction map is associated with a video, which is composed of a sequence of frames. The frame is composed of blocks.

Block (i, j) of any video frame is characterized by the mean motion vector $\overrightarrow{MMV_p}\,(i,\ j)$. To calculate this vector, we use the history of previous p frames. For each of these frames, we compute the average motion vector and thus the mean of all the average motion vectors for the p frames.

$$MMV_p^{\vec{h}}(i,j) = \frac{1}{p} \sum_{k=n-p}^{n} \left(\frac{1}{NV_k} \sum_{l=1}^{NV_k} \overrightarrow{V_l}(i,j) \right) \qquad (2.21)$$

where:
n is the number of current frames.
p is the number of considered previous frames
NV_k is the number of vectors in block (i, j) of frame k.
$\overrightarrow{V}_l(i,j)$ is to the vector l situated in block (i, j) of frame k.
The formula can be broked down as follows:
$V\,(i,j)$ corresponds to the mean motion situated in block (i, j) of frame k.

$$\overrightarrow{V(i,j)} = \frac{1}{NV_k} \sum_{l=1}^{NV_k} \overrightarrow{V_l}\ (i,j) \qquad (2.22)$$

And $\overrightarrow{MMV_p}\,(i,\ j)$ the motion mean in p frames, previous to the current one (frame n).

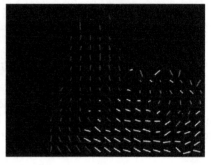

(a) both escalators have the same direction: bottom to top

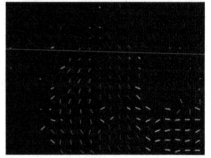

(b) Top to bottom for the left escalator, bottom to top for the right one

Fig. 2.6 Representation of direction maps obtained from two video sequences.

$$MM\overrightarrow{V}_p^h (i, \ j) \ = \ \frac{1}{p} \sum_{k \ = n \ -- \ p}^{n} \overrightarrow{V(i, j)} \tag{2.23}$$

Figure 2.6 presents the average motion vector $\overrightarrow{V}_k(i, j)$ computed for block (i, j) of frame k using all motion vectors of this block ($\overrightarrow{V}_1, \overrightarrow{V}_2, \overrightarrow{V}_3, \overrightarrow{V}_4$).

Using p frames, a new mean motion vector is computed using the p average motion vectors computed previously (see Figure 2.7). To calculate the mean motion vector for block $B(i, j)$, we only take into account p frames for which the average motion vector is not equal to zero.

2.3.2.6 Difference of Direction Map

Difference DDM between the average direction to frame m and the instant map corresponding to current frame p increases in case of abnormal events.

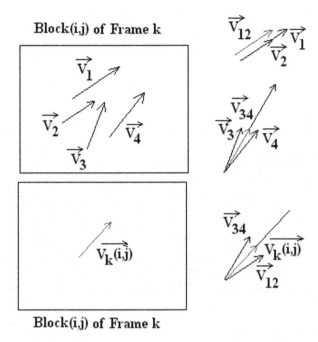

Fig. 2.7 Example of the computation of the average motion vector in the frame

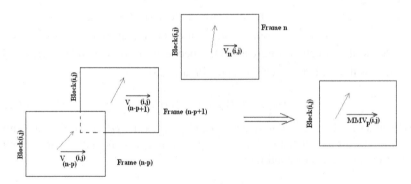

Fig. 2.8 Example of the computation of the mean motion vector for a block over frames

$$DDm = \frac{\sum\limits_{i=1}^{N}\sum\limits_{j=1}^{M}(MM\overrightarrow{V_p^h}(i,j) - MM\overrightarrow{V_1^{n+1}}(i,j))}{N \times M};; i = 1\ldots N, \; j = 1\ldots M \quad (2.24)$$

The average direction considers last l frames. And the instant map considers current $p\text{-}th$ frame. $N{\times}M$ represents the number of blocks in a frame. The right image in figure 2.6 shows the mean direction in each block of the view field of an escalator camera. Some tendencies can be seen: in the blue region, for example, the motion is from top to bottom. In the yellow region, the motion is from right to left.

2.3.3 Other Intermediate-Level Features

2.3.3.1 Motion Continuity Factor

The Motion Continuity Factor (*MCF*) measures the continuity of the motion of one block. This factor will be computed and used only when normal traffic flow has been defined. People are moving in some areas of the scene, and the *official* motion direction of each area is unique. Therefore, any motion which does not conform to the official direction has to be detected. The continuity of the motion is characterized by the continuity of direction to be computed in relation to the direction difference between the vectors of current and previous frames. This difference is computed as the angle between them. The continuity in magnitude motion that will be computed in relation to the difference between the magnitudes of the motion vectors.

Direction Continuity Measure

Let us consider:
  - $MM\vec{V}_p(i,j)$ is the mean motion vector of block (i, j) at frame n,
  - $\vec{V}_{n+1}(i,j)$ is the average motion vector of block (i, j) at frame (n+1)
  We define the direction difference (DD) between the vectors $MM\vec{V}_p(i,j)$ and $\vec{V}_{n+1}(i,j)$ as the angle between them (see Figure 2.9).

$$DD = MM\vec{V}_p(i,j), \vec{V}_{n+1}(i,j) \tag{2.25}$$

DD values are comprised of between *0* and *Π*. Measure *DCM* (Direction Continuity Measure) is associated with block *(i, j)* of frame *n* so as to distinguish continuity in direction from discontinuity.

$$DMC = \begin{cases} 0, if DD \leq \frac{\pi}{3};; \\ 1, if \frac{\pi}{3} < DD \leq \frac{\pi}{2};; \\ 2, if \frac{\pi}{2} < DD \leq \pi \end{cases} \tag{2.26}$$

Possible values of DCM are then 0, 1, 2 where:

- 0 indicates the continuity in motion direction
- 1 indicates a low discontinuity in motion direction
- 2 indicates a high discontinuity in motion direction

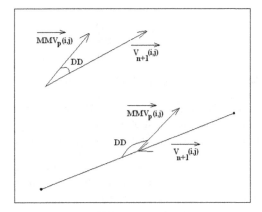

Fig. 2.9 Example of the computation of difference direction

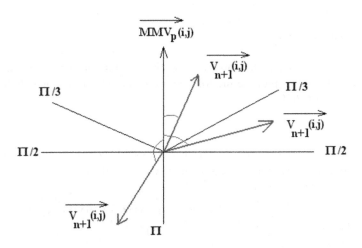

Fig. 2.10 The three main directions

Motion Magnitude Continuity Measure

We define the magnitude difference (MD) between vectors $MM\overrightarrow{V}_p(i, j)$ and $\overrightarrow{V}_{n+1}(i, j)$ as the difference between their magnitudes.

$$MD = \|vecV_{n+1}(i, j)\| - \|MM\overrightarrow{V}_p(i, j)\| \tag{2.27}$$

MD values pertain theoretically to the interval: $[-\|MM\overrightarrow{V}_p(i, j)\|, +\infty]$.

In order to distinguish continuity in motion magnitude from discontinuity, we associate with block *(i,j)* the following measure *MMCM* (Motion Magnitude Continuity Measure):

$$MMCM = \begin{cases} 0, if \text{ MD} < 0;; \\ 4, if \text{ MD} = 0;; \\ 8, if \text{ MD} > 0. \end{cases} \quad (2.28)$$

Possible *MMCM* values are the interval *0, 4, 8* where:

- *0* indicates a discontinuity in magnitude motion corresponding to deceleration
- *4* indicates continuity in magnitude motion (same values)
- *8* indicates continuity in magnitude motion corresponding to acceleration

In the case where there is no motion in block $B(i, j)$ of the previous frame, even if there is motion in the same block of the current frame (beginning of the motion), we consider the value of direction difference *DD* to be equal to *zero*, and magnitude difference *(MD)* to be equal to the motion magnitude of the average motion vector of this block.

Motion Continuity Factor

In order to characterize both continuity and discontinuity of motion direction and motion magnitude, we propose the following relation which measures the motion continuity factor *(MCF)*:

$$MCF = DCM + MMCM \quad (2.29)$$

The following table indicates *MCF* values, where *9* values are possible, with each one indicating a specific state of motion in the considered block.

	MMCM=0	MMCM=4	MMCM=8
DCM=0	0	4	8
DCM=1	1	5	9
DCM=2	2	6	10

Table 2.1 Values of the motion continuity factor

We then associate with each frame an *MCF (N x M)* matrix where *MCF (i, j)* is the motion continuity factor of block *(i, j)*. In cases in which there is no motion in the current and preceding frames of block *B (i, j)*, the *MCF (i, j)* value is set to *3* (see Figure 2.11).

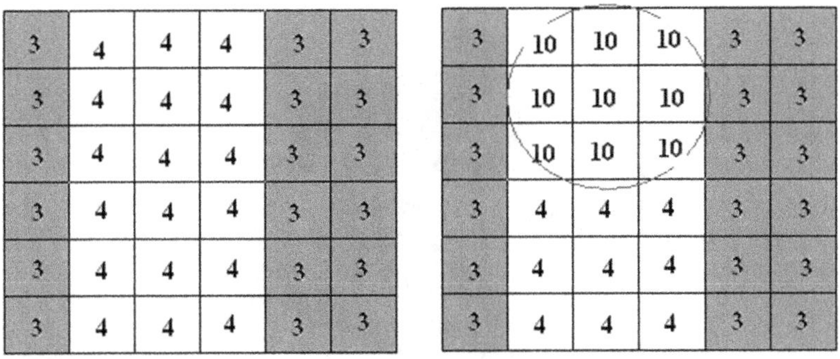

3	4	4	4	3	3
3	4	4	4	3	3
3	4	4	4	3	3
3	4	4	4	3	3
3	4	4	4	3	3
3	4	4	4	3	3

3	10	10	10	3	3
3	10	10	10	3	3
3	10	10	10	3	3
3	4	4	4	3	3
3	4	4	4	3	3
3	4	4	4	3	3

Fig. 2.11 2 matrices of motion continuity factor values

How to Use the Motion Continuity Factor

2.3.3.2 Motion Description Factor

Whenever it is possible to extract blobs and optical flows which correspond to moving objects, we define the motion description factor, which is more accurate than the motion continuity factor, since it describes how the blob moves within the frame.

Mean Motion Vector

Blob Bi of frame p is characterized by the mean motion vector $MM\vec{V}_n(i)$ which indicates the average motion vectors $\vec{V}_n(i,j)$ in this blob Bi (see Figure 11).

$$MM\vec{V}_n(i) = \frac{1}{NV_k} \sum_{j=1}^{NV_k} \vec{V}_n(i,j) \qquad (2.30)$$

where:
- n is the number of current frame
- NV_k is the number of vectors in block Bi of frame n.
- $\vec{V}_n(i,j)$ corresponds to vector j of blob Bi of frame n.

Motion Direction

Let α be the orientation angle of the mean motion vector $MM\vec{V}_n(i)$ (see Figure 2.12). The direction measure (D_M) based on the orientation angle α is associated with the mean motion vector D_M, $D_M = MM\vec{V}_p(i)$ of blob $B(i)$. Its value is computed as follows:

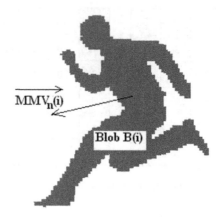

Fig. 2.12 The mean motion vector of the blob

$$
DM = \begin{cases}
0, & \text{if } 0 \le (\alpha) \le \pi/4 \\
1, & \text{if } \pi/4 < (\alpha) \le \pi/2 \\
2, & \text{if } \pi/2 < (\alpha) \le 3\pi/4 \\
3, & \text{if } 3\pi/4 < (\alpha) \le \pi \\
4, & \text{if } \pi < (\alpha) \le 5\pi/4 \\
5, & \text{if } 5\pi/4 < (\alpha) \le 3\pi/2 \\
6, & \text{if } 3\pi/2 < (\alpha) \le 7\pi/4 \\
7, & \text{if } 7\pi/4 < (\alpha) \le 2\pi
\end{cases}
\tag{2.31}
$$

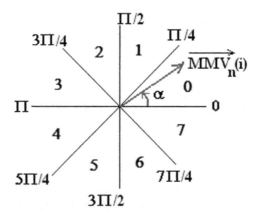

Fig. 2.13 Eight principal directions

Magnitude Motion Measure

We define the magnitude difference MD(i) of blob B(i) as the difference between magnitudes of its mean motion vectors $MM\vec{V}_n(i)$ and $\overrightarrow{MMV_{n+1}}(i)$ computed, respectively, at frames (n) and (n+1).

$$MD = \|MM\vec{V}_{n+1}(i)\| - \|MM\vec{V}_n(i)\| \qquad (2.32)$$

MD values are theoretically in the interval: $[-\|MM\vec{V}_n(i)\|, +\|MM\vec{V}_{n+1}(i)\|]$.

MMM measure (Magnitude Motion Measure) is associated with blob B(i) at each frame and computed as follows:

$$MMM = \begin{cases} 0, if\ \mathbf{MD} < 0;; \\ 8, if\ \mathbf{MD} = 0;; \\ 16,\ if\ \mathbf{MD} > 0. \end{cases} \qquad (2.33)$$

Possible MMM values are 0, 8, 16 where:
- 0 indicates a discontinuity in the magnitude motion corresponding to a deceleration
- 8 indicates a continuity in magnitude motion (the same values)
- 16 indicates a continuity in the magnitude motion corresponding to an acceleration

Motion Description Factor Measure

In order to describe the most accurate motion of *blob B(i)* at frame **n**, **MDF** factor, which uses the direction measure and the magnitude motion measure, is defined as follows:

$$MDF = DM + MMM \qquad (2.34)$$

Table 2.2 indicates the MDF values where each one of these values describes the motion of the blob between the previous and current frames.

2.3.3.3 Motion Trajectory of the Blob

We define the Motion Trajectory of blob MT as a set of motion description factors (MDF) for blob B(i) corresponding to a sequence of n frames.

$$MT(Bi) = \{MDFn - p, MDFn - p + 1, \ldots, MDFn\} \qquad (2.35)$$

The different $MDFp+i$ values describe the trajectory of the blob semantically (variation in the magnitudes of the motion and its different directions). For example, in Figure 2.14, we give the (DM, MMM) values of the blob corresponding to six

	MMM=0	MMM=8	MMM=16
DM=0	0	8	16
DM=1	1	9	17
DM=2	2	10	18
DM=3	3	11	19
DM=4	4	12	20
DM=5	5	13	21
DM=6	6	14	22
DM=7	7	15	23

Table 2.2 Values of the motion description factor

frames. The set of computed values for corresponding motion description factors are 19, 11, 11, 12, 4, 11. These values clearly indicate the motion trajectory of this blob:

- 19: increase in the motion magnitude with direction number 3
- 11: consistency of the motion magnitude with same direction number 3
- 11: consistency of the motion magnitude with same direction number 3
- 12: consistency of the motion magnitude with new direction number 4
- 4: decrease in the motion magnitude with same direction number 4
- 11: increasing of the motion magnitude with new direction number 3

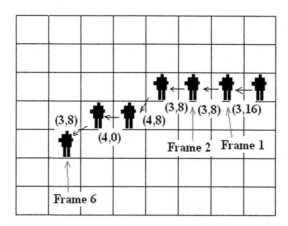

Fig. 2.14 (*DM, MMM*) values for different positions of the blob for six frames

2.3.4 High-Level Features

High-level features determine whether the event in the current frame is normal or abnormal. This chapter presents the high-level feature involved in collapsing event detection. Another high-level feature will then be outlined regarding opposite flow event detection. Our goal is to demonstrate that intermediate-level features used for collapsing event detection can also be used to handle other challenges.

2.3.4.1 Detecting Collapsing Events

Entropy

Entropy is the term that defines high-level features. It is used to determine whether a collapsing event happens or not. Function E extracting the feature at frame p has been developed. Function E depends on the following: motion area ratio (M_R), direction variation variance (V_θ), motion magnitude variance (V_M), peak cardinality in direction histogram (PC_α), and difference in direction map behavior at frame p. p is not explained in the formula for reasons of simplicity. E is calculated at each frame. All intermediate features have been well detailed in previous paragraphs. They individually characterize certain aspects of the abnormal event and are in general proportionally higher when collapsing events occur in crowded environments. High-level feature E makes immediate use of certain intermediate-level features for collapsing, as presented above. This does not mean that other intermediate-level features are inappropriate or that other options do not exist to detect collapsing events through alternative combinations of intermediate-level features. It simply means that current measure E has a good shape and is suitable for collapsing event detection, as proven by empirical demonstrations based on on-going experiments. When a collapsing event occurs at the exit of an escalator, the crowded motion density (motion area ratio (M_R)) increases instantly, as any trouble at this particular point increases the collision between running people. Someone who stands still at the exit will make those people behind, who are moved by the escalator, come to a sudden and abnormal halt. In normal situations, when the number of people is limited at the escalator exit, the sudden increase observed will lead to disorder. The resulting motion is generally disordered due to the high number of people in the same region. Let us now consider direction variance (V_θ). The direction variance calculates the variance of angle θ. The observed collapsing events show an increase in the direction variance. For a few seconds, people are suddenly stopped at the exit and try in vain to move in all directions. The variance direction is therefore increased. With abnormal events such as collapsing or panic, the motion magnitude variance (V_m) triggers various motion magnitudes so that the variance is relatively high in comparison with normal event situations. In the case of collapsing events, the magnitude of certain points of interest is high, while they are low for others. As a result, the magnitude variances are high, this characteristic being typical of disorder motions. The number of peaks (PC_α) for direction histogram DH is higher during collapsing events than during normal situations. Indeed, collapsing events involve many optical flows with various directions, which are typical of disordered motion. Therefore, there is an increase in the direction cardinalities, and the number of peaks is important. However, in normal event situations at the escalator exit, the optical flows tend to go in the same direction, which is normal for escalator exits. The number of peaks is then limited.

DD_M calculates the difference mean between previous frames' average direction and the current frame's directions. This value is high when there are sudden changes of direction. In our challenge, a person is walking towards the escalator exit, and stops or falls instantly, causing a sudden change of direction.

Intermediate-level features increase when the collapsing event occurs at the exit, contributing to different characteristics of the collapsing event. We believe that entropy E defines collapsing events as follows:

$$E = M_R * V_\theta * V_m * PC_\alpha * DD_M \tag{2.36}$$

For an event to be considered normal or abnormal based on entropy E, threshold th - which lists events in normal and abnormal classes - must be computed. If E is greater than threshold th, then the event is abnormal; otherwise, it is normal. Entropy E depends on the controlled environment, namely, the distance from the camera to the scene, the orientation of the camera, and the type and position of the camera. The greater the distance from the camera to the scene, the lower the number of low-level features (optical flows and blobs). There is a growth in entropy when object movement in the images increases. Dependency between entropy and controlled environment does not directly impact the measure itself, as entropy measure is invariant in a controlled environment. However, it impacts the threshold that determines the normality or abnormality of the event. A controlled environment means a video stream. As said before, the controlled environment is defined by the position of the camera, the type of the camera, the distance from the camera to the scene, and the orientation of the camera. For this reason, at least one threshold per video stream is expected. There are n video streams - in airports, shopping malls, banks, playgrounds etc. - for n thresholds. If there is any change in the environment, the threshold should then be regenerated.

Threshold

The theoretical principle of the method is the following: the threshold is greater than the maximum of entropies in large videos containing exclusively normal events:

$$th = \frac{\max E\left(frame_p\right)}{p = 1 \ldots f} \tag{2.37}$$

nf is the number of frames in the video database. The theoretical principle is too time-consuming, $O(nf)$. If nf is considered over three months of video recording, then the running time is huge. Three months of video stream involves three months of processing. Thus, we propose a method reducing the processing time. The input is a video stream *vd*, composed exclusively of normal events. So *vd* does not contain any collapsing events. The method output is threshold *th* associated with *vd*.

The method relies on sampling and consists of drawing a video stream sample, applying entropy to that sample, and determining the maximum sample entropy. The point is that, if the sample is drawn in a sufficiently random way, the sample entropy will approximate the entropy of the entire video stream. In order to arrive at better approximations, the method draws multiple samples and gives the maximum entropies as the output.

Example

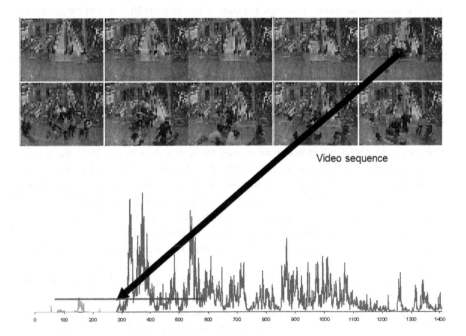

Fig. 2.15 Sudden variation of the entropy *E* when collapsing event happens

Experiments realized in a more general way and reported in [64] indicate that five samples of size *z* (less than one hundred) give satisfactory results.

The above example illustrates a case in which a trolley wheel suddenly breaks off owing to the resulting friction when it passes over an escalator near the exit point. This causes an abnormal emergency situation at the exit point. The figure contains the video frames and the curve of *E*. The first line in the top of the figure contains normal events, while the video frames in the second line contain abnormal

---

Algorithm 1

(input: vd, size of sample: s, ouput: th)
Begin
For i = 1 to 5, repeat the following steps:
Draw a sample of s frames randomly from the entire video database
$th = Threshold_s = \max \left(E(frame_p)_{p=1...card(s)} \right)$
End

---

events. E is greater than the threshold in the fifth frame of the figure. Green and red curves represent the frames of normal and abnormal events, respectively. The point at the beginning of the red curve represents threshold th. Once again, a threshold is used to label and differentiate this fact. The blue line in the figure represents the threshold. Below the blue line, behavior is considered normal, while above that line, it is considered abnormal. The blue horizontal line depicts the chosen threshold for this video. Any peak above this blue line for a given duration is treated as abnormal. There is a high peak with various durations reflecting the abnormal situation. From the video data sets, our method detects the perilous and inconsistent circumstances which occur in a certain place during a particular period of time.

2.3.4.2 Detecting Opposing Flow Event

The aim is to detect when someone moves through a door opposite to the normal traffic flow. We assume that normal traffic flow has been defined. Let us remember that each frame is decomposed into blocks, and that the mean motion vector is computed for each block $B(i, j)$. For each frame, matrix MCF(NxM) of motion continuity factors is computed when $MCF(i, j)$ indicates the motion continuity factor of block $B(i,j)$. Figure 2.16 illustrates an example of such a matrix, indicating that people are moving in the same general direction with few differences in the magnitude motions.

For the current frame, the average motion vectors of all blocks $B(i, j)$ are computed.

In any block $B(i, j)$, when the MCF value is equal to 2, 6, or 10, the mean motion vector of this block is not computed for this frame because the motion goes in the opposite direction of the normal flow. Consequently, when people are moving in the opposite direction, elements $MCF(i, j)$ whose values are 2, 6 or 10 are moving in the matrix and their number may increase from one frame to another. Figure illustrates the evolution of MCF values for the blocks that correspond to the motion in the opposite direction.

To detect this event, we propose the following method:
Let:
- NBIP be the average number of blocks that correspond to one person in the frame

3	3	3	4	4	4	4	4
3	3	4	4	4	4	8	4
3	8	0	8	0	4	0	4
3	8	4	4	0	3	3	3
4	4	4	0	3	3	3	3
4	4	3	3	3	3	3	3

Fig. 2.16 Example of matrix of motion continuity factors

3	3	3	3	4	4	10	6
3	3	4	4	4	6	10	4
3	0	0	4	0	4	0	4
3	0	4	8	0	4	0	3
4	4	4	3	3	3	3	3
4	4	3	3	3	3	3	3

Frame 1

3	3	3	3	4	4	10	4
3	3	4	4	4	6	6	4
3	0	0	4	6	10	4	4
3	0	4	8	0	4	0	3
4	4	4	3	3	3	3	3
4	4	3	3	3	3	3	3

Frame 2

Fig. 2.17 Evolution of motion continuity factors which correspond to the opposite flow

- NFrMin be the minimum number of frames used to detect the opposing flow event
- Found be the logical variable which indicates if there is an opposing flow event or not
- NumFrStart be the number of frames for which the opposing flow event starts
- NumFrEnd be the number of frames for which the opposing flow event terminates

The basic principle of the following function consists of computing the matrix of motion continuity factors *MCF (NxM)* for each frame. In this matrix, we are searching for the existence of an area (a set of neighbouring blocks) in which the motion is opposing the flow direction. If this sub-area persists for a significant number of frames with no decrease in size, then the opposing flow event is detected.

Algorithm 2

Function EventOpposingFlow(VideoStream, NFrMin, NBlP, Found, NumFrStart, NumFrEnd)
Begin
$NumFr = 0$
$NumFrStart = 1$
$NbFr = 0$
$Found = false$
repeat
  #Pass to the following frame#
  $NumFr = NumFr + 1$
  - Compute the matrix of motion continuity factors $MCF(N \times M)$
  - Compute the maximum number of neighboring elements $MCF(i, j)$ whose values are *2*, *6* or *10*. Let *NBl* be this number.
  if $NBl = NBlP$ **then**
    $Found = True, NbFr = NbFr + 1$
  else
    $Found = false, NbFr = 0, NumFrStart = NumFr + 1$
  end if
until $Found And NbFr = NbFrMin$
$NumFrEnd = NumFr$
End

2.4 Group Detection and Tracking

We will describe an algorithm that detects crowd related events. The proposed algorithm comprises several steps (Figure 2.18): It starts by extracting a set of Points of Interest (PoIs) in the current frame, then tracking them over the next frame through optical flow computation. Static and noise points are removed to focus on moving points. The scene is divided into blocks, and each motion vector is attached to the suitable block.

The block-clustering step consists of gathering neighboring blocks that have similar orientation and magnitude into groups. These groups are tracked over the next frames. Finally, the events are detected by using information obtained from group tracking, the magnitude model and the direction model.

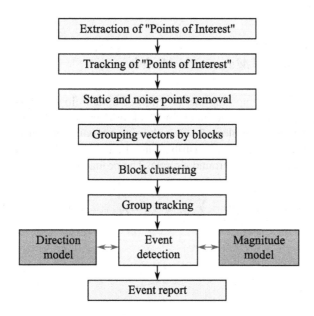

Fig. 2.18 Detection Algorithm Steps

2.4.1 Detection and Tracking of PoIs

Once the points of interest have been defined, they are tracked over subsequent frames using optical flow techniques. For this, we use a Kanade-Lucas-Tomasi feature tracker [84]. The Shi-Tomasi algorithm [119] utilizes the smallest eigenvalues of an image block as the criterion for ensuring that features which can be tracked reliably by a Lucas-Kanade tracking algorithm are selected.

After matching the features between frames, the result is a set of vectors:

$$V = \{V_1...V_N | V_i = (X_i, Y_i, A_i, M_i)\} \tag{2.38}$$

Where:

X_i: X coordinate of feature i,
Y_i : Y coordinate of feature i,
θ_i direction of feature i.

This step also allows the removal of static and noise features. Static features are the ones which move less than a minimum magnitude. Noise features are isolated and have more random angles and magnitude differences in comparison with their close neighbors owing to tracking calculation errors. Finally, the camera view is divided into $Bx * By$ blocks. Each motion vector is attached to the suitable block following its origin coordinates.

2.4.2 Direction and Magnitude Models

This step consists of computing the direction of optical flow vectors within each block. These directions are the input for block orientation distribution. The local probability distribution for block $B_{x,y}$ is built using a mixture of Von Mises distributions (also called circular normal distributions). Figure 2.19 illustrates a mixture of two Von Mises distributions around a circle. The probability of an orientation θ is given by:

$$P_{x,y}(\theta) = \sum_{i=1}^{K} \omega_{i,x,y} \cdot V\left(\theta; \mu_{i,x,y}, m_{i,x,y}\right) \tag{2.39}$$

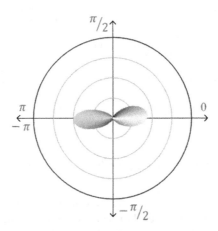

Fig. 2.19 Representation of a mixture of Von Mises distribution

where K is the number of distributions and represents the maximum number of major orientations to consider. $\omega_{i,x,y}, \mu_{i,x,y}, m_{i,x,y}$ are respectively the weight, mean angle and dispersion of the ith distribution for block $B_{x,y}$. $V(\theta; \mu, m)$ is the Von Mises distribution with mean orientation μ and dispersion parameter m, over angle θ, with the following probability density function:

$$V(\theta; \mu, m) = \frac{1}{2\pi I_0(m)} \exp[m \cos(\theta - \mu)] \tag{2.40}$$

where $I_0(m)$ is the modified Bessel function of the first kind and order 0 defined by:

$$I_0(m) = \sum_{r=0}^{\infty} \left(\frac{1}{r!}\right)^2 \left(\frac{1}{2}m\right)^{2r} \tag{2.41}$$

2.4.3 Block Clustering

This step concerns the grouping of similar blocks to obtain block clusters. The idea is to represent a group of people moving in the same direction at the same speed by the same block cluster. By *similar*, we mean same direction, same speed and in neighboring locations. Each block $B_{x,y}$ is defined by its position $P_{x,y} = (x, y); x = 1..Bx, y = 1..By$ and orientation $\Omega_{x,y} = \mu_{0,x,y}$ (see section 2.4.2).

The merging condition consists of a similarity measure D_Ω between two blocks $B_{x1,y1}$ and $B_{x2,y2}$ defined as:

$$D_\Omega(\Omega_{x1,y1}, \Omega_{x2,y2}) = \min_{k,z} |(\Omega_{x1,y1} + 2k\pi) - (\Omega_{x2,y2} + 2z\pi)|$$
$$(k, z) \in Z^2 \tag{2.42}$$
$$0 \le D_\Omega(\Omega_{x1,y1}, \Omega_{x2,y2}) < \pi$$

Based on these definitions, two neighboring blocks $B_{x1,y1}$ and $B_{x2,y2}$ are in the same cluster when:

$$D_\Omega(\Omega_{x1,y1}, \Omega_{x2,y2}) < \delta_\Omega$$
$$0 \le \delta_\Omega < \pi \tag{2.43}$$

where δ_Ω is a predefined threshold. In our implementation, we choose $\delta_\Omega = \pi/10$ empirically. Figure 2.20 shows a sample output of the process.

Mean orientation X_j of cluster C_j is given by the following formula:

$$X_j = \arctan \frac{\sum_{x=1}^{Bx} \sum_{y=1}^{By} \mathbb{1}_{C_j}(B_{x,y}) \cdot \sin(\Omega_{x,y})}{\sum_{x=1}^{Bx} \sum_{y=1}^{By} \mathbb{1}_{C_j}(B_{x,y}) \cdot \cos(\Omega_{x,y})} \tag{2.44}$$

where $\mathbb{1}_{C_j}$ is the indicator function.
Centroid $O_j = (ox_j, oy_j)$ of group C_j is defined by:

$$ox_j = \frac{\sum_{x=1}^{Bx} \sum_{y=1}^{Bx} \mathbb{1}_{C_j}(B_{x,y}) \cdot x_i}{\sum_{x=1}^{Bx} \sum_{y=1}^{By} \mathbb{1}_{C_j}(B_{x,y})} \tag{2.45}$$

Fig. 2.20 Group clustering on a frame

we obtain oy_j by analogy.

2.4.4 Group Tracking

Once the groups have been built, they are tracked over subsequent frames. The tracking is achieved by matching the centroids of the groups in frame f with the centroids of frame $f+1$. Each frame f is defined by its groups $\{C_{1,f}, C_{2,f}, ..., C_{n_f,f}\}$ where n_f is the number of groups detected in frame f. Each group $C_{i,f}$ is described by its centroid $O_{i,f}$ and mean orientation $X_{i,f}$. Group $C_{m,f+1}$ matching group $C_{i,f}$ must have the nearest centroid to $C_{i,f}$ and has to be in a minimal area around it. In other words, it has to satisfy the two following conditions:

$$\begin{cases} m = \underset{j}{\operatorname{argmin}}(D(O_{i,f}, O_{j,f+1})) \\ and \\ D(O_{i,f}, O_{m,f+1}) < \tau \end{cases} \tag{2.46}$$

Where τ is the minimal distance between two centroids (we choose $\tau = 5$). If there is no matching (meaning that there is no group $C_{m,f+1}$ satisfying the two conditions), then group $C_{i,f}$ disappears and is no longer tracked in the next frames.

2.5 Detecting Multiple Flows and Events in a Crowd Scene

Further results are presented in this section. Multiple Flows can be deduced directly from the direction model. However, event detection requires additional processing which is described in the next subsections.

2.5.1 Multiple Flow Detection

In public places, people generally go in different directions. However, certain areas have a typical motion pattern which contains two or more major orientations. For example, there are four major orientations in a footpath, two opposite orientations for pedestrians who cross the footpath and two others for cars which are orthogonal to the pedestrians' orientations. It would be interesting to know which of the pedestrians or cars pass over that area. This is done by the Direction Model. In fact, each block has a mixture Model that contains up to four major orientations. The dominant orientation of the block is the first orientation of its mixture.

We consider a flow vector that represents a block $B_{x,y}$ defined by the four dimensional vectors $Vb_{x,y}$:

$$Vb_{x,y} = (Xb_{x,y}, Yb_{x,y}, Ab_{x,y}, Mb_{x,y}) \qquad (2.47)$$

where

- $(Xb_{x,y}, Yb_{x,y})$: is the origin of flow vector $Vb_{x,y}$ which is the center of the block $B_{x,y}$.
- $Ab_{x,y}$: is the motion direction of flow vector $Vb_{x,y}$ which is equal to $\mu_{0,x,y}$, the mean of the first Von Mises distribution in the mixture model of the block $B_{x,y}$.
- $Mb_{x,y}$: is the motion magnitude of flow vector $Vb_{x,y}$ which is the mean motion magnitude of block $B_{x,y}$

2.5.2 Event Recognition

The events described in PETS'2009 are listed in three categories:

- Motion speed related events: these can be detected by exploiting the motion velocity of the optical flow vectors across frames (e.g. running and walking events).

- Crowd convergence events: these occur when two or more groups of people get near to each other and merge into a single group (e.g. crowd merging event).
- Crowd divergence events: these occur when people move in opposite directions (e.g. local dispersion, split and evacuation events).

Events from the first category are detected by fitting the mean optical flow magnitude of each frame against a model of the scene's motion magnitude. Events from the second and third categories are detected by analyzing the orientation, distance and position of the crowd. Convergence is when two groups of people go to the same area. Divergence, however, is when they take different directions. A more detailed explanation of adopted approaches will be given in the following sections.

2.5.3 Running and Walking Events

As described earlier, the main idea is to fit the mean motion velocity between two consecutive frames against the magnitude model of the scene. This gives a probability for running P_{run}, walking P_{walk} and stopping P_{stop} events. In this work, we process motion flows, thus $P_{stop} = 0$ and $P_{run} = 1 - P_{walk}$.

Since a person has a greater chance of staying in his/her current state rather than moving suddenly to another state (e.g. someone walking and gradually increasing his/her speed until he/she starts running), then the final running or walking probability is the weighted sum of current and previous probabilities. The result is thresholded to infer a walking or a running event. Formally, a frame f with mean motion magnitude m_f contains a walking (resp. running) event if:

$$\sum_{l=f-h}^{f} w_{f-l} \cdot P_{walk}(m_l) > \vartheta_{walk} \qquad (2.48)$$

where ϑ_{walk} (resp. ϑ_{run}) is the walking (resp. running) threshold. h is the number of previous frames to consider. Each previous state has a weight w_l (in our implementation we choose $h = 1$, $w_0 = 0.8$ and $w_1 = 0.2$). $P_{walk}(m_l)$ is the probability of observing m_l. It is obtained by fitting m_l against a magnitude model. This probability is thresholded to detect a walking (resp. running) event. We choose a threshold of 0.05 for the walking event and 0.95 for the running event, since there is a 95% probability for a value to be comprised between $\mu - 2\sigma$ and $\mu + 2\sigma$ where μ and σ are the mean and standard deviation of the Gaussian distribution, respectively.

2.5.4 Crowd Convergence and Divergence Events

Convergence and divergence events are first detected by computing circular variance $S_{0,f}$ of each frame f considering the following equation :

$$S_{0,f} = 1 - \frac{1}{n_f} \sum_{i=1}^{n_f} \cos\left(X_{i,f} - \overline{X_{0,f}}\right) \tag{2.49}$$

where $\overline{X_{0,f}}$ is the mean angle of clusters in frame f defined by:

$$\overline{X_{0,f}} = \arctan \frac{\sum_{i=1}^{n_f} \sin(X_{i,f})}{\sum_{i=1}^{n_f} \cos(X_{i,f})} \tag{2.50}$$

$S_{0,f}$ is a value comprised between 0 and 1 inclusive. If the angles are identical, $S_{0,f}$ will be equal to 0. A set of perfectly opposing angles will give a value of 1. If the circular variance exceeds a threshold β (we choose $\beta = 0.3$ for our implementation), we can infer the realization of convergence and/or divergence events. The position and direction of each group in relation to other groups is examined in order to figure out which event happened. Convergence is when two groups are oriented towards the same direction and are close to each other (figure 2.21). Divergence, however, is when they are going in opposite directions and are close to each other. More formally, let $\overrightarrow{v_{i,f}}$ be a vector representing a group $C_{i,f}$ at frame f. $\overrightarrow{v_{i,f}}$ is characterized by origin $O_{i,f}$ which is the centroid of group $C_{i,f}$, orientation Ω_i and destination $Q_{i,f}$ with coordinates $qx_{i,f}, qy_{i,f}$ defined as:

$$qx_{i,f} = ox_{i,f} \cdot \cos(\Omega_i) \tag{2.51}$$

$$qy_{i,f} = oy_{i,f} \cdot \sin(\Omega_i) \tag{2.52}$$

2 groups are converging (or merging) when the two following conditions are satisfied:

$$\begin{cases} D(O_i, O_j) > D(Q_i, Q_j) \\ and \\ D(O_i, O_j) < \delta \end{cases} \tag{2.53}$$

where $D(P,Q)$ is the Euclidean distance between points P and Q, and δ represents the minimal distance required between the centroid of two groups (we took $\delta=10$ in our implementation).

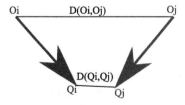

Fig. 2.21 Merging clusters

Similarly, two groups are diverging when the following conditions are satisfied:

$$\begin{cases} D(O_i, O_j) < D(Q_i, Q_j) \\ \text{and} \\ D(O_i, O_j) < \delta \end{cases} \tag{2.54}$$

However, for this situation, three cases are distinguished:

1. The groups do not stay separated for a long time and have a very short motion period so they are still forming a group. This corresponds to a local dispersion event.
2. The groups stay separated for a long time and their distance grows over the frames. This corresponds to a crowd split event.
3. If the first situation occurs while the crowd is running, this corresponds to an evacuation event.

To detect the events described above, another feature is added to each group $C_{i,f}$ which corresponds to its *age*, represented by the first frame where the group appeared, noted $F_{i,f}$. There is a local dispersion at frame f between two groups $C_{i,f}$ and $C_{j,f}$ if the conditions in (2.54) are satisfied. In addition, their motion has to be recent:

$$\begin{cases} f - F_{i,f} < v \\ \text{and} \\ f - F_{j,f} < v \end{cases} \tag{2.55}$$

where v is a threshold representing the number of frames since the groups have started moving (because group clustering relies on motion). In our implementation, it is equal to 28, which corresponds to four seconds in a 7fps video stream.
Both groups $C_{i,f}$ and $C_{j,f}$ are splitting at frame f, if they satisfy the conditions (2.54). Moreover, one of them exhibits recent motion, while the other exhibits older motion.

$$\begin{cases} f - F_{i,f} \geq v \wedge f - F_{j,f} < v \\ \text{or} \\ f - F_{i,f} < v \wedge f - F_{j,f} \geq v \end{cases} \tag{2.56}$$

There is an evacuation event between both groups $C_{i,f}$ and $C_{j,f}$ at frame f if they satisfy the local dispersion conditions (2.54) and (2.55), as well as the running conditions (2.48).

2.5.5 Results

The approach described in the previous sections has been evaluated on PETS'2009 datasets. This dataset includes multisensor sequences containing different crowd activities. Several scenarios involving crowd density estimation, crowd counting, single person tracking, flow analysis and high level event detection are proposed. A set of training data is also available.

We processed the Flow Analysis and Event Recognition sequences which are organized in dataset S3. We selected "VIEW_001" for flow analysis and "VIEW_002" for Event Recognition. Other views were not considered for processing since one view was sufficient for each subsystem to operate. The system was run directly on the JPEG images that make the PETS 2009 dataset up. The algorithm processed nine 720×576 video streams.

We have processed five 'S3.MultipleFlow' sequences described in Table 2.3. Figure 2.22 shows multiple flow representation in sequence 'S3.MultipleFlow/Time_14-13/View_001' on frame 112. Direction tendencies can be observed: in yellow regions, the typical motion goes from West to East. In the orange region, the typical motion goes from North to South-East.

Time Stamp	Short Description
Time_12-43	Seven persons are moving by performing a zigzag
Time_14-13	Crowd moving and avoiding human obstacles
Time_14-37	3 groups merging into a single group
Time_14-46	3 persons entering a crowd and passing through
Time_14-52	them by moving in their opposite direction

Table 2.3 Description of S3.MultipleFlow sequences of PETS'2009 dataset

Fig. 2.22 Multiple flow representation on a frame

The four sequences in S3.HighLevel highlight crowd-related events. Events were successfully detected, Figure 2.23 shows a splitting event represented by a white line between the splitting groups. Some false detections appear, mainly due to the shadows which generate false groups of people and the lack of depth resulting in an imprecise distance between clusters. Table 2.4 shows the most relevant detected events in each sequence.

T.S.	Walk	Run	Disp.	Split	Merge	Evac.
14-16	•	•				
14-27	•		•		•	
14-31	•			•		
14-33	•	•			•	•

Table 2.4 Most relevant detected events

Fig. 2.23 Split event detection: before and after splitting

2.6 Method Adaptation to Context

2.6.1 Overview

The cluster measure is the current method output used. The analysis of the value and variations of this measure throughout time allows us to decide if the situation is normal or abnormal (the term *abnormality estimation* can also be used), which is also an output of our method.

2.6.2 Context Factors

We can find here some factors of potential context variations in escalators that will help to adjust the method to different contexts:

1. Day/night, peak time are factors that will influence the final method results. For example, it is necessary to adapt (increase) the thresholds to detect real collapsing situation instead of simple overcrowding situation at peak time. The opposite action (decreasing the thresholds) is performed for night where there is no motion. This can be achieved using a *Periodic Motion Heat Map*, but it has to be treated as a context-related factor: for instance, a heat map for the day, another one for the night, etc., as presented in Figure 2.6.2.

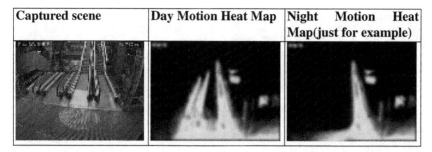

Captured scene	Day Motion Heat Map	Night Motion Heat Map(just for example)

Fig. 2.24 Day and night motion heat maps

2. The escalator typology is also important. For example, to ensure that all escalators go in the same direction (or if there is only one escalator), every motion in the opposite direction is prohibited. This is not the case when the escalators travel in two directions. Even if we can extract this information by a learning period to build the Direction Histogram, it has to be treated as a context-related factor.
3. The position of the camera is also an important factor. Some positions are indeed better than others as far as the quality of the final results is concerned. It depends on:

   a. Perspective,
   b. Orientation : *Top camera* or *Front camera*,
   c. Distance from the escalator: subjects are near or far,

Fig. 2.25 Escalator typology

Fig. 2.26 Different camera positions.

2.6.3 Method Extensions

Let's imagine that a video stream is characterized by several context-related thresholds. Suppose that in a certain period of time, due to a contextual factor, the density is very high, and in another period of time, the density is very low. Therefore, entropy may be influenced by contextual information (period). The higher the density, the higher the threshold. So, we can consider, for example, several categories of densities (e.g. low, medium, high) and then several thresholds associated with suitable density categories of normal events. The definition of several entropies would then be necessary.

The method, as outlined previously, relies on sampling, since finding representative frames of density categories in normal situation for the entire video database is extremely time-consuming. Thus, the algorithm draws a sample of the database, applies a K-medoid algorithm to that sample, and finds the medoids of the sample. Each medoid corresponds to a density. The point is that, if the sample is drawn in a sufficiently random way, the medoids of the sample would approximate the medoids of the entire video database. To come up with better approximations, the algorithm draws multiple samples and gives the best clustering as the output. Here, for the sake of accuracy, the quality of a clustering is measured based on the average dissimilarity of all videos in the entire database, not only those in the samples. The video database is composed of frames. Each frame is represented by the motion ratio area (density). As a result, the method appears as follows:

Algorithm 3

Algorithm (input: vd, size of sample: s, output: threshold-density-j /j=1..3)
Begin
For i = 1 to 5, repeat the following steps:
Draw a sample of s frames randomly from the entire video database, and call Algorithm K- medoids to find k medoids of the sample.
For each frame f in the entire data set, determine which of the k medoids is the most similar to f.
Calculate the average dissimilarity of the clustering obtained in the previous step. If this value is lower than the current minimum, use this value as the current minimum, and retain the three medoids found in step 2 as the best set of medoids obtained so far.
Return to step 1 to start the next iteration.
j=1..3 corresponding respectively to low, medium and high densities. C_{ij} is the cluster j
$$Threshold - density - j(C_i) = \max \left(E(frame_p)\right)_{p=1...card(C_j)}$$

K-medoids of $O(n^2)$, by applying K-medoids to the samples only, each iteration is of $O(k^2 + k(n - k))$, $\sim O(n)$. The complexity is reasonable, as the n value (n = number of frames) is not high. K is the number of clusters.

2.6.4 Experiments

2.6.4.1 Some examples

We present two examples related to three different video streams, where sudden and important variations of entropy E are observed during a collapsing event. We can also point out how much entropy varies over time. The curved green color indicates normal events and the curved red line indicates the collapsing event.

2.6.4.2 Data Set

Datasets are videos from a video surveillance system at escalator exits. They have been provided by a video surveillance company. Data sets are divided into two kinds of events: normal and abnormal. The total video length is about 60 hours with 16 abnormal events. In normal situations, the crowd flows with no collapsing event in the escalator exits. Generally, in the videos, there are two escalators travelling in

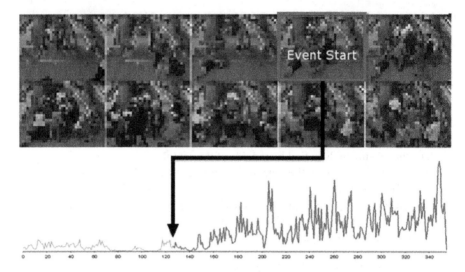

Fig. 2.27 Abnormality estimation (Case 1)

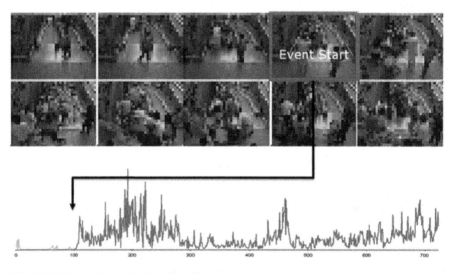

Fig. 2.28 Abnormality estimation (Case 2)

opposite directions. In videos depicting abnormal situations, collapsing events occur in an escalator exit. The original video frame size is 640×480 pixels.

In the Table 2.5, the identification of video sequences corresponds to abnormal events, annotated manually by the video surveillance expert.

2.6.4.3 Methodology

Regarding features detection and tracking, low-level features are extracted per frame (optical flows in points of interest), with five intermediate-level features, as defined in the previous sections. We also define the high level of features, namely entropy, which is specific to this experiment, where abnormal events correspond to collapsing in the escalator exits of the airport. Collapsing events detected by the system are compared with collapsing events annotated manually (references). Event observations can occur at any moment and for any duration. Each event detected for the evaluated detection system will be to the reference annotations. Therefore, an optimal *one-to-one* mapping is needed between *the system* and *reference observations*. The mapping is required as there is no pre-defined segmentation in the streaming video. The alignment will be performed using the Hungarian solution to the Bipartite Graph [70] matching problem by modeling event observations as nodes in the bipartite graph. The system observations are represented as one set of nodes, and the reference observations are represented as a second set. The time congruence formula below assumes that the mapping is performed for one event at a time.

$$(O_s, O_r) = \frac{\text{Min}\left(\text{End}\left(O_r\right), \text{End}\left(O_s\right)\right) - \text{Max}\left(\text{Beg}\left(O_r\right), \text{Beg}\left(O_s\right)\right)}{\text{Max}\left(\frac{1}{25}, Dur(O_r)\right)} \tag{2.57}$$

With:
O_r: Reference observation of the event.
O_s: Observation of the event for the system.
$End(\ )$: End of the observation's time span.
$Beg(\ )$: Beginning of the observation's time span.
$Dur()$: Duration of the event.

The function for observation comparisons is composed of two levels. The first level, indicated by Ø(*empty*) values, differentiates potentially mappable observation pairs from non-mappable observation ones. The second level takes into account the *temporal congruence* (state of agreement) of the system and reference event observations, as well as the observation's detection score in relation to the system's range of detection score. The Figure 2.29 shows the mapping idea, as presented in this subsection.

The list of the evaluation methodology's inputs and outputs is summarized below.
Inputs:
O(s) Events Detected: Start Frame, End Frame
O(r) Events Annotated: Start Frame, End Frame
Outputs:
Number of relevant events (mapped events) detected
Number of events returned
Recall
Precision
Number of False Alarms

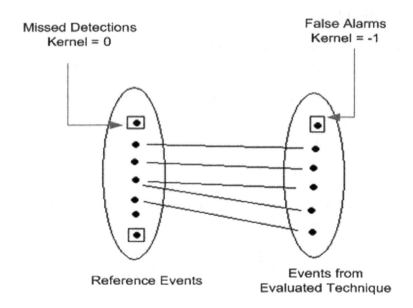

Fig. 2.29 Matching of Bipartite graph

Number of missed detections

The recall is the ability measure of the system to detect all relevant events. It is the fraction of the documents that are relevant to the query that are successfully retrieved. In binary classification, recall is called *sensitivity*. So it can be considered as the probability that a relevant document is retrieved by the query. It is trivial to achieve recall of 100 percent by returning all documents in response to any query. Therefore recall alone is not enough but one needs to measure the number of non-relevant documents also, for example by computing the precision.

$$\text{Recall} = \frac{\text{Number of relevant events detected}}{\text{Number of relevant events in the dataset}}$$

Precision is the system's ability to detect only relevant events (no false alarms). It is the fraction of the documents retrieved that are relevant to the user's information need. In binary classification, precision is analogous to positive predictive value. Precision takes all retrieved documents into account. It can also be evaluated at a given cut-off rank, considering only the topmost results returned by the system. This measure is called *precision* at n or Pan. Note that the meaning and usage of *precision* in the field of Information Retrieval differs from the definition of accuracy and precision within other branches of science and technology.

$$\text{Precision} = \frac{\text{Number of relevant events detected}}{\text{Total number of events returned}}$$

2.6.5 Results

The results of the experiments show that abnormal events have been detected successfully. The result is satisfactory overall. In the table below, three events have not been detected. When examining them carefully, we notice that two of them correspond to video streams in which the escalator stopped, as a collapsing event occurred on the other side of the escalator, which was not visible in the video stream. Therefore, we didn't consider these two events to be an omission. The only omission concerns a case in which a person falls down in the middle of the escalator and the motion is relatively weak, since there is a certain distance between the scene and the middle of the escalator. So, our method is efficient when the targeted scene is relatively close and the motion ratio is relatively important. The table 2.5 shows that there is no false alarm over three hours of video. Recall = 0,928 Precision = 100%

Sequence	Manual Annotation		Algorithm Result		Result	Score	Remark
	First frame	Last frame	First frame	Last frame			
060210_C1atascopasillo-11.24.55-11.26.09_vs	866	-	not a collapsing situation		x		The event occurs in the other side of the escalator
060210_C2atascopasillo-11.24.56-11.26.09_vs	645	1451	720	-	√	0,9069	
060216_C1atascopasillo-16.04.21-16.05.39_vs	366	1738	336	1860	√	0,9538	
060218_C1atascosubidapasillo-22.18.39-22.19.48_vs	571	-	351	-	√	0,0896	
060303_C1atascosubidapasillo-12.26.38-22.50.00_vs	104	2359	1617	-	√	0,3290	Slow motion
060304_C2atascofinalpasillo-22.57.06-22.58.11_vs	370	1446	78	-	√	0,9727	
060305_C1atascoenpasillo-21.08.49-21.09.46_vs	100	-	-	-	x		Slow motion
060305_C2atascoenpasillo-21.08.49-21.09.45_vs	1200	-	-	-	x		The event occurs in the other side of the escalator
060308_C2caidaseñores-14.32.14-14.33.37_vs	220	1277	308	-	√	0,9167	No normal situation videos available
060309_C2caidavarios-13.04.45-13.05.27_vs	160	-	340	-	√	0,8655	No normal situation videos available
060309_C2enganchedecordon-23.13.15-23.13.45_vs	249	707	285	-	√	0,9214	
060326_C1caidaseoras-17.35.50-17.38.44_vs	1420	-	1311	-	√	0,9186	
060416_C2taponytorta-16.00.37-16.02.04_vs	336	2075	381	-	√	0,7698	
060424_C2taponalasalida-00.11.24-00.12.45_vs	558	-	609	-	√	0,9619	
060430_C2taponycaida-16.07.58-16.08.52_vs	250	1335	309	-	√	0,9456	
060505_C1carroencaidalibre-07.29.27-07.32.16_vs	1080	3280	996	-	√	0,5703	

Table 2.5 Results of the experiments

2.7 Conclusion

At this stage, our intention is to keep the methods suitable for the real-time requirements of processing. The selected approach consists of extracting some portions of
videos coinciding with abnormal event detection, applied to collapsing detection.
It performs calculations on information such as density, direction and velocity of
motion, and decides whether the content is normal or abnormal. Our approach was
tested on various videos in real-world conditions, namely, recorded incidents in airport escalator exits. We developed a method for detecting abnormalities in crowd
flows, by relying on a framework based on three levels of features: low, intermediate and high. Low- and intermediate-level features are not specific to collapsing
detection. The framework is designed to support massive increases in the number of
features on these two levels. High-level features depend on the application domain.
We defined an entropy function suitable to detect collapsing situations in airport
escalators. Entropy is sensitive to crowd density, velocity and direction.

One of the our major contributions is formulating a method based on a framework
with three levels of features, which tackles the application challenge: the detection
of collapsing events in real time and in a crowded environment. The targeted application is the escalator exits of an airport. However, it can be adapted to collapsing
events for any other applications (e.g. doors, exits). One interesting contribution is
the construction of a framework composed of three levels of features, including two
levels of application-independent features. By application-independent features we
mean low (points of interest, blobs, optical flows) and intermediate level features
(motion ratio, direction map, etc.). They are certainly useful in tackling the challenge of collapsing event detection. However, they are not exclusively limited to
collapsing events. They may be applied to other abnormal events or challenges related to security, such as the detection of opposite flow events - as presented above
-, sudden motion variations (typical behaviour in panic situation) or other security challenges. Therefore, we do not claim that our method, based on the 3-level
features framework, is a generic method for detecting abnormal events in video
streams. Indeed, our objective is not to present any evidence to demonstrate that the
system is generic and application-independent. However, we consider our method
to be a contribution in the following way: although this falls outside of the scope
of the book, further experiments on the detection of other events are necessary to
assess the generic aspect of the framework. Again, we do not claim that the system
is generic or that it can be adapted to other abnormal events. For this, we have to
develop high-level features to detect several abnormal events. We simply assert that
our framework may be extended by intermediate-level features to deal with new
abnormal events (high-level features).

The experimental results are promising, and we certainly need much more data
to make a definitive decision on the soundness of our method. We underline the fact
that this data is confidential, and the owner is very reluctant to provide us with large
quantities of video surveillance data on escalator exits. However, the method applied
to available videos (60 hours) showed promising results on the basis of the statistical
evaluation (detection accuracy and recall) that we used. Video surveillance data used

in our work is confidential. That is why we had some difficulties in obtaining a large quantity of video data for our experiments. We need prior agreement from their customer (the data owner) to use their videos in our experiment.

Intermediate-level features are based on the results of low-level features (optical flows, points of interest, blobs). The quality of intermediate-level features, then, depends on the quality of low-level features. The noise in low-level features is limited as follows: firstly, the method analyzes the scene in certain regions defined by the heat map, so that only the regions characterized by motion are taken into account. Secondly, the scene is broken down into blocks of equal sizes, and the points of interests are extracted from each block. Generally, the blocks contain several persons. We thus avoid problems arising from situations in which intermediate-level features are sensitive to textures. If a person wears grid-like clothes, there will be many corner points detected from his/her region, but they will be limited to a few parts of the block. As a result, the motion directions in this frame are the same as the movement direction of the person, but limited to a small part of the block. Features like direction histogram will not be overly distorted in this case. Therefore, the size of the block is enough to limit the consequence of this situation. Thirdly, the blobs are only extracted when the motion ratio is low. In this case, the matching between blobs and related persons is optimized.

There are several parameters used for intermediate-level features (e.g. block size, direction histogram size, number of previous frames analyzed in the direction map, etc.). The settings of these parameters are held on two levels. The first one relates to application: collapsing events in a crowded environment. For example, the direction histogram size is the total number of considered angles: $[-\pi, +\pi]$. We may consider four angles: East, North, West and South. They can be extended to North-East, North-West, South-East and South-West. In the direction map, only four directions were considered - East, North, West and South. It is enough to show the direction map of the motions in the escalator exits. Another application (e.g. Mall traffic) will consider the suitable number of directions (8 as a minimum). The number of previous frames analyzed in the direction map turns around a few seconds, noted empirically. The range of peak intervals is generally low; we believe that we should have at least three peaks to be significant for collapsing detection. The second level of settings relates to video streams: block size $N \times M$ depends on the video stream and, more precisely, on the distance between the camera and the observed scene. Any learning process will be carried out on these two levels. In short, the settings of these parameters depend on two levels of context - application and video streams - and are set empirically.

If the method is based on a framework composed of three levels of features, the high-level feature - called entropy - is the most visible part. It is calculated on the basis of the following intermediate-level features: motion ratio, direction variance, motion magnitude variance, peak cardinality in the direction histogram and difference of the direction map behavior. These features have one dimension and are normalized between 0 and one. Each feature distinguishes one aspect of the collapsing event. They generally increase individually when there is disorder in the motions, such as a collapsing event. Therefore, the product of these features results in entropy. We showed empirically that collapsing events are distinguished by entropy.

Chapter 3
Flow Estimation

Abstract The aim of this chapter is to describe a new people counting technique based on spatio-temporal optical flow analysis. Using a single vertical overhead or oblique-mounted camera, our technique counts the number of people crossing a virtual line via an online blob detector and a linear classifier. In addition to the counting information, this technique identifies the speed of the observed blobs: fast, slow and stationary. It also identifies the nature of the blob: one person, two persons and group of persons. The suggested technique was validated by several realistic experiments. We showed the real-time performance and the high counting accuracy of this technique in indoor and outdoor realistic dataset.

3.1 Introduction

Automated people counting is a major issue. Indeed, in order for supply to meet demand, as well as to enhance resource management and ensure security by limiting the number of entries at given place, it is necessary to accurately quantify the number of people entering or leaving. In other words, it is necessary to constantly measure people flows at different spots of a place so as to meet a certain number of requirements. These requirements varies depending on the application: people counting in public places, transportation networks and event places, as well as pedestrian counting for road traffic management.

There are various reasons to count people within stores, one of the most important being the estimation of the conversion rate, that is, the percentage of customers completing a purchase. This rate is the main performance indicator for a store since - as opposed to traditional methods which only take the sales data into account - it allows for a real interpretation of the evolution of the turnover. For instance, if sales are declining, checking the evolution of the conversion rate permits to determine whether there is a decrease in the number of customers or in the number customers completing a purchase. In this particular case, the managers may change their strategies by performing a commercial campaign in order to attract more custumers, or by adapting the prices to encourage them to purchase more.

Considering that the needs in terms of employees are directly linked to the number of customers, getting precise counting information is essential in the optimization process of staff deployment. In a lot of places such as factories, it is crucial to know how many persons are inside a building at a given time. Indeed, if an accident occurs, requiring for the building to be evacuated, everyone can be taken into account. As a result, this type of application obviously requires a very precise counting system.

As far as transportation operators are concerned, the implementation of automated counting systems for passenger flows has to meet a certain number of requirements:

- Measuring the distribution of traffic in order to optimize the transportation offer.
- Determining the characteristics related to people traveling without tickets: estimating the efficiency of the fighting means depends on the evaluation of fare-dodging.
- Distributing the receipts between the various operators of a same transportation network.
- Supporting commercial studies or traffic forecasts to meet the requirements.

To meet this objective, many approaches exist and can be compared in terms of cost, intrusiveness, result relevance or type of sensors (e.g., infrared, thermal or weight sensors, cameras, etc.). Computer vision-based approaches are the most appropriate for this application because they use cameras as capturing devices. In fact, surveillance cameras deliver a richer signal than other sensors. However, sophisticated approaches are necessary to get relevant counting results from captured videos. For example, the previous counting methods designed for a particular camera configuration failed when a change occurred in parameter settings such as camera height and view point.

This chapter presents a view-invariant methodology to count the number of persons crossing a virtual line. It is organized as follows: Section 3.2 briefly describes the state-of-the-art of person-counting methods. Then, section 3.3 details the approach consisting of two main stages: *blob detection* and *count estimation*. In Section 3.4, we present the experiments and the obtained results. We conclude and describe future work in Section 3.5.

3.2 Related Works

Counting-people approaches have been explored in many different ways. We present in Table 3.1 a comparison between counting approaches relying on sensors other than camera.

In the following section, we will focus on approaches that resort to cameras and can be divided into the following classes:

Technology	Forces	Weaknesses
Passive Heat	- Does not count rigid objects or anything that is not at the temperature of a human body. - Non-intrusive.	- Affected by rapid changes of temperature or light. - Blind in hot environments. - Affected by immobile persons.
Active Infrared	- Oblivious to rapid changes of temperature or light. - Oblivious to immobile persons or passengers. - Mass installation allows to cover large inputs. - Non-intrusive.	- Does not count children. - Affected by immobile persons.
Passive Infrared	- Adjustable sensitivity increasing precision. - Mass installation allows to cover large inputs. - Non-intrusive.	- Affected by background changes. - Affected by crowds.
Ultrasound Prensence Detector	- Low cost. - Non-intrusive	- Nondirectional. - May induce wrong counting from detrimental stimulus.
Light Rays	- Low cost. - Non-intrusive.	- Limited detection zone. - Dead angles may allow someone to pass without being detected. - Requires a non-obstructed destection zone
Hybrid Technologies Contact Carpet	- Each technology compensates for the weaknesses of the other ones. - Non-intrusive	- May produce overcounting when a person is detected twice by two technologies. - Often damaged by weather conditions and daily utilization. - High installation and customization cost. - Low reliability.

Table 3.1 Comparison between counting approaches that do not rely on camera.

3.2.1 Methods based on Motion Detection and Analysis

These methods follow a succession of two stages. The first one involves the detection of moving regions in the scene corresponding mostly to individuals. The second one uses the detection result to rebuild the trajectories of moving objects over time.

The trajectory analysis enables us to identify and count the people crossing a virtual line or a predefined area [82], [153], [149].

3.2.1.1 Approach Proposed by Xu and al. [149]

This approach proposes a rapid counting method using a scene model, a human model and a ground model by taking into account the constraints on the models.

The scene model is defined using homogeneous coordinates and satisfies the following equation:

$$sm = PM = K[R|t]M \tag{3.1}$$

Where M is a world point defined by the following coordinates $[XYZ1]^T$ and m its point on the image plane with coordinates $[uv1]^T$. P is a 3×4 projection matrix. s is an unknown scale factor. The projection matrix P is decomposed as the matrix K of the intrinsic parameter system and (R,t) that denote the orientation and the position of the camera with respect to the world coordinate system. The parameters can be computed either by using the approach described in [154] or by using coarse camera parameters provided by the camera manufacturer.

The human and ground models are perspective models based on the assumption that the camera is approximately vertically-mounted as described in Figure 3.1. This figure represents the human head as a sphere, and the body as cylinder. The different parameters and coordinates use optimized triangle geometry.

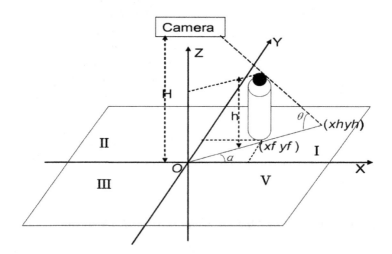

Fig. 3.1 Human model using an overhead camera

Resorting to a block background subtraction method and a hole-filling operation, the blobs of moving persons are extracted as illustrated in Figure 3.2. Then, a coarse segmentation is applied to detect single persons based on the number of pixels in a blob. Next, a fine segmentation is applied to detect multi-persons using the Niblack binarization method. Figure 3.3 shows the coarse and fine segmentation steps.

The detected persons are tracked between consecutive frames. The tracking algorithm consists of a detection-matching method with current frame groups O_c and previous frame groups O_p defined as:

$$O_c = O_t \bigcup O_i \bigcup O_e \bigcup O_l \qquad O_p = O_t \bigcup O_m \bigcup O_l. \qquad (3.2)$$

where O_t are the objects in the tracked area, O_i are the objects in the connected area, O_l are the objects leaving the area, O_m and O_e are respectively the missed and error objects.

The matching between objects is performed by combining a nearest object matching function with a character matching function.

This system whose process gray level images is fast, obtains good results and can manage up to 15 pedestrians at the same frame. However, it requires manual parameter computation for each camera configuration and has restrictive assumptions on the camera position and the head color.

3.2.1.2 Approach Proposed by Zhang and Chen [153]

This approach is designed for counting people from video sequences captured by a monocular camera located with an angle less than $45°$ towards the ground. This results to the variation of human height in an image along the depth direction (or the Z axis). Figure 3.4 illustrates the approach diagram, which can be divided into three main modules: motion detection, multiple human segmentation and group tracking.

The first module, motion detection, consists of estimating the foreground pixels. First a single Gaussian model [144] is used in order to detect moving pixels. Then, the shadows are removed by applying the algorithm described in [96]. The authors propose to use normalized RGB to cope with illumination change. Normalized chromaticity is defined by:

$$r = R/(R+G+B) \qquad (3.3)$$

and

$$g = G/(R+G+B) \qquad (3.4)$$

The second module is human segmentation. Its role is to distinguish the persons from the foreground. The considered assumption is that most of the time, the human head is visible. Hence, the authors can improve and optimize the segmentation method described in [156]. It consists of detecting the heads which are defined as local peak points in the foreground image as illustrated in figure 3.5. False detections are avoided by using a vertical projection silhouette. If the projection value of a candidate's head top is larger than a given threshold, it is considered as a real head top.

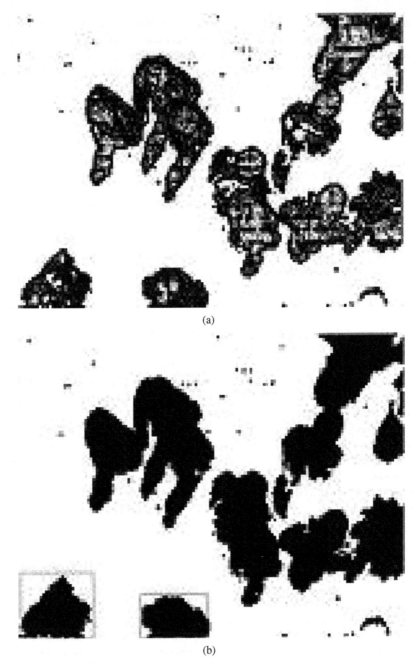

(a)

(b)

Fig. 3.2 Blob detection. (a) Background subtraction. (b) Hole filling.

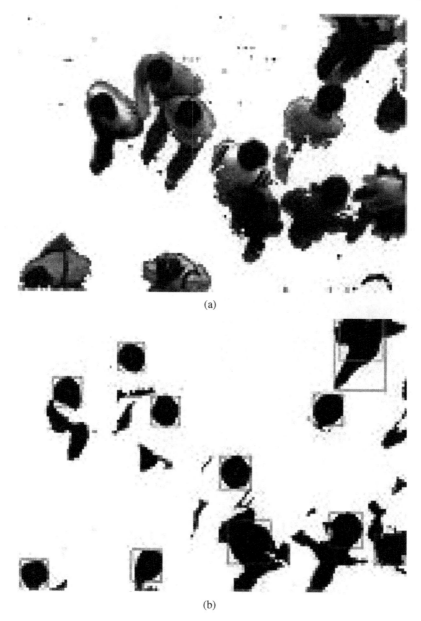

(a)

(b)

Fig. 3.3 Segmentation results in a frame. (a) Detetcted blobs. (b) Segmentation results.

The threshold is related to human height in an image and it is not easy to fix. Since the camera is placed at an angle less than $45°$ towards the ground, his image height is larger when close to the camera. Therefore, this problem is solved by setting the

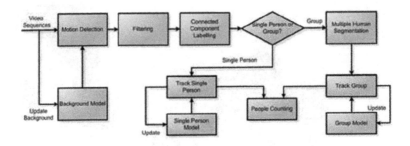

Fig. 3.4 People couting diagramproposed by [153]

smallest and largest height in an image. This is done using linear interpolation that
returns the image height at any position in a scene.

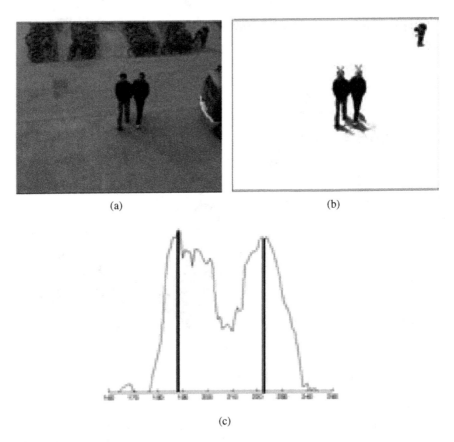

(a)   (b)

(c)

Fig. 3.5 Multiple human segmentation. a) original image. b) foreground. c) boundary analysis in
the region

The last module is the group tracking for people counting. Human segmentation provides the number of persons in a group. However, when partial or complete occlusion occurs, defining the number of people by segmentation is incorrect. Therefore, group tracking records the history of the number of persons in the group. In this approach, assume that complete occlusions do not exist. Hence, human segmentation can lead to a correct number of people in the group, except a few frames (for example, in ten frames, three frames are missegmented because of occlusion). Then, confidence coefficients are introduced to improve the tracking. The tracking module is able to manage the merging, splitting and overlapping of groups. Figure 3.6 shows group segmentation and splitting over time.

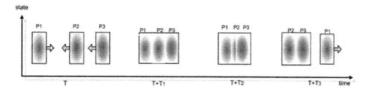

Fig. 3.6 Group creation and splitting

The approach has been validated on the PETS'2002 dataset and has obtained less than five percent errors. The experiments show the fast processing of the method. However, this approach assumes a static background since a single Gaussian is used. In addition, it is also sensitive to sudden illumination changes. Finally, the assumption on the camera is very restrictive and the interpolation between image position and real depth needs to be defined for each scene.

3.2.2 Methods Based on Contour Analysis

These methods consist of extracting objects of interest which correspond to contours with a particular shape and organization. These objects are then used for the counting. For example, a head can be assumed to be a region of interest, corresponding to a contour with a circular shape [19], [38], [152].

3.2.2.1 Approach Proposed by Bozzoli and al. [19]

This approach counts people in crowded environments. It uses a single commercial low-cost camera vertically mounted on the ceiling. Figure 3.7 illustrates the main steps of the approach. It estimates firstly the optical flow between each two successive frames. Next, motion detection by gradient images detects the foreground and is insensitive to illumination changes. Connected edge segments are used to correct optical flow errors and annihilate human artifacts.

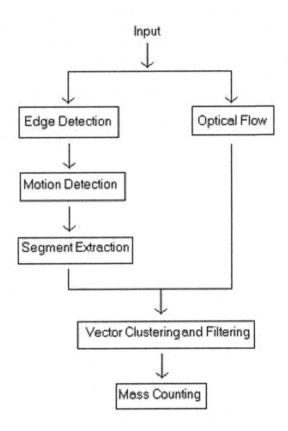

Fig. 3.7 Flow chart of Bozzoli and al. [19] approach

While popular motion detection approaches are based on recursive background modeling, one of the most used recursive techniques for background adaptation is the running average [25], in which the intensity value of the background model at time t with respect to pixel (x,y), $B_t(x,y)$ is updated using:

$$B_t(x,y) = \alpha B_{t-1}(x,y) + (1-\alpha)I_t(x,y) \tag{3.5}$$

where $I_t(x,y)$ is the intensity of pixel (x,y) at instant t, and parameter $\alpha \in [0,1]$ regulates the adaptation speed. The mixture of the Gaussian approach improves the previous method since it involves the multi-modality of the pixel color. Nevertheless, the running average is computationally much faster and provides a more accurate foreground detection in dynamic scenes. However, the running average fails with sudden lighting condition changes like those occuring when the doors of a bus or of a station are opened and closed as shown in Figure 3.8.

Fig. 3.8 Reaction of typical background subtraction methods after sudden lighting change

This approach proposes to use gradients in order to overcome these problems. The Gradient image-based motion detection step is a combination of a running average-like background model applied to the edge images and a background subtraction of the current edge image from the background model. Figure 3.9 shows the static and the moving edges of an image. Before detailing the related equations, we define E_t the (binarized) edge image of frame t, obtained when using the standard Canny algorithm [23] (Figure 3.9(a)),with $E_t(x,y) \in [0,1]$, then the background model is updated using:

$$B_t(x,y) = \alpha B_{t-1}(x,y) + (1-\alpha)E_t(x,y) \qquad (3.6)$$

The foreground pixels F_t are selected as follows:

$$F_t(x,y) = \begin{cases} 0, if |E_t(x,y) - B_t(x,y)| \leq 2\sigma_t(x,y) \\ 1, otherwise \end{cases} \qquad (3.7)$$

where:

$$\sigma_t(x,y) = \alpha\sigma_{t-1}(x,y) + (1-\alpha)|E_t(x,y) - B_t(x,y)| \qquad (3.8)$$

Figure 3.9(b) shows the foreground edges F_t and its coresponding edge map shown in Figure 3.9(a).

(a)

(b)

Fig. 3.9 Static and moving edges of an image. (a) Static edge map. (b) Moving edges.

After obtaining moving edge images, connected line segments are grouped and considered as belonging to the same objects (by object we mean individuals, animals, moving trolleys or any animated entity). This choice is motivated by the results of the Gestalt experiments [67]. However, segments composed of straight lines are considered artifacts and are annihilated. Figure 3.10 illustrates the results of this step where only the retained segments are visible.

Formally, a line segment s is as an ordered sequence of 8-connected edge pixels representing an image line and interrupted at line junctions: $s = (p_1, ..., p_n)$, where: $F_t(p_i) = 1 (1 \leq i \leq n)$, p_j and p_{j+1} are adjacent $(1 \leq i \leq n)$ and p_i and p_n are the only elements in s having either zero or more than two adjacent edge pixels. Short line segments are deleted.

In the first place, line segments are used to remove potential human artifacts such as doors which disturb the counting process and which can usually be distinguished from human beings because they are composed of straight lines. For this reason, the segments which can be approximated with a straight line are annihilated. To do so, if $s = (p_1, ..., p_n)$ this can be simple checked:

$$Dist(p_i, R) \leq \lambda, 1 \leq i \leq n \tag{3.9}$$

R being the straight line passing through p_i and p_n, $Dist(p, R)$ the distance between point p and line R, and λ a fixed threshold value $(\lambda = 1)$.

Let $S_t = \{s_1, ..., s_m\}$ be the set of remaining line segments in frame t. These remaining segments are considered for the next step.

Next, optical flow vectors are computed between each two successive frames using the algorithm proposed by [85]. However, some errors appear and are corrected by clustering and filtering via the connected segments.

This is first performed via the introduction of context information by associating each movement vector in I_t with the closest segment s of S_t, and then by using this vector/segment association to filter out incoherent vectors. In fact, since the segments, by construction, represent connected lines in the image interrupted at line junctions, it is very unlikely that the same segment belongs to more than one moving object. Thus, when two or more people touch each other or touch another object (e.g., a door), the lines possibly connecting them are usually interrupted by a T junction. Thus, movement vectors which are not coherent with the other movement vectors of the same segment can be removed. $PV(S_t)$ is the set of all the movement vectors remaining after this phase.

Finally, the counting is performed by computing the number of pixels inside a predefined counting region which has the shape of a closed and connected polygon.

$TL_1, TL_2, etc.$ are the target lines drawn by a human operator in the system installation phase, and assume that the GUI system forces the user to draw a unique, closed, connected polygon P as the target *exit-enter* area. Then, to compute the amount of *people mass* passing through P, the pixels belonging to the closed polygon are defined only once by the system as a boolean matrix B where $B(p) = true \Leftrightarrow p \in P$. Afterwards, the people mass passing at time t in both directions (respectively, Min_t and $Mout_t$) is defined as:

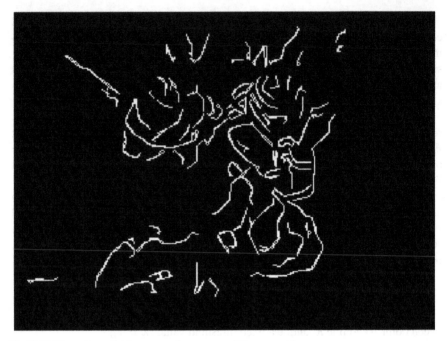

Fig. 3.10 Line segments after computing connected line segments

$$Min_t = \#\{v = (f,l) : v \in PV(S_t) \wedge B(f) \wedge \neg B(l)\}$$
$$Mout_t = \#\{v = (f,l) : v \in PV(S_t) \wedge \neg B(f) \wedge B(l)\}$$
(3.10)

where $\#A$ is the cardinality of the set A.

It is then necessary to associate these values with the number of people actually transiting during all the video sequence. This is done using a *VPR* which is the average number of movement vectors corresponding to a single person. Its value is set by the human operator who indicates the system when the first ten persons have passed.

Although this system is efficient, it requires manual initialization of certain parameters such as *VPR*. The background subtraction method requires more tests and validation.

3.2.3 Template-Based Methods

These methods attempt to find the regions in the processed images that match predefined templates [120], [39]. These templates (models) are either characteristic models or appearance models. The disadvantage is that these approaches usually require a large learning database and/or cause a problem of model generalization.

3.2.3.1 Approach Proposed by Sidla and al. [120]

This approach is able to detect, track and count people in crowded situations. Figure 3.11 shows the result of the tracking module for a subway scenario. The blue line is called *virtual gateway* used to perform the counting. People are detected by applying a region of interest (ROI) filter built from a background model and Ω-like shape detector. The people's trajectories are maintained using a Kalman filter. The counting is performed using a predefined virtual gateway and simple trajectory-based heuristics.

Fig. 3.11 People detection and tracking for a subway platform scenario

ROI consists of all foreground pixels on which all further computations take place and are computed as follows. For every new video frame, a simple foreground mask is created which decides whether the underlying pixel is part of a pedestrian or not. The algorithm uses a histogram for each pixel on a reduced set of 64 grey values. The histogram is accumulated for every new frame and its highest grey value frequency is selected as the background. At regular intervals, the pixel-wise histograms are divided by a constant factor to reduce the absolute numeric values of the histogram entries. New dominant grey values can significantly facilitate the control gain of the histogram in case of illumination changes or new stable background objects. In addition to the background computation, 1,200 salient image points are constantly tracked frame to frame using the Kanade Lucas Tomasi (KLT) algorithm [85]. These points provide motion information for the whole image and they are used in two

ways: (i) clustering the points which move in the same direction with similar speed
are added to the ROI, and (ii) projecting the location of detected pedestrian shapes
into future video frames.

Pedestrian detection is divided into two parts. A fast contour searching method
detects the candidates for ω-like shapes within the ROI based on the principles
described by Zhao and Nevatia [155]. A pedestrian contour is represented as a model
which consists of 23 points. A local angle of a model point is defined as the direction
of the vertex on its right side when the contour is crossed in the clockwise direction.
The detection process starts by applying a Canny edge detector to the input color
image, masked by the ROI. A wide hull of gradient values exponentially decaying
eight pixel is spread on the edges. The result is a gradient image map O. An angle
map R is computed directly from O by calculating the local pixel's wise orientations
on it. Then, for every possible location (xs, ys) of the reference shape in the input
image, a cost function S is computed. Figure 3.12 illustrates the main steps of the
detection algorithm.

The results are further analyzed by fitting active shape models (ASM) in order to
retain only the candidates that match well. The ASM implementation is described
by [26].

Fig. 3.12 Zhao shape matching algorithm. The images are displayed in a clockwise order from
top-left: input image, computed cost function, final head candidates, edge orientation image and
expanded gradient image map O.

The authors summarize the tracking algorithm as follows:

1. Create Zhao candidates within the foreground mask.
2. Remove false positives with ASM.
3. Merge very similar shapes computed in Steps 1, 2.
4. Compute co-occurrence features of remaining shapes.
5. For each ASM shape.

   a. Project the shape into the next frame using either KLT motion information or a Kalman filter.

   b. In an area around the prediction obtained from Step 5a, find the most similar co-occurrence feature vector for shape. Unmatching shapes keep their predicted locations.

   c. Merge the results of Step 5b with the candidates from Step 3 to avoid shapes tracked redundantly.

   d. ASM iteration at the location from step 5c with the initial shape model from the previous frame, as the new shape is only allowed to differ slightly from the previous frame.

6. Link the new shape locations to their respective trajectories.
7. Head candidates from Step 3 start new trajectories.
8. Remove the trajectories which have been predicted more than 5 times with the Kalman filter.

For counting purposes, a heuristics is used for a virtual gate G by defining the following conditions for a video frame n:

1. A point p of trajectory T is in virtual gate G.
2. No other point of T has been in G for frames i, for all $i < n$.
3. No other trajectory points have been in G for k frames.

If all of the three conditions hold, the pedestrian counter associated to G is incremented. The third condition avoids multiple counts for an individual which has been associated with multiple trajectories. k depends on the frame rate and is usually set to 5 for out data. The counting direction is based on the position of the starting point of T relative to G.

Figure 3.13 shows the detection and tracking results after some frames. Although this approach is very efficient, it is not effective and requires for the parameters to be introduced manually.

3.2.4 Stereovision-Based methods

They use in-depth information provided by several cameras to detect and count people [15], [130], [150]. Indeed, the three-dimensional representation of the scene allows to detect concealed objects, turning them into robust methods to manage complex situations. However, the use of multiple cameras is not favored since a calibration stage and as a lot of computing time are necessary.

Fig. 3.13 Tracking and counting results

3.2.4.1 Approach Proposed by Terada and al. [130]

This approach counts people passing through a gate by using a stereo camera. The stereo camera is hung from the ceiling of the gate as illustrated in Figure 3.14, while Figure 3.15 shows some obtained frames. The optical axis of the camera is set up so that the passing people could be observed from overhead only. Because of this system arrangement, the image data of the passing people does not overlap with itself on the obtained images when the gate is crowded. In addition, the height of each passing person is measured by applying the triangulation-based algorithm.

Figure 3.16 shows a diagram of the system. The first step in the process of counting passing people is to obtain the series of input images each time the camera captures two frames corresponding to the the left eye and the right eye. Next, on the left eye image, only pixels on the measurement line are picked up. This measurement line is set on the floor at a right angle with the moving directions of the passing people. Then, these pixels are arranged along the time axis and transformed into the space-time image. In a similar manner, from a right eye image, only pixels on a measurement line are picked up and transformed into a space-time image. By analyzing both space-time images for both eye, the height of each passing person is detected.

Next, on the right eye image, the pixels on another measurement line are picked up and the space-time images are generated. Then the moving direction of each passing person is detected by applying the template matching process.

This is performed by firstly applying the triangulation. The three dimensional location of point P, which is projected at (z_L, y_L) and (z_R, y_R) on the image planes, is calculated by following three equations:

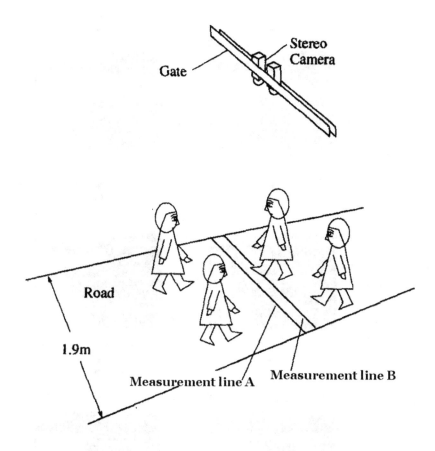

Fig. 3.14 Counting system where the stereo camera is on the top of the gate

$$x = \frac{x_L l}{x_L - x_R}$$
$$y = \frac{y_L l}{x_L - x_R}$$
$$z = \frac{fl}{x_L - x_R}$$
(3.11)

To calculate the three-dimensional locations, it is necessary to detect the positions of (x_L, y_L) and (x_R, y_R) accurately. These points are detected by applying template matching, as shown in Figure 3.17. In general, the problems arising from template matching are related to long processing times because of the many pairs of stereo images, owing to the fact that the template matching process is carried out at each of the many stereo images. Therefore, the space-time image on the measurement line is used. Spatio-temporal images of people passing through the left measurement line and the right measurement line are constructed. The template matching method is carried out between the spacetime image generated by left eye images,

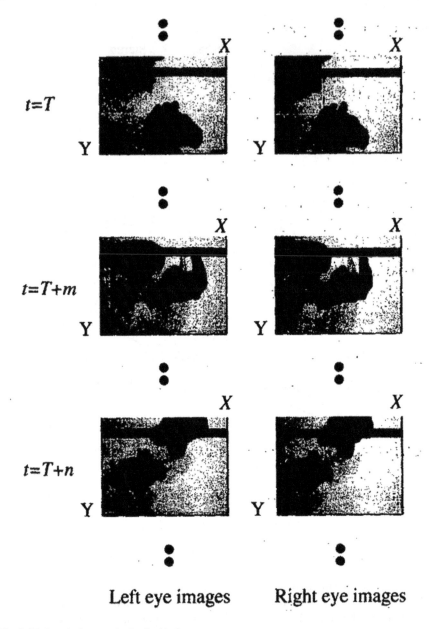

Fig. 3.15 Sample frames obtained with the stereo camera

and the space-time image generated by right eye images, in order to obtain three-dimensional shape data.

Finally, the incoming and outgoing persons can be measured by counting the people data on the space-time image with the information of each moving direction

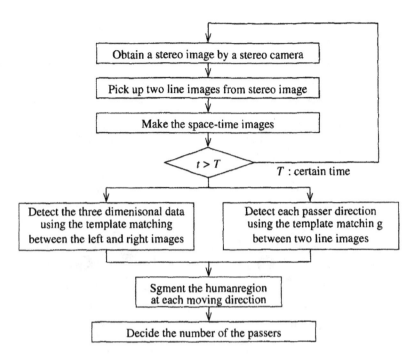

Fig. 3.16 Diagram for counting passing people

and each height. The direction cannot be estimated using one spatio-temporal image only from one measurement line. Hence, an outside measurement line is added, as illustrated in Figure 3.18. The process of the template matching is carried out between the spatio-temporal images constructed from instant t to instant $t + n$. The positions of the interest points between spatio-temporal images inform the direction of that point. Then the counting is performed by analyzing the passing speed of the person. If the person walks slowly, the area of the data is thick along the time axis, and if fast, the data area is thin. Therefore,the counting of passing people is carried out, allowing the passing speed which is decided by template matching.

3.2.5 *Spatio-Temporal Methods*

involve selecting virtual lines in the acquired images and building a space-time map on each line by stacking the lines in time. Statistical models are then used to derive the number of persons crossing the line, and to analyze the discrepancies between the space-time maps, in order to determine the direction [1], [12], [151]. These methods have the advantage of being fast and simple to implement. However, works based on these methods have not provided concrete solutions to teh problem of

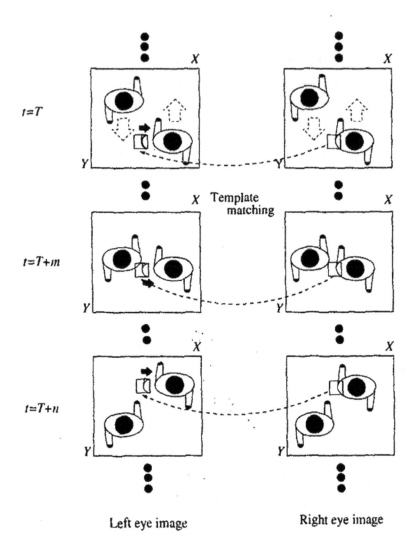

Fig. 3.17 Template matching method

interpreting a significant number of cases. For example, when a person stops on the virtual line, a huge blob will be generated and misinterpreted as being a group of people.

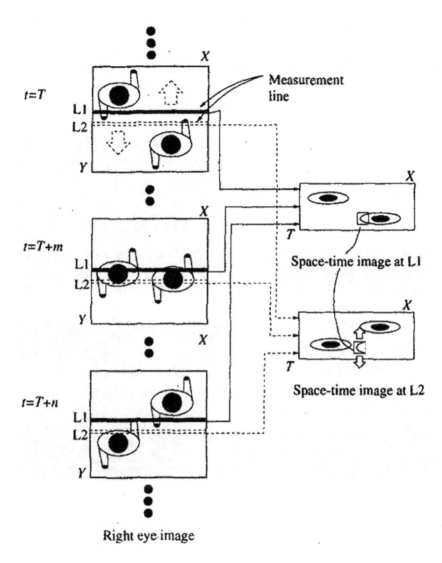

Fig. 3.18 Template matching between two spatio-temporal images in order to estimate the direction

3.2.5.1 Approach Proposed by Albiol and al. [1]

This approach focuses on counting the persons that enter or leave a train, regardless of the crowdedness and illumination changes using a delayed real-time algorithm. This means that the algorithm processes the data until it is fully acquired. For this reason, the approach is composed of three states. Firstly, the initial state is when the doors are closed and the camera is covered. In this state the system is idle and waits for the doors to open.

Secondly, there is the acquisition state, when the doors are opened and people enter or leave the train as shown in Figure 3.19. In this state, different stacks of people crossing the virtual line on the door are constructed: they are the white, gradient, and black stacks respectively, as illustrated in Figure 3.20.

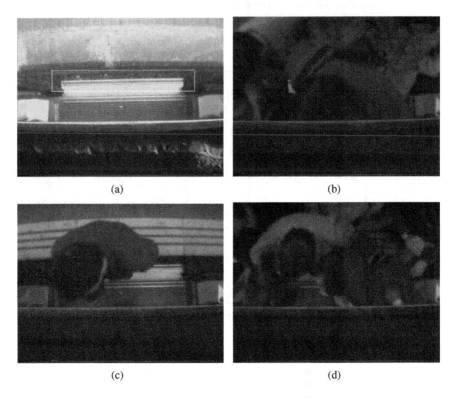

(a)   (b)

(c)   (d)

Fig. 3.19 Sample shots at the acuisition state. (a) No persons, (b) Isolated person, (c) and (d) Crowded situations

Lastly is the counting state which is triggered when the doors close. It processes the constructed stacks in order to retrieve the number of crossing people. The first operation consists of detecting the presence (or foreground pixels) by applying a background subtraction. Next, the persons are isolated by segmenting the foreground image by taking into account the following situations.

1. Isolated person, passing quickly. This can be determined from the short vertical size of the print.
2. Two People passing side by side.

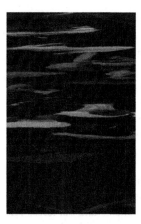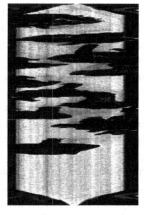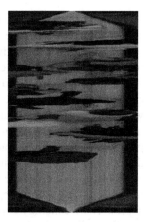

Fig. 3.20 Example of stacks. From left to right: black, gradient, and white stacks.

3. A single person passing directly below the camera. The camera height is low so wide angle lenses are used. In this case, the print can be as wide as for two people if the person passes directly below the camera.
4. Two People passing immediately one after the other, leaving no frame (row of the stack) of gap between them.
5. One person. Print with branches. This is a very common situation. Legs, arms, bags, etc. appear normally as narrow branches.
6. One person passing slowly. Irregular print. One person passing slowly takes many frames to completely cross the door. This causes a large vertical print size. The shape of the real prints has irregularities as those shown.

The directions of the people are estimated by applying an optical flow to the people's centroids. The speed obtained from the optical flow equation gives one value per stack pixel. For each label of the segmentation, the weighted average speed value is computed.

3.2.6 Commercial Applications

3.2.6.1 Cognimatics

Cognimatics is a cognitive vision company whose objective is to provide efficient and innovative tools in business segments such as mobile communication and intelligent surveillance. Founded in 2003, Cognimatics host a group of researchers from the Mathematical Sciences Center, Lund University, Sweden. 50 percent of the members are PhD researchers who are internationally recognized for their expertise in the cognitive vision field.

Working in close partnership with the university and researchers, Cognimatics successfully develops state-of-the-art products and solutions, as shown by the number of units shipped worldwide: more than 1,000 for intelligent surveillance, and over 1,000,000 for mobile communication.

Cognimatics uses the camera as a sensor. Cognitive vision algorithms (close to computer-aided vision) are then applied so the computer can analyze videos in the way most similar to human analysis. The video records a large amount of information, although extraction may sometimes be difficult to perform. The technology proposed by Cognimatics adresses this challenge and proposes solutions for object detection and people tracking.

Object detection: this technology is based on the learning techniques for detecting objects with various appearances, shapes and sizes, and from different viewing angles. The technology applies to the detection of heads, chests and vehicles. The FaceWarp^{TM} solution is now available for lots of mobile phones and digital cameras.

People tracking: Cognimatics offers solutions for people tracking in real time, allowing for various applications such as the counting of people crossing a doorway, or the number of persons within a defined zone.

3.2.6.2 Infodev

Infodev is specialized in electronic people counting, for all types of locations: in retail sales environments (shopping malls, stores), casinos, train and bus stations, airports and vehicles (buses, light rail, trains, tramways). They design and manufacture automated people counting systems that are reliable and easy to install, and provide customer service.

People counting sensors work horizontally and vertically on doors and wide transiting zones. They can be integrated into both wire and wireless networks. The company has thousands of sensors and data acquisition tools installed in hundreds of places worldwide.

Infodev is a distributor and integrator which design electronics, optics, boxes and software. They manufacture and install all of their products, and offer other related products to the transportation business: preemption of traffic light signals and automated localization of vehicles.

Infodev mainly focuses on two business sectors: transportation and buildings.

Transportation

Counting the passengers in vehicles represents a particular challenge for Infodev: the products proposed work in a lot of environments under various lighting, vibration and movement conditions, as well as in various types of vehicles.

Counting people within vehicles also involves counting vehicles when they are moving. Infodev has developed a refined system with data transfer and GPS-tracking applicatin tools. This automated counting system shows the number of people in a vehicle, as well as the place and time.

Additional systems enable us to control traffic light signals, provide information for preventive maintenance, analyze the speed of vehicles and provide a complete representation of the territory, in compliance with the hours and provision of the carrier's stocks. An application for online connections allows us to make data available, avoiding long software installations on the users' workstations.

Buildings

With regard to people counting within buildings, Infodev works for various clients such as casinos, museums, stores, airports, and shopping malls. Products are non-intrusive and customized for each installation location.

People counting systems developed by Infodev can also be integrated to existing Ethernet networks using serial networks and wireless communication.

Online software presents analyses and stocking reports. Complexes belonging to networks may also centralize their data within a single database to perform comparisons.

3.2.6.3 Eurecam Sarl

At the heart of a high technology business center in Palaiseau, France, Eurocam was founded in 2005 and focuses on its expertise in electronics. Aiming at diversifying the people counting market by offering innovative products, the company offers tailored services in electronic engineering.

To collect data, Eurecam offers a range of solutions which are designed for applications such as temporary audience analysis, store customer counting to measure the transformation ratio, and passenger flow measurement in public buildings.

Eurecam's proposed solution is based on intelligent cameras whose on-board processing systems can count the number of people crossing a virtual counting line.

This unique and innovative system has been specially designed to count people in public places in order to study occupancy. It is supported by an exclusive video processing system and benefits from the latest technological developments, turning it into a reliable and cost-effective product.

3.2.7 Contribution

Our approach belongs to the category of spatio-temporal approaches. It has the particularity of avoiding the misdetection of persons stopping on the virtual line. This is done by considering only the pixels on the virtual line that have a non-zero optical flow vector. Optical flow vectors also provide the orientation of the blobs efficiently.

In addition, the proposed approach uses blob features (motion velocity, orientation, position and dimensions) in order to improve the prediction regarding the number of persons inside a blob. Our approach is able to detect in real time the blobs crossing the virtual line as opposed to previous approaches proposed by [1] and [12] which require waiting for the space-time map to be completely built before starting the blob detection.

3.3 Approach Steps

In this study, our goal is to design an approach to count the people crossing a virtual line which can be adapted to different scene configurations. In fact, the majority of video surveillance systems use oblique cameras to get an overview of the scene, as well as details such as faces and clothes. However, to avoid occlusions and respect the anonymity of people, the cameras are installed vertically above the persons' heads. Figure 3.21 shows two configurations that are suitable for our approach.

Our approach can be divided into two major blocks as depicted in Figure 3.22. The block called *blob detection* includes four steps which are used to extract the blobs of the persons crossing the virtual line. The second block, *count estimation*, includes the two last steps. Each blob is associated with a direction as well as a number representing the people count. This number can vary from 0 in the case of non-countable objects (car, truck), to n people for a group .

3.3.1 Blob Detection

First, a line of interest called a *virtual line* is defined on the input video, and the changes that occur in that line over time are analyzed. The pixels on the virtual line form a slice. The virtual line accumulation step stacks the slices over consecutive frames. We then obtain a colored spatio-temporal map (or a spatio-temporal map) representing the variations of the three RGB color components over time on the virtual line. This step is illustrated in Figure 3.24 which is the spatio-temporal map obtained when a person crosses the virtual line in red.

The next step involves computing the optical flow vectors of the pixels on the virtual line over the next frame of the input video. For this, we resort to the Lucas and Kanade [85] method. It is a differential method which estimates the relative motion of pixels between two consecutive frames using the following illumination constraint, where $I(x,y,t)$ is the illumination of the pixel at position x,y at the frame t.

$$I(x,y,t) = I(x+\sigma x, y+\sigma y, t+\sigma t) \qquad (3.12)$$

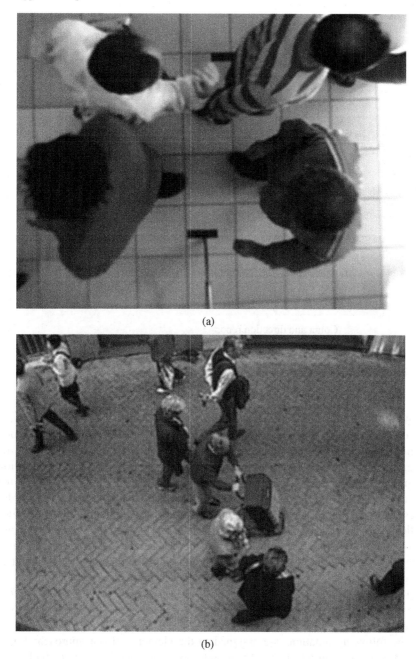

(a)

(b)

Fig. 3.21 Examples of suitable configurations: (a) Vertical overhead camera, (b) Oblique camera.

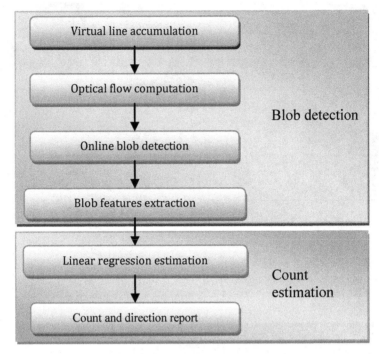

Fig. 3.22 Architecture of the proposed system.

As an input, this optical flow algorithm requires an initial frame as well as the set of pixels of that frame to estimate the motion. Then, by providing a second frame, a set of vectors is estimated. The origin of these vectors coincide with the origins of the previously specified pixels, and their end corresponds to the position of these pixels at the second frame. In our approach, the pixels used as inputs for the optical flow algorithm always correspond to the pixels on the virtual line, in order to estimate the motion on the virtual line over time. The orientations and velocities of the resulting vectors are stacked over time so as to build spatial maps of velocity and orientation. Figure 3.23 shows the spatio-temporal map of orientations obtained when two persons cross the virtual line. All this information represents the input of the next step.

The online blob detection step detects the blobs and updates their respective features (size, coordinates, orientation and velocity) in time until the blobs have completely crossed the virtual line.

The following notations are assigned to the elements of our approach: L is a virtual line with length l. $p_{i,t}$ is a pixel in the spatio-temporal map map_L built from line L at frame t with $i = \overline{0..l-1}$. $OF(p_{i,t})$ is the optical flow vector whose origin is pixel $p_{i,t}$. Each optical flow vector is defined by its velocity and orientation:

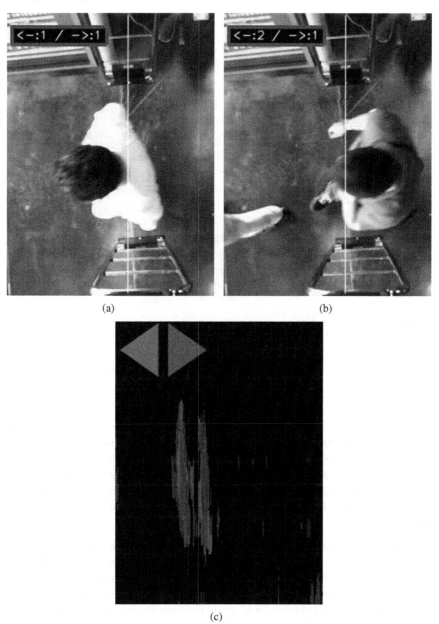

(a)   (b)

(c)

Fig. 3.23 Representation of the spatio-temporal map of orientations. (a) A first person crosses the virtual line. (b) A second person crosses the virtual line after 20 frames. (c) Spatio-temporal map of orientations obtained after 80 frames.

$$OF(p_{i,t}) = \begin{pmatrix} velocity(p_{i,t}) \\ orientation(p_{i,t}) \end{pmatrix} \qquad (3.13)$$

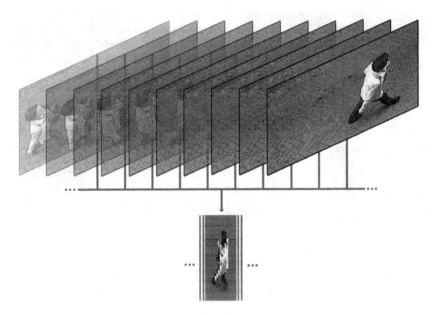

Fig. 3.24 Virtual line accumulation over time.

The set of blobs is noted S. A blob with identifier Id is defined by the following vector:

$$B(Id) = (P, N, \alpha, \beta, w, h, Hist, O, V) \tag{3.14}$$

Where P is the set of pixels in the blob, and N is their number. w and h are respectively the width and height of the smallest rectangle containing all the pixels of the blob. α and β are the coordinates of the rectangles top left corner. $Hist$ is the color histogram of the blob. O is the orientation of the blob, and V is its velocity.

The online blobs detection and the updating of their parameters are done in the following way:

- Each new point having non-zero velocity is considered to be a new blob.
- The spatially related points having similar velocity and an orientation difference of less than $\pi/2$ are grouped in the same blob according to the law of common fate; flow vectors with similar orientation should be considered a unit.
- The temporally related points having similar velocity and an orientation difference of less than $\pi/2$ are grouped in the same blob.
- Hypothesis to manage temporal blobs merging are applied and blobs features are updated.
- Blob's velocity, orientation and histograms are updated as follows:

$$B(Id).P = B(Id).P \cup \{p_{i,t}\} \tag{3.15}$$

$$B(Id).N = B(Id).N + 1 \tag{3.16}$$

$$B(Id).V = \frac{\sum_{p \in B(id).P} velocity(p)}{B(Id).N} \tag{3.17}$$

$$B(Id).O = arctan\left(\frac{\sum_{p \in B(id).P} \sin(orientation(p))}{\sum_{p \in B(id).P} \cos(orientation(p))}\right) \tag{3.18}$$

$$B(Id).Hist = B(Id).Hist + Hist(p_{i,t}) \tag{3.19}$$

The blobs are saved by the algorithm so as to be updated in the next iterations. However, if a blob has not been updated after two iterations, as we consider one neighboring pixel, then this blob is considered to be an entity that has completed the crossing of the virtual line. In this case, the blob features extraction step extracts the features described in formula 3.14 from such blobs. These features are the input of the next block.

3.3.2 Count Estimation

We propose to use a linear regression model to estimate the number of people inside a blob. The linear regression model is given by the following formula:

$$y = H(x) = \sum_{i=0}^{n} \theta_i x_i = \theta^T x \tag{3.20}$$

Where y is the estimation of the number of people inside a blob. $H(x)$ is called *hypothesis*, which is a linear regression model in this work. n represents the number of blob features as described in formula 3.14. x is a vector of n dimensions containing the blob features. Figure 3.25 shows a linear regression model that predicts the values on the y axis given a value on the x axis. The n dimensional coefficient vector θ is estimated by supervised learning. For each different configuration, a coefficient vector θ is trained offline using a ground truth annotated manually by an expert. It consists of a set of blob features with respective people counting. The advantage of using a distinct coefficient vector for each configuration is the possibility for the approach to support new configurations easily. A regression analysis is performed on the training data in order to fit a linear model. The pace regression method is used since it has two main advantages over other standard linear modeling methods: it evaluates the effect of each variable and includes this information in the evaluation of the regression model. Further details on pace regression can be found in [140]. The learning step results in a coefficient vector θ for a given configuration. This vector is a plugged in formula 3.20 which returns a count estimation y of a blob given its feature vector x obtained from the previous block.

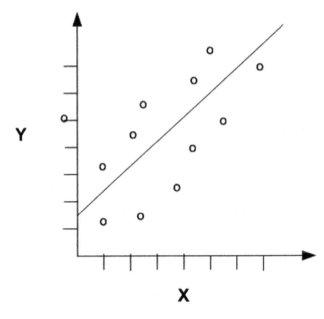

Fig. 3.25 A linear regression that estimates the value of Y given X.

The blob direction (*left* or *right*) for the oblique camera, and *enter* or *leave* for the overhead camera) depends on the orientation of the virtual line. In this work, we assume that the virtual line is vertical (with an orientation of $\pi/2$ or $-\pi/2$). However, the following method can be generalized to any orientation of the virtual line. The direction of the blob is obtained by comparing its orientation with values 0 and π. In order to retrieve the direction of blob i, the following set must be computed:

$$\arg \max_{\theta \in \{0,\pi\}} \left(\cos(B(i).O - \theta) \right) \tag{3.21}$$

If the set is equal to $\{0\}$, then the blob goes in the right direction. If the set is equal to $\{\pi\}$, then the blob goes in the left direction. For specific cases whose set is equal to $\{0, \pi\}$, the orientation of the blob is equal to $\pi/2$ or $-\pi/2$. In other words, the blob is moving along the virtual line. Therefore, the blob is not considered in the final counting result since it does not cross the virtual line.

When using the rounded estimation and the direction of the blob, the total count for the corresponding direction is incremented. Figure 3.26 illustrates the key steps described earlier. Figure 3.26(a) shows a sample frame where the scene is captured using a vertically-mounted overhead camera. The virtual line is vertical and represented in white. Figure 3.26(b) shows the spatio-temporal map of orientations, the red color representing the pixels that move to the right and the blue color representing the pixels that move to the left. Figure 3.26(c) shows the results of the online blob detection step. Each blob has a different color, and blobs having a count estimation equal to 0 are annihilated. Figure 3.26(d) shows a spatio-temporal map

where the blobs are bounded and their orientations are specified with an arrow at
their bottom.

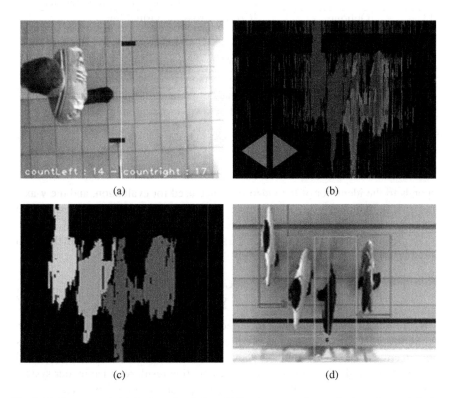

Fig. 3.26 Key steps (a) Original overhead view, (b) Spatio-temporal map of orientations, (c) Online
blob detection (d) Representation of the spatio-temporal map with the orientation of the blobs.

3.4 Experiments and Results

The performance of our system was evaluated on two datasets. The first one corresponds to the videos recorded with an overhead-mounted camera. The total duration
of the sequences is two hours with a frame rate of 30 frames/second. The frame dimensions are 240×320 pixels. The second dataset is obtained using an oblique
camera. The total duration of the sequences is 30 minutes with a frame rate of 25
frames/second. The frame resolution is 640×240 pixels. The number of passing
people in the whole datasets exceeds 1000. Table 3.2 describes the sequences targeted by our experiments.

Figure 3.27 shows the counting results with the oblique camera, and Figure 3.28
shows those corresponding to the overhead camera. For both figures, the x-axis cor-

Sequences	Camera configuration	Description
1-2	Oblique	People cross the virtual line individually
3	Oblique	Crowds cross the virtual line
4-5	Oblique	Sequences with vehicles
6	Oblique	Rainy weather and people with umbrellas
7-10	Overhead	Some persons have trolleys and strollers
11	Overhead	Scenarios, from the basic case of a single file to crowds crossing in both directions

Table 3.2 Dataset description.

responds to the identifier of the video sequence used for evaluation, and the y-axis represents the number of people counted. The ground truth is represented in blue and the counting system results in red.

The global accuracy of the system for a set of sequences Q and a certain direction d is given by the following equation:

$$A_{Q,d} = 1 - \frac{|\sum_{i \in Q} GT_{i,d} - \sum_{i \in Q} CS_{i,d}|}{\sum_{i \in Q} GT_{i,d}} \tag{3.22}$$

Where d is a value representing the direction. $d = 0$ represents the right direction or the entries. $d = 1$ represents the left direction or *leave* situation. $d = 2$ represents both directions. The following table shows the obtained results. $GT_{i,d}$ is the ground truth of video i with direction d. $CS_{i,d}$ is the counting result returned by our system for video i with direction d. Table 3.3 shows the accuracy of our approach.

Sequences	Direction	Accuracy
1-6	(0) Right	94,03%
1-6	(1) Left	98,73%
1-6	(2) Both	96,71%
7-11	(0) Enter	97,33%
7-11	(1) Leave	85,19%
7-11	(2) Both	93,39%

Table 3.3 Global accuracy of the counting system.

The results show that the system is very robust with a global accuracy of $96,71\%$ for the first dataset and $93,39\%$ for the second one. The significant difference between $A_{7-11,0} = 97,33\%$ and $A_{7-11,1} = 85,19\%$ is explained by the fact that the customers present in our dataset have generally filled their bags when leaving the store, which generates a bigger blob. However, our linear model could not adapt suf-

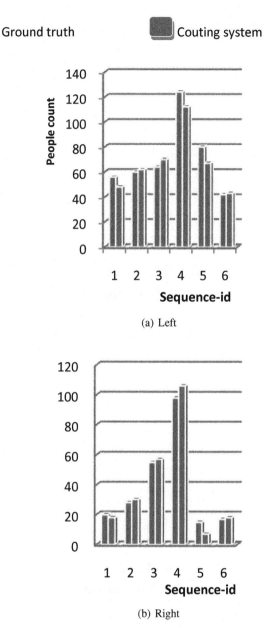

(a) Left

(b) Right

Fig. 3.27 Counting results with the oblique camera.

ficiently to this situation. We also remark that the system tends to overcount people, which leads us to consider a correction factor so as to improve the global accuracy. However, false positives are more tolerated than false negatives in most applica-

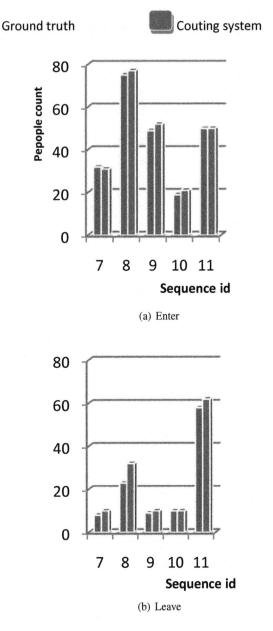

Fig. 3.28 Counting results with the overhead camera.

tions. In the security field, for instance, it is preferable to report false detections than real missing detections. The same applies to the marketing domain in which the estimation of the number of customers is of particular interest.

Approach	Architecture	Execution frame-rate
[103]	SGI Indy Workstation	14 fps
[149]	P4 2.66G CPU and 1GB ram	8 fps
[19]	Pentium M 1.4G CPU	17 fps
Our	Intel Celeron 1.86G and 1GB ram	45 fps

Table 3.4 Execution speed comparison data.

Table 3.4 shows a comparison of the execution speed between different approaches. We note that our approach is faster than [149] which is theoretically explained using the complexity. Our approach has $O(2L+B)$ complexity where $2L$ is the number of pixels of the virtual line for the current and previous frames, and B is the number of non-complete blobs in the current frame. However, the approach described in [149] has complexity of $O(N)$ with N the number of pixels of an image. Hence, we have $2L + B < N$. This is demonstrated as follows:

- Since we consider one neighboring pixel for blob construction, the number of non-complete blobs is always less than $L/2$.

$$B < L/2 \qquad (3.23)$$

- As stated earlier, a virtual line can be a column or a line of an image and $N = W * H$, where W and H are respectively the width and height of the image. If we assume that W and H are higher than 3, then the following is always true.

$$3L <= N \qquad (3.24)$$

- Using 3.23 and 3.24 we can infer that:

$$2L + B < N \qquad (3.25)$$

This approach is attractive as it involves a low computational cost and a decent accuracy with respect to more complex systems. However, using a single virtual line is a weakness in certain situations (e.g., someone turning around or wandering, total occlusion when passing the virtual line, etc.).

3.5 Conclusion

In this chapter, we have presented a new approach to counting the people crossing a virtual line. The main stages of our methodology are the detection of blobs crossing the virtual line, and the estimation of the number of persons in the blobs detected . The proposed approach has three particularities: (i) avoiding the misdetection of static people on the virtual line; (ii) online blob detection algorithm; (iii) fast adaptability to different camera configurations using a linear regression model for each configuration. We have tested our approach on a large dataset that contains realistic videos in both indoor and outdoor environments. The global accuracy of the system is 96,71% for the videos with an oblique camera, and 93,39% for the videos with a vertical overhead camera. We believe that our results are very promising. Therefore, we intend to improve our approach by modeling the blobs in the spatio-temporal map. In addition, we will consider combining the results obtained from multiple virtual lines.

Chapter 4
Estimation of Visual Gaze

Abstract Studying gaze direction is useful for the completion of visual tasks. It is well known that the visual gaze is a product of two contributing factors: head pose and eye location. In general, the visual gaze can be determined from head pose when standing at some distance from the visual target [76]. Starting from this general statement, the present chapter will first detail the human visual system and the steps that are necessary to generate the gaze. An account of the completed works on gaze tracking will then be presented along with selected techniques according to the different types of systems (intrusive or non-intrusive). A few applications will be introduced afterwards to illustrate how data collected from the gaze are processed. Finally, we will examine how the head pose contributes to visual gaze estimation, and also how to estimate the gaze based on eye position only.

4.1 Human Vision System

Eyesight is one of the five human senses. It enables people to see and describe objects which are part of their surrounding world. This facility of perception results from a complex process that is carried out by two organs: the eye and the brain. The eye receives light signals forming about one million dots on the retina [21]. These dots contain information on the quantity of light and colors coming from the environment. Then, they form a 2D image which is taken along neuronal paths in the form of signals towards the cortical analysis device. Finally, the brain interprets the different signals received to describe what is surrounding us in order to give meaning to the perceived image. Figure 4.1 shows broadly a horizontal cut of the human eye in which translucent tissues (cornea and crystalline lens) allow for the formation of a clear image on the retina.

Various physiological studies show that the gaze can be inferred from the combination of head pose and eye position. Langton and al. [76] establish that an observer who is interpreting the gaze is influenced by the head pose of the person observed.

C. Djeraba et al., *Multi-Modal User Interactions in Controlled Environments,*
DOI 10.1007/978-1-4419-0316-7_4, © Springer Science+Business Media, LLC 2010

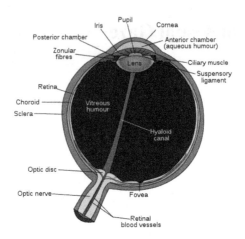

Fig. 4.1 Schematic horizontal cut of the human eye

A striking example of this effect is illustrated by an image from the 19th century presented in Figure 4.2 [142].

Fig. 4.2 Wollaston illusion: although the eyes are strictly identical in both views, the way the gaze direction is perceived, is influenced by head direction.

In this figure, two views of the same person's face are presented following a similar configuration of the eyes, but with two different head orientations. The analysis of these views shows the influence exerted by head orientation on how the viewing direction is perceived. Indeed, if we remove the lower part of the face (keeping the eyes only), the gaze direction is perceived as if the head had a frontal configuration.

4.2 History of Gaze Tracking

Visual gaze estimation is an old practice dating from long before the emergence of the first computers and the development of information technologies. Indeed, the first works in this field go back to the late 19th century. Javal [60] used a mirror system to observe the visual movement of a person reading. However, these works were technically limited as the subjects were invited to transcribe by themselves the points they were looking at. Therefore, the validity of the results is highly disputable.

In 1901, Dodge and Cline [33] designed a system using the reflection of a vertical light beam on the cornea to record the horizontal movements of the eye through a photographic plate positioned behind a horizontal slot. Although it required the subject to be totally motionless, this method would become a landmark reference in the history of gaze tracking, as it was used up to the 1970's with some improvements. In 1905, Judd and al. [62] used a photographic capture system (a forunner to the camera) to record eye movement. In 1921, Gilliland [40] performed the first 2D recording of ocular movements, breaking down the corneal reflection of a light beam into horizontal and vertical components. This method enabled Buswelle [22] in 1935 to get the first ocular tracks (i.e. the gaze position overlaying the visual support which created it at a particular instant). During this period, most of the studies were carried out within the framework of physiology and cognitive psychology in order to study the ocular movements while reading [56], or the eye movements produced by pilots when landing [36].

With the arrival of the television, the first system allowing an ocular track to be overlaid onto a visual mobile scene was created in 1958 [88]. In the early 1970's, the research started to focus on collected data analysis, to the detriment of new acquisition system design. Then, new theories linking eye movements to cognitive processes began to appear [97]. In the late 1970's, IT developed the calculation capacities necessary to process data in real time. Eye movement was then used as a new way to interact with computers [6]. The 1980's saw the first studies regarding the analysis of gaze information. Indeed, technological progress enabled oculometric systems and computers to work in tandem to track cognitive processes in real time, as well as to observe user behavior when confronted with a visual scene. The first applications were, in particular, aimed at disabled people [57].

The 1990's were influenced by the emergence of new application domains focusing on Computer-Assisted Cooperative Work, and virtual and augmented realities [137]. In the 2000's, within the digital era, devices are able to record precise ocular movements. They are used in cognitive ergonomics to validate interfaces and in marketing to measure the impact when presenting products. Currently, the tendency is to use simple webcams to estimate the gaze direction [72].

4.3 Gaze Tracking Techniques

Since the first studies in the 1900's, the methods for measuring ocular movements have advanced hugely. Various measuring tools do exist, each having particular features adapted to its utilization. Generally, the most discriminating constraint concerns the capturing tool not disturbing the user when moving. Indeed, any system requiring that the users carry some equipment which generates visual or sound disturbance is considered intrusive. The following sections will present techniques for estimating the visual gaze according to the type of system used: intrusive or nonintrusive.

4.3.1 Intrusive Systems

Intrusive systems usually give precise results. Some are presented below:

4.3.1.1 Electro-Oculography

This technique is based on a particular eye property: the presence of an electrostatic field whose characteristics are linked to the position of the cornea with regard to the retina. Thus, when positioning a certain number of electrodes around the eye (see Figure 4.3) and recording the potential differences, it is possible to measure eye orientation with a precision of $0.5°$ to $1°$ on a wide domain of orientations ($\pm$ $70°$) [45]. However, this technique does not permit projecting the position of the gaze point (or fixation point) onto a visual support. Movement is measured with regard to the head position, and not to any outside marker. This method is tedious to implement, as it involves applying electrodes to the face, and is relatively painful for the subject. It is still widespread in the medical field, as it enables ophtalmologic symptoms such as juvenile strabismus to be diagnosed.

4.3.1.2 Contact Lenses with Magnetic Coils

This technique was invented by Robinson [113] in 1963 and allows eyeball movements to be directed directly. It requires two specific contact lenses of large diameter to be applied onto the eyes of the subject. These special lenses contain a small receptacle forming a ring, in which a thin coil of electrical lead is inserted. Each lens is connected by a very thin lead to an instrument which measures the current in the coil, which is itself generated by the magnetic forces produced by the two big electric coils positioned perpendicularly to each other around the head of the subject. It is then possible to record the exact position of the lens after calibrating the system (the current depends on eye position with regard to the two larger coils). Although this measure may be the most precise, it is reserved for clinical use. The lens is ex-

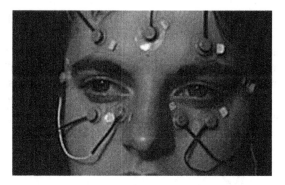

Fig. 4.3 Electro-oculography electrodes

tremely uncomfortable for the subject and applying it is still tricky (see Figure 4.4). In addition, it may cause some allergic reactions in the eye.

Fig. 4.4 Application of contact lenses with magnetic coils

4.3.1.3 Localization of the Limb

The limb is the frontier between the sclera and the iris. The luminosity difference between these two parts of the eye enables the limb to be detected and tracked easily. Using a simple luminosity-measuring tool made of diodes and infrared sensors placed on glasses, it is possible to create a cost-saving measuring tool. Marketed systems, having a precision of 0.1 degree (horizontal or vertical measure only), or of 0.5 degree for horizontal and 1° for vertical (when measured simultaneously), are available. However, the eyelids occasionally conceal the upper and lower parts of the limb, leading to instable measures [42]. Moreover, the subject must stay still since this technique does not allow the head position to be measured.

4.3.1.4 Analysis of Eye Images

This technique consists of analyzing the eye image captured by a camera in order to localize one of its components (e.g. the pupil or the iris). Tracking a component enables the eye movements to be measured with regard to the head of the subject, who stands still with regard to the camera. For this, it is possible to fix the camera to the head or use a semi-reflecting mirror. The most commonly used technique requires an infrared light to be projected onto the eye. This results in four reflections of the light source: the first two are from the cornea, and the last two are from the cristalline lens. These light reflections are called *Purkinje images* after their discoverer, and are shown in Figure 4.5.

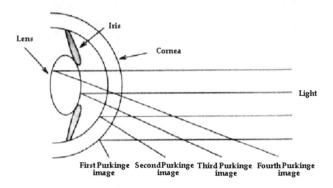

Fig. 4.5 A light ray reflects in four different ways on the eye. These reflections are named *Purkinje images* after the researcher who discovered them in 1832.

These reflections are processed in two ways:

1. **Cornea reflection/pupil**: This technique consists of positioning, under a computer screen and towards the eyes of the subject, a camera equiped with an infrared diode at the center of its lens. Figure 4.6 shows the configuration of such system. With this diode, an infrared ray (invisible) lights up the eye of the user. This ray produces various distinct phenomena which enables gaze direction to be determined.

   The infrared ray is reflected by the cornea, causing a small, relatively intense and easily detectable reflection called the *First Purkinje* or *Glint* image. This ray also crosses the various components of the eyeball and is reflected by the retina. The pupil turns red, which is an aspect that will be familiar to all photography enthusiasts. This phenomenon enables the pupil to be distinguished from the surrounding iris due to the heightened contrast between these two elements.

   A program specializing in image processing identifies the positions of the pupil and iris, and calculates the relative position of one with regard to the other (see Figure 4.7). Indeed, a change in the gaze direction involves minor viariation in the position of the corneal reflection. This is an excellent reference marker for calculating the pupil position. In the opposite, the gaze direction follows the pupil and determines the localization of the point observed. Therefore, calculating the relative position between these two elements at every instant allows the successive positions of the eye to be determined. It is then necessary to combine each

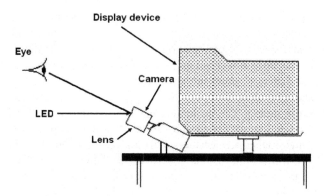

Fig. 4.6 Scheme of an *Eye tracking* system

captured position (corneal position/pupil) with a point of the targeted scene or screen observed by the subject. For this, a short calibration phase is required.

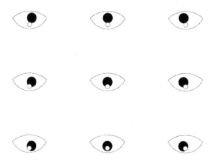

Fig. 4.7 Calculating the gaze position by detecting the pupil and the first Purkinje image

The calibration phase enables the relative pupil position and corneal reflection to be linked to on-screen coordinates. To do this, the user focuses on a point displayed at different positions in order to divide the screen into squares. Once the correspondence between the pupil positions and the relevant on-screen coordinates is known, it is necessary to extrapolate the coordinates depending on the intermediary pupil positions. The position of the fovea (central part of the macula, which is the retinal zone where the details can be seen more precisely) on screen covers about 1 to 1.5 degrees. Therefore, the spatial position of the observed zone cannot be considered a point but a surface, so that the evaluation is limited by the size of that surface. Recent studies show the possibility of avoiding this calibration phase by using a second camera as well as an image of the other eye via the calculation of the crossover point of the eyes.

This technique is probably the most commonly used in commercial eye tracking systems, which are also called *oculometers* [93]. However, these systems tolerate very gentle movements of the head only. Indeed, the subject must stay almost motionless. The margin of error is two to five degrees depending on models, and is bigger than with other intrusive methods. This error decreases with the improvement of cameras.

2. **Dual Purkinje image**: This technique is based on the same principle as that for corneal reflection, except that in this method the position of the first and fourth Purkinje images are detected. This allows the rotation of the eye to be evaluated, regardless of horizontal or vertical translations. Using a mobile mirror dedicated to these translations enables an image of the eye to be kept centered with regard to the camera. However, the fourth Purkinje image is hard to track, in particular when the pupil is too small. It is important, then, to control the light conditions when performing the measures. The systems based on this technique are more precise than those based on the corneal reflection/pupil (1 degree margin of error), but they require a specific equipment which is more expensive.

4.3.2 Non-Intrusive Systems

Non-intrusive systems can be listed according to the number of cameras. Systems including a single camera are *monocular* while those including two cameras are *binocular*. A recent survey on works in this field is available in [46].

4.4 Applications

Information produced by somebody's gaze is important in a lot of fields. It enables us to analyze the behavior and develop an enhanced understanding of the target scene. Some applications using or analyzing information produced by somebody's gaze will be presented below, by focusing on those that were used to validate our results.

4.4.1 Interaction During Meetings

Gaze plays a significant role in human interaction. Interaction has been studied in social psychology for many decades [95] as the gaze performs various tasks (e.g. establishing relationships through mutual gaze, expression of intimacy [8], and the practice of social control [75]). People tend to look at objects which grab their interest immediately. Vertegaal and al. [136] show that, in a conversation between four persons, when the gaze of the person speaking meets the eyes of another, there is an

80-percent chance that the person observed is the target of the conversation. In addition, when the person listening looks into the eyes of another, there is a 77-percent chance that the person observed is the speaker. Therefore, information provided by the gaze of other people is used to determine when they have to speak or if the message delivered is directed to them. For instance, the gaze is used to find the appropriate moment to ask for an order of speaking [102], while at the end of a sentence, it may be understood as a request for an answer [61]. This theme is deemed so important that CLEAR evaluation campaigns were dedicated to the subject in 2006 and 2007 [143].

4.4.2 Driver Monitoring

Advanced systems to assist driving can save a lot of lives by helping drivers to make quick security decisions when manoeuvering. Every year, traffic accidents cause the death of about 1.2 million people throughout the world. 80 percent of these accidents are due to driver inattention [5]. To counter the effects of inattention, assistance systems have been designed to provide drivers with a warning when a dangerous situation is imminent, as well as to help them to react appropriately. Nevertheless, the type and position of the sensors (see Figure 4.8) for optimizing performance are still under examination. They are often combined with a particular application [34]. The sensors must detect what is happening within the three main components of a driving system: the environment, car and driver. Recent research indicates that sensors should be built into the vehicle, following a holistic approach [131], so as to observe driver behavior.

4.4.3 Virtual Reality

Most virtual reality approaches, based on the gaze as a means of navigation and interaction, use Head Mounted Displays. Knowing the gaze direction may help in the optimization of systems in real time or off-line, allowing for a significant visual improvement in 3D renderings. Hillaire and al. [50] show how online gaze tracking can be used to enhance visual effects (e.g. depth of the visual field, movements of the camera, etc.). The experiment performed by Tanriverdi and Jacob [129] demonstrates that the selection of objects for on-screen visualization is achieved faster when using a gaze-oriented approach than when just pointing a finger. The gaze is quite widely used in virtual cooperative environments to perform precise tasks (e.g. solving a puzzle [124] as illustrated in Figure 4.9). An evaluation of binocular systems dedicated to eye tracking in relation to gaze interaction in virtual reality environments is available in [107].

Fig. 4.8 (Image on top) Approximate distribution of zones where the gaze is fixed for labeling. (Bottom images) Examples corresponding to the gaze fixing nine labeled zones.

Fig. 4.9 Resolving a puzzle in virtual reality

4.4.4 Human Computer Interaction

Using the gaze to interact with a computer is currently a popular topic. Gaze estimation has become a very interesting tool, in particular for improving the interaction between disabled people and computers. Hirotaka and al. [7] examine the learning process of eight students using their gaze to capture 110 sentences, while Kammerer and al. [63] evaluate the efficiency of two approaches in making a selection from menus using the gaze.

4.4.5 Extraction of Saliency Maps in Images

In graphic and design applications and in indexing and information searching, it is essential to determine where the person is looking within the scene, whether for image cropping [115], image and video compression into multiple resolutions [141], detail detection for non-realistic image rendering [32] (see Figure 4.10), or seam carving.

Fig. 4.10 Non-realistic image rendering

An eye tracking system is often integrated into the process of recording the fixations of a user sitting in front of a computer equipped with an *eye tracker*. The collected data is then transmitted to the selected method using a learning model to create a saliency map [83, 66]. However, because an eye tracking system is not always available, it is necessary to have a means of predicting where the users will look without resorting to such a system. There are alternative models that have been used to measure the visibility of a region, or the probability of a region catching the attention of an observer [9, 20, 51, 58]. These models are inspired by biology and bottom-up calculation methods. For this, various low-level features (e.g. color intensity, orientation, texture, etc.) are extracted from the image at different scales. A saliency map is built for each feature. These maps are then standardized and combined in a linear or non-linear manner into a single general saliency map representing the importance of each pixel. For instance, Ehinger and al. [35] propose a model based on the combination of three factors (saliency map combined with low-level features, target features and scene context) to predict the zones that people are looking at when searching for pedestrians.

4.4.6 Store Marketing

Increasing competition encourages retail stores to get more and more interested in understanding their customers' behavior and buying-decision processes. Usually this kind of information can only be obtained through direct observation of the customers or, indirectly, through discussion groups or specialized experiments in a controlled environment. However, computer vision has the potential to answer these questions by analyzing videos of test-customers exploring a store. This type of application is more profitable than for loss-prevention. Getting a glimpse at customers' movements and behavior is of huge interest to marketing, special offer campaigns and data processing. It is particularly interesting to analyze the decision-making process and answer questions such as: what caught the attention of a customer? Which products went unnoticed? What does a customer look at before making a decision? Rather than tracking the path of customers as most surveillance camera installed in stores used to do, new technologies try to estimate the direction of customers' gaze. This application category was used to validate our different approaches.

Various approaches attempting to track customers within retail-sale environments have been proposed. Haritaoglu and al. [47] used stereoscopic cameras positioned overhead and pointing downwards to track the positions and actions of customers. Stereovision offers the advantage of easily dividing the customers from the shopping trolleys among the moving *blobs*, but requires the presence of dedicated stereo sensors rarely available in stores. Another approach used to count customers using stereovision is presented in [16]. Krahnstoever [68] uses a stereovision system to track the interaction between customers and products via the position of their heads and hands. This system also uses information obtained from RFID sensors inserted in the products to detect and track their movements. Mustafa and Sethi [100] resort to an approach based on moving edges to track the sellers entering or leaving the backshop. The attention of customers waiting in a queue with regard to the advertising billboards is examined in [48]. Liu and al.[81] examine what people are looking at in a store.

4.5 Contribution of Head Pose in Visual Gaze

In order to determine where a person is looking at, it is necessary to estimate the direction of his/her gaze and then to project it in this direction on the target scene. The gaze is often defined as the spatial direction of the eyes. It is, therefore, a combination between head and eye orientations. This means that it is necessary to estimate these two orientations in order to determine the gaze direction precisely.

Detecting the eyes cannot be achieved easily when someone is standing far from the camera, depending on the resolution. In this case, the only information regarding the gaze is provided by head orientation. This raises the following question: how is it possible to predict where a person is looking on the basis of head orientation only?

To answer this, a study on gaze analysis [125] was performed for four persons attending a meeting. Special equipment was used to measure head orientation and gaze direction. The goal of this study is to determine how head orientation contributes to gaze direction, as well as to calculate the precision with which it is possible for a person to look at someone else on the basis of head orientation only.

4.5.1 Database

The scenerio proposed for this study consists of placing four persons around a table. A data session of about ten minutes is collected for each participant. During each session, a participant wears a head-mounted device[1]. The system also resorts to a magnetic tracking subsystem to track the position and orientation of the head, as well as subsystem equiped with a head-mounted camera to record images of his/her eyes. The following data can be recorded by the software provided with this system at a frequency of 60 Hz with a precision lower than one degree: head position, head orientation, eye orientation, eyes blinking, and global gaze direction (viewing line). Figure 4.11 [125] shows an image captured during the experiment.

Fig. 4.11 Image of collected data

---

[1] made by ISCAN Inc (http://www.iscaninc.com)

4.5.2 Calculating the Contribution of Head Pose

Calculating the contribution of head orientation to head direction consists of analyzing its contribution with regard to the contribution of the eyes on the horizontal
axis. It was observed that, in 87 percent of the images, the direction of head orientation was similar to the eyes (right or left). For images having similar direction, the
contribution of head orientation to gaze direction is calculated. The horizontal component of the viewing line, los_x, is the sum of horizontal movements produced by
head orientation ho_x and eye orientation eo_x. The contribution percentage of head
orientation HC with regard to the global gaze direction is calculated as follows:

The results obtained during the four experimental sessions are presented in Table
4.1:

Subject	Nb Images	Blinking	Same Direction	Contribution of the Head
1	36003	25.4%	83.0%	62.0%
2	35994	22.6%	80.2%	53.0%
3	38071	19.2%	91.9%	63.9%
4	35991	19.5%	92.9%	96.7%
Average	-	21.7%	87.0%	68.9%

Table 4.1 Contribution of head orientation in the global gaze direction

Based on the results of this experiment, various interesting remarks can be made:

- Most of the time, the participants turn their heads and eyes in the same direction,
  and look at what interests them.
- Resorting to head orientation to change the gaze direction varies a lot depending on the participants (from 53 percent for Participant No. 2 to 96 percent for
  Participant No. 4, with an average of 68.9 percent), although it stays rather high
  (more than half of the global gaze direction).
- Winking occurs in around 20 percent of the total number of images. This information is important as it shows the limits of commercial equipment which
  estimates the global gaze direction from the eyes. Indeed, they do not work for
  about one fifth of the times (eye position unknown).

These observations allow us to conclude that head orientation is a determining
factor, and is sometimes sufficiently available, to estimate gaze direction.

4.5.3 Prediction of the Target

Gaze direction is used in Stiefelhagen's [126] experiment to calculate how often
a person observed by a participant is properly detected, based on head orientation

only. Figure 4.12 presents the horizontal component's histograms for the gaze direction of two participants. The three peaks appearing on the histograms correspond to the orientation used by a participant to look at the position where the three other ones are sitting. These peaks are automatically determined by using a K-means algorithm [89]. Each image is labeled based on the shortest distance between the line related to gaze direction, and the one related to the three targets (other three participants).

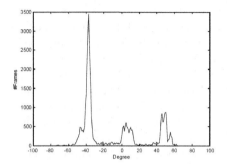 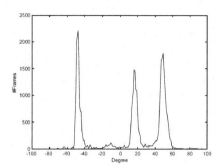

Fig. 4.12 Horizontal component's histograms for the gaze direction of two participants

A modeling approach with a mixture of Gaussians is used to estimate gaze direction based on head orientation only [127]. The results are compared with the labels obtained from the gaze direction data. Table 4.2 shows the precision obtained when resorting to head orientation only.

Sujet	Precision
1	85.7%
2	82.6%
3	93.2%
4	93.2%
Average	88.7%

Table 4.2 Detecting visual focus of attention based on the horizontal component of head orientation

This experiment shows that head orientation is a significant factor in estimating gaze direction. The precision reaches an average of 88.7 percent, encouraging the use of this information when the position and orientation of the eyes are unknown.

4.6 Estimating Gaze Direction Based on Eye Localization Only

Estimating the gaze direction based on the eyes only is usually performed when a person is in front of a computer screen, since head movements are limited. The proposed state-of-the-art methods tend to simplify the problem by assuming that the eye does not turn but that it just moves. This simplification comes from the hypothesis that the person maintains a frontal position with regard to the screen so as to eliminate the estimation of head orientation. The estimation of head orientation is then ignored as this calculation is too time-consuming. Information related to the position of the eyes and corners is then required [133]. The most commonly used method is the one suggested by Zhu and Yang [158]. The two of them use a method based on linear mapping. A calibration step, consisting of displaying a set of datapoints on a screen, is then necessary. These points shall be observed by the user. A 2D mapping is performed from a vector positioned between the eye corners and the iris center. The mapping is recorded for the known positions on-screen. This vector is then used to make an interpolation on the known on-screen points.

For instance, when taking two calibration points $P1$ and $P2$ from on-screen coordinates α et β, as well as the vector for the central point of the eye x and y, the following interpolation is used to get the on-screen coordinates of a new vector:

$$\alpha = \alpha_1 + \frac{x - x_1}{x_2 - x_1}(\alpha_2 - \alpha_1)$$

$$\beta = \beta_1 + \frac{y - y_1}{y_2 - y_1}(\beta_2 - \beta_1)$$

The advantages of this approach are that it is time-saving in terms of calculation and has an acceptable precision with regard to other systems that are more complex. Unfortunately, this method does not allow head movement. Every significant movement, whether horizontal or vertical, requires for the system to be recalibrated. However, if the distance between the screen and intrinsic parameters of the camera are known, it is possible to compensate for this problem by performing another mapping of the points used for calibration, depending on eye movement. Therefore, the precision of this system is only limited by the camera resolution. This results to a grid-effect on data. As for the precision, it is limited by the quality of the camera and its distance from the user. This type of system is used for specific applications which do not require a high level of precision (like changing an active window, or a particular action when the user is looking beyond the screen edges).

4.7 Head Pose Estimation

The ability to estimate head orientation is a huge challenge for computer vision systems. As opposed to face detection or person recognition using facial features, which have been the main research axes of the computer vision community, head

pose estimation is a recent active area. Detecting head position consists of localizing someone's head in an image, while *estimating* head position applies to head
orientation. When someone's eyes are not visible, detecting head position and estimating its orientation combined with pupil position analysis offers a more precise
estimation of gaze direction.

4.7.1 State of the Art

We will describe below how to estimate head orientation and what are the inherent
difficulties in the various existing approaches.

4.7.1.1 Definition

Estimating head orientation consists of determining, from an image, the angle values
depending on the three degrees of freedom defined in Figure 4.13 as follows:

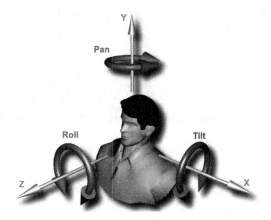

Fig. 4.13 Representation of the three degrees of freedom of the head

- **Tilt (Pitch)**: corresponds to head movement from top to bottom around X-axis
  (*yes* axis).
- **Pan (Yaw)**: corresponds to head movement from left to right around Y-axis (*no*
  axis).
- **Roll (Slant)**: corresponds to head movement from left shoulder to right shoulder
  around Z-axis (the axis which allows the subject to put an ear on his/her shoulder).

4.7.1.2 Human Capacity for Estimating Head Orientation

The psychophysical foundations of the human capacity for estimating head orientation are still largely unknown. We do not know if human beings have a natural ability to estimate the degrees of freedom of the head, or if they gain this knowledge through experience. However, some data do exist and allow the human capacity for performing this task to be measured. Indeed, Kersten and al. [65] use frontal and profile poses as key-poses, since the brain activates them unconsciously, while being unable do that with other poses. Figure 4.14 shows the image used by the authors. It represents a cylindrical facial projection for pose competitions, as all horizontal head orientations are present.

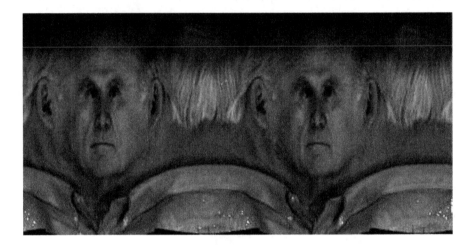

Fig. 4.14 Cynlindrical flattened projection of a human face

Gourier [44] performs an experiment which consists of asking a group of people to estimate head orientation in *Pointing'04 Head Pose Image Database* [43]. The experiment is performed on a group of 72 persons, including 36 men and 36 women between 15 and 80 years old. Everyone was asked to examine an image showing a face, and circle the related head orientation among various suggestions. The experiment follows a random order and was divided into two phases: *Pan* angle estimation and *Tilt* angle estimation. 65 images for pan and 45 images for tilt angles (i.e. five images per angle) from *Pointing'04 Head Pose Image Database* were presented in a random order for seven seconds per image. Figure 4.15 shows an example of the images presented during the experiment, where "+" and "-" indicate right and left orientations respectively, avoiding any possible confusion.

The subjects were divided randomly into two subgroups - *Trained* and *Untrained* - to evaluate the impact of training on their ability to estimate head orientation. Before starting the experiment, calibrated subjects can examine as long as they wanted

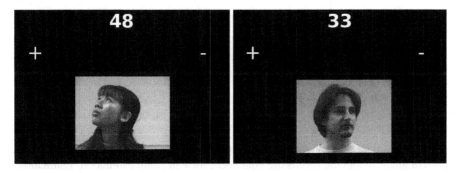

Fig. 4.15 Examples of test images presented during the experiment

image samples previously labeled according to their orientations before starting the experiment. However, non-calibrated subjects did not see any training image.

The experiment ends with the presentation of an image from Kersten works previously showed in Figure 4.14. The subjects are asked to circle the angles they saw on the image. The aim of such a question is to confirm that frontal and profile poses are actually key-poses for the human brain, since all Pan angles are visible on this image.

Three metrics were selected to measure the human ability to estimate head orientation. The theoretical position of Image k is marked $p(k)$, while the position estimated by the subject is marked $p^*(k)$. They are stated in degrees. The total number of images on each axis is marked by $p^*(k)$.

$$\text{Average Error} = \frac{1}{N} \sum_{k=1}^{N} \|p(k) - p^*(k)\|$$

$$\text{Maximal Error} = Max_k \|p(k) - p^*(k)\|$$

$$\text{Correct Classification} = \frac{Card\{\text{correct image classification}\}}{Card\{\text{Images}\}}$$

The results of the metrics applied to Pan and Tilt angles estimations are reported in Tables 4.3 and 4.4 respectively.

Measures	Mean Error	Maximal Error	Correct Classification
All subjects	11.85°	44.79°	41.58%
Trained Subjects	11.79°	42.50°	40.73%
Untrained Subjects	11.91°	47.08°	42.44%

Table 4.3 Results of Pan angle estimation.

Measures	Mean Error	Maximal Error	Correct Classification
All subjects	11.04°	45.10°	53.55%
Trained Subjects	9.45°	39.58°	59.14%
Untrained Subjects	12.63°	50.63°	47.96%

Table 4.4 Results of Tilt angle estimation.

Trained subjects are significanltly better than untrained subjects at estimating the Tilt angle, while the results are equivalent for Pan angle estimation. Estimating the Pan angle seems to be more natural than for Tilt. This results from the fact that people turn the head from left to right more often than from top to bottom when interacting socially. The frontal pose is the most recognized. This is confirmed when presenting the cylindrical image of Kersten face at the end of the experiment. Indeed, 81 percent of the subjects just saw the frontal and profile poses in that image.

These results show that frontal and profile poses are the most used by the human visual system as key-poses. It also shows that human beings are more likely to estimate horizontal orientation.

4.7.1.3 Problems Encountered when Estimating Head Poses

Estimating head orientation in an image is relatively complex due to the huge variability in the following parameters: facial appearance, pose, viewing angle, lighting conditions, etc. Indeed, building a robust system which is capable of performing this task, shall face variations in these parameters in terms of persons, environments and images.

- **Scale variation**: the size of the face changes in the image when someone is getting closer to/further from the camera.
- **Lighting conditions**: lighting sources have an influence on head orientation estimation when someone is standing at a given place. For instance, the analysis of skin texture is different under two different lights, and right/left lighting may significantly influence the estimation due to assymetry problems in the facial image.
- **Intrapersonal variations**: for the same person, the head and mainly the face (but also hair arrangement, presence of beard or moustache, etc.) are subject to variations. Facial expressions or make-up has an influence on a system's ability to determine head orientation, and even head position (especially for approaches that are based on global appearance).
- **Interpersonal variations**: anthropometric facial features depend on each person. The estimation of head orientation is based on the following hypothesis: several persons having the same pose are more similar than the models made for a person observing various poses (interpersonal similarity hypothesis). In modeling, it is

then necessary to decorrelate individual features from those that are common to everyone with regard to a given pose.

- **Self-occlusions**: ordinary movements like turning around (i.e. presenting the back of the head), running a hand down the face, or readjusting glasses, would be enough to produce estimation errors. Also, the presence of a cap, scarf or band-aid may obstruct facial detection in an image.
- **Image dimension**: this is the difficulty for an image to represent the high number of available data. For instance, a 300×200 image has 60,000 pixels to which 180,000 color-related values are combined in the RGB color space.

We propose taking the following prerequisites into consideration [71] when analyzing a method for head pose estimation:

- **Precision**: the mean absolute error shall be as low as possible when in the presence of a correct or incorrect head position.
- **Type of camera**: head orientaton estimation shall be performed from images provided by one camera only.
- **Number of people**: head orientaton estimation for various persons shall be performed from one image only.
- **Distance**: head orientaton estimation shall be performed from images taken closely or from a distance regardless of their resolutions.
- **Identities of the persons**: head orientaton estimation shall be performed regardless of the identities of the persons.
- **Calculation time**: head orientaton estimation for various persons shall be performed in real time.

It is to be noted that some systems require prior head detection. These methods need pre-processing and can be considered as hybrid, which makes the clasiffication of the methods even more complex. The studied methods are also characterized by discriminativity and generativity concepts. Although generative models are efficient to estimate head orientation, they are not recommended to estimate the head position in an image. This results to the emergence of methods based on linking discriminative methods to one or various generative ones.

Shape-Oriented Approaches

A set of specific facial features like eyes, nose and mouth, are used to estimate head orientation. The designed model can either be flexible or geometrical.

Flexible Models

The method adapts a non-rigid standard model (mask) to the analyzed image. The model is used as strategic point cores like mouth corners, eye positions and some

facial angles. Besides annotating the various poses, a learning basis including the local facial features shall be created. Three model subgroups can be identified: Elas-
tic Graph Matching (EGM), Active Shape Model (ASM) and Active Appearance
Model (AAM). These models are generative by nature, as a virtual mask shall be
applied to the image to get adapted to physiological features and head orientation.

The EGM [69] has the ability to represent distorted or non-rigid objects. Head
orientation estimation is performed via the creation of a graph for every object.
Each one is compared with the image including the face through iterative distortion
that allows finding minimum distances between each core, as well as each detected
feature point. The position related to the graph maximizing the similarity is then
selected [145]. EGM is used since interpersonal anthropometric variations are neg-
ligible compared with the variations of feature points induced by head position.
Indeed, all individuals have approximatively the same distance between the eyes,
the same face height (about 23 cm), etc.

The ASM [28] is the most widely used model. A model that distributes points
allowing to analyze and represent a shape is processed. It consists of an average-
shape prototype (see Figure 4.16) with modular variation modes gained from learning datasets that are composed of instances from the studied shape. Two steps are
necessary to design an ASM. The first one corresponds to initialization, and a set
of images is selected when entering the system. These are normalized images in
which the mean positions of relevant points are located within the predicted zones.
The ASM is based on an algorithm detecting relevant points, and it memorizes their
positions. Therefore, due to the analysis of a relatively large number of images, it is
possible to estimate the correlations between the points, as well as to calculate their
positions' mean values in order to establish the mean position of the model with
regard to the image. The second step, which is active, resorts to a sequence of images as inputs (a video sequence, for instance). The relevant point positions are then
detected. Head pose estimation is finally performed via a geometrical calculation
algorithm using these data to infer head orientation.

Fig. 4.16 Example of ASM for facial application

The AAM [27] is the most advanced flexible model. The ASM only learns the first variation modes of facial shapes whilst the AAM also learns texture. This allows to compensate for the perspective problems induced by the localization of relevant facial points. The design of the AAM starts by generating an ASM from a learning dataset. Then facial images are distorted so that the feature points correspond to the average shape. Images are normalized to design the model. At last, the correlations between shape and texture are learned so as to generate an appearance model combining the two of them. Once the model converge to the position of the feature points, head orientation estimation is obtained by mapping appearance parameters and head orientation.

Advantages

- Invariance of head localization errors.
- Precise estimation of head orientation.
- Less interpersonal variations.

Disadvantages

- Very long initialization phase.
- Low robustness to occlusions (the presence of all eye corners are generally required in the image to estimate the orientations).
- Hard to use when the subject is remote from the camera or with low-resolution images.

Geometrical Models

They are based on the detection of facial feature points, like flexible models. The difference occurs when analyzing the position of these points. Indeed, a geometrical model is created with a segment whose symetrical axis is traced from the eye center to the middle of the mouth. The position of the eyes and mouth corners are added to this axis, as well as the position of the nose. It is then possible to estimate the three degrees of freedom via geometrical calculations. The significant difficulty of this model consists of localizing the facial feature points precisely. Other problems may occur with occlusions (e.g. wearing glasses, scarf, etc.). The detection of feature points is first performed. The difference between the face and the model is then calculated based on statistical information. The example above [105] shows the estimation of Roll angle γ. It is estimated via the following formula:

$$\gamma = \frac{\gamma_1 + \gamma_2 + \gamma_3}{3}$$

with:

$$\gamma_1 = \arctan\left(\frac{y_{ell} - y_{elr}}{x_{ell} - x_{elr}}\right)$$

$$\gamma_2 = \arctan(\frac{y_{erl} - y_{err}}{x_{erl} - x_{err}})$$

$$\gamma_3 = \arctan(\frac{(y_{ell} + y_{elr})/2 + (y_{erl} - y_{err})/2}{(x_{ell} + x_{elr})/2 - (x_{erl} + x_{err})/2})$$

Points *ell*, *elr*, *erl*, *err*, *em*, *nm* and *mm* used in the calculations are identified in Figure 4.17.

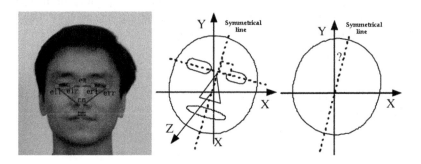

Fig. 4.17 Roll angle estimation

Advantages

- Calculation is performed quickly.
- Simplicity.
- Reasonable estimation with few information.

Disadvantages

- Localizing the feature points is a source of error.
- Head orientation can only be estimated when close to a frontal view.
- Feature points are hardly identifiable in occlusions cases.

Approaches Based on Global Appearance

Instead of focusing on facial features, the global appearance of the head is modelized from the learning image database. Various methods can be used to achieve this:

Template-Based Methods

They consist of comparing the input facial image with a collection of labeled images so as to find the most similar pose. The image database is a set of images corresponding to various poses taken by a same person. This database is extended - for the same sequence of poses - to a large number of persons by giving the same labels to every similar poses. Image comparison metrics, such as the Mean Squared Error [101] or Support Vector Machines (SVM), can be used to map the analyzed image with the one appearing in the dataset. Therefore, it is possible to infer the possible head orientation.

Advantages

- Simplicity.
- The image database can be extended easily.
- No negative learning is required.
- Resolution is independent.

Disadvantages

- The region in which the head is located within the image requires prior detection.
- Errors in head detection involve strong deteriorations in the precision of head orientation estimation.
- A large image database engenders a large number of calculations.
- The biggest disadvantage is that two different persons who are analyzed observing the same pose will be more unlikely mapped than a person taking two different poses (the similarity hypothesis is not observed). However, to solve this problem, the most similar facial outlines can be highlighted with the image convolutions via a Laplace-filter, while the identity-related textures can be removed.

Methods Based on Detector Arrays

These methods resort to detector arrays combined with specific head orientation to refine the quality of classification (one detector = head orientation). This method is the natural extension of a large number of successful models for frontal detection [138]. It then consists of specializing various face detectors corresponding to subtle head orientations. The position is selected depending on a single degree of freedom. The first prototypes [54] for this type of methods were limited to the recognition of three different head orientations (3 detectors) following a vertical axis. Currently, about 12 detectors (to the maximum) can identify the different head orientations. The process is identical for the three degrees of freedom (the consequences in the quantity of generated data can easily be imagined). These detectors are trained following a learning algorithm (SVM or Adaboost) or neural networks. The position related to the detector with the biggest support (highest relevance) is assigned to the image. In order to infer the calculation time, a classification router is often used.

Advantages

- Head detection and orientation estimation can be performed simultaneously on the same classifier.
- Very good results for one degree of freedom.
- Immobility to changes of appearance does not correspond to changes of poses.
- Resolution is independent.

Disadvantages

- Necessity to learn on a negative basis (example of images with no heads).
- The image database and creation process are heavy.
- The increase in classification problems is proportional to the number of detectors.
- Significant time of calculation.
- Difficulty to estimate the three degrees of freedom simultaneously (estimations are generally limited to one degree with less than 12 detectors).
- Possibility of ambiguities when an image is listed as positive by several detectors.

Methods Based on Manifold Embedding

These methods search for a reduced set of dimensions, modeling the continuous variations of head orientation. A manifold is an abstract topological space designed by endowing other simple spaces. It allows to change the dimensions of image rendering. The positions have well-defined values within an interval of this new dimension. It is then necessary to perform an undersizing to estimate head orientation while ignoring other image variations. When the manifold is linear, the Principal Component Analysis (PCA) [118] is the most commonly used method. However, it does not take the available label into account, since the method resorts to non-supervized learning.

An alternative approach consists of normalizing the image and projecting it to every proper pose-eigenspaces and find the pose inferring the biggest projection energy [122]. This approach is based on linear approximaition such as Locally Embedded Analysis (LEA) [37]. There is a variant to linear methods that is based on cores such as the Principal Component Analysis (in KPCA) or Linear Discriminant Analysis (in KLDA) [145]. Another non-linear undersizing seems more appropriate due to the image variations caused by the change of pose. There are various techniques showed in Figure 4.18 such as: Isometric Feature Mapping (Isomap) [52, 112], Locally Linear Embedding (LLE) [114], and Laplacian Eigenmaps (LE) [13]

Advantages

- Very good results when applying the Gabor filter to the image.

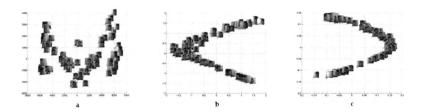

Fig. 4.18 Embedding facial images with various facial orientations in two dimensions. (a) Isomap, (b) LLE, (c) LE.

Disadvantages

- Tendency to create injective applications for both identity and head orientation.
- Heterogeneity of the database.
- Limited adaptation capacity for non-linear techniques.

Methods Based on Non-Linear Regression

These methods resort to non-linear regression tools to perform a functional mapping between the image (or rather its features) and a measure of head orientation. Indeed, the large number of image dimensions represents a challenge for regression tools. The success of these methods was proven by using machines with Support Vector Regressors (SVR) after dimension reduction by the PCA [78], or on facial features [87].

The most commonly used non-linear regression tools are neural networks, in particular the Multi-Layer Perceptron (MLP) [128]. These tools can either be trained on a continuous interval of positions with an output for each degree of freedom (output activation is proportional to related orientation), or with a MLP set with an output for each core learned for each degree of freedom. It is also possible to resort to a sequential combination of a filter selecting characteristics, and a neural network via a boosting process [11].

The Locally-Linear Map (LLM) approach is another neural network composed of various linear maps. The construction of the network requires to compare input data with a barycenter sample for each map. It is used to learn a mass matrix. A convolutive network can also be used [104].

Advantages

- Rapidity.
- Efficiency.
- Zoom insensitivity.

Disadvantages

- Important estimation errors when head localization is incorrect.
- Difficulty to learn the mapping based on a specific regression tool.

Hybrid Approaches

This type of approach is a combination of two or various methods mentioned above in order to compensate for the limit inherent in the utilization of a single method. The most commonly used approach consists of completing a static estimation of head orientation via a tracking system. The static system is in charge of the initialization, and the tracking system is in charge of maintaining the estimation of head orientation throughout time. If the tracking system starts diverting, it can be reinitialized by the static system. These methods lead to more precision than with tracking-only approaches. A lot of combinations were used to estimate head orientation resorting to: a geometrical method with feature point tracking [53], a mapping based on integrated models using PCA with optical flow [159] or a hidden Markov model based on continuous density [55], an appearance model based on grey scale and depth consistency [99].

These tracking methods are performed by observing the head movements between the consecutive images of a video flow. These models can resort to a model-oriented approach in order to focus on a known position. In practice, the tracking methods are always followed by a reinitialization step to compensate for occlusion effects or the loss of the tracked object (e.g. a hand readjusting glasses).

Advantages

- High level of precision.
- Detection of all variations in analyzed images.
- Less errors related to appearance variations.

Disadvantages

- Initialization required: the subject shall maintain a frontal pose before the system starts, and shall recenter if the pose is lost (it is necessary to use a face detector).
- Lack of robustness.

Synthesis

We have gathered in Table 4.5 the advantages and disadvantages of shape-oriented approaches as well as approaches based on global appearance.

After analyzing the various states-of-the-art of methods in terms of advantages and disadvantages, we decided to resort to a hybrid approach. It will be composed

	Shape oriented	Global appearance
Low resolution	-	+
Global illuminations	+	-
Partial occlusion	-	+
Good face localization	-	+
Face features localization	+	-
Extreme head orientations	-	+
Distance from the camera	-	+

Table 4.5 Comparison between shape-oriented approaches and approaches based on global appearance

as follows: (i) estimation method for head orientation based on global appearance, as this type of method is appropriate when the user is remote from the camera, and (ii) head tracking method based on a cylindrical model. The first method will be used for both head tracking initialization and reinitialization in diversion cases.

4.7.2 Image Datasets

To build and evaluate the estimation tools for head orientation, a ground truth is necessary. We will first present the methods to get image databases, and then the most commonly used state-of-the-art image databases.

4.7.2.1 Building Image Datasets

The methods for building a ground truth are presented here following an increasing precision order (from the most to the less precise).

Directional Suggestion

A series of markers is placed in specific positions of the target scene with regard to the location of the subject. Every subject is invited to successively look at these markers by making head movements rather than eye movements. A camera is positioned in front of the subject and records different images of the head for each marker the subject is watching. This method generates a gound truth which is not very reliable. Indeed, it assumes that each head is located at the same physical place within a 3D space, so that all head directions correspond to the same position. In addition, it assumes that each subject has the ability to direct his/her head precisely towards an object. However, this task is imprecise and the subject meets some difficulties to perform it, especially when moving eyes only.

Directional Suggestion with Laser Pointer

This method resorts to the same process as directional suggestion, a laser pointer is installed on the head of the subject. This allows him/her to spot the locations he/she has to look at with higher precision due to *virtual feedback*. This method also implies that each head is located in the same physical 3D space, which is hard to guarantee as the subject tends to move naturally during the image recording process.

Manual Annotation

Head images are examined by one person. The annotator assigns a facial pose in the image, depending on his/her own perception of head orientation. This process is often used to estimate head orientation for only one degree of freedom with an approximate set of poses. However, it is not appropriate to precisely estimate head orientation.

Series of Cameras

Various cameras installed at specific positions record images of someone's face from different angles simultaneously. This method offers a very precise ground truth if the head of each subject is positioned at the same place. However, it is only adapted to images taken from a short distance. It is hardly applicable to real-case videos.

Magnetic Sensors

The sensors measure the magnetic force they produce. The sensors can be placed on the head of the subject, and determine the head position and orientation. The theoretical precision of these sensors is high (less than one degree of error). However, they are very responsive to surrounding noise and metals (even in minimal quantities) when collecting data. This method is widely used. The most well-known sensors are *Polhemus FastTrak* and *Ascension Flock of Birds*.

Systems Capturing Optical Movements

These systems are robust but costly to deploy. They are mainly used for professional cinematographic captures of articulated body movements. A series of infrared cameras installed at a short distance resort to various stereo views to track the markers attached to a person. These markers may be fixed behind the head of a subject. The best known system is *Vicon MX*.

4.7.2.2 Utilized Image Database

Over the last few years, various image databases dedicated to head orientation estimation have been created. Some of them will be presented here-below, and we will
detail the ones we used in this thesis.

Pointing'04 Head Pose Image Dataset

Building the *Pointing'04 Head Pose Image Database* [43] required the intervention
of 15 persons. Each one was taken twice in 93 different poses depending on two
degrees of freedom. There was a calibration every 15 Pan degrees, and every 15/30
Tilt degrees over a half-circle of poses from -90 degrees to +90 degrees on the two
axes. The Pan angle can then reach the following values: (0, 15, 30, 45, 60, 75, 90),
where negative and positive values correspond to right and left poses respectively.
The Tilt angle can reach the following values: (0, 15, 30, 45, 60, 75, 90), where
negative and positive values correspond to low and high values respectively. Figure
4.19 shows the 93 poses taken by one person in this image database.

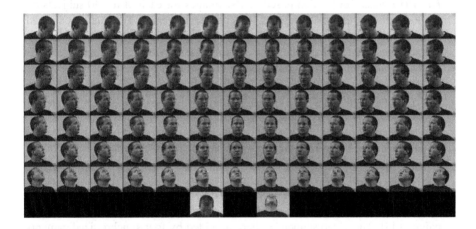

Fig. 4.19 Example of all head orientations associated to one person

Boston University Head Pose Dataset

The *Boston University Head Pose Dataset* [24] is composed of 45 video sequences.
Five subjects were asked to perform nine different movements with their heads
within a standard office environment under uniform lighting. The head is always
visible with the presence of some insignificant self-occlusions. The videos have a
low resolution (320x240 pixels). A *Flock of Birds*-type magnetic sensor is used to

record head position and orientation. This system has 1.8 mm of translation precision, and 0.4 degree of rotation precision. When collecting data, electromagnetic noise interfered with the precision of the capturing system. However, the recorded measures are rather low to be used as ground truth. Figure 4.20 shows the five persons who performed the experiment under different orientations.

Fig. 4.20 Examples of persons captured during data collection

Other Image Datasets

- *FacePix dataset* [80] is composed of 181 images for each of the 30 subjects on the Pan axis within a [-90 degrees, +90 degrees] interval. The images captured by a camera installed on a revolving platform were reframed manually to ensure that the eyes and face have the same position in each view.
- *CMU PIE dataset* [121] is composed of 68 facial images resorting to 13 poses under 43 lighting conditions with four different expressions. A series of 13 cameras were used: nine cameras on the Pan axis within a 22.5 degree interval, one above the center, and two at each corner of the room.
- *Hermes Head direction dataset* [109] contains four videos (2 of them were captured inside, and two others outside). Two different persons appear in the videos (but one is available at a time). Besides, 25 learning images per person are available, at the rate of five images per pose. Poses are within a 45 degree interval on the Pan axis, between -90 degrees and +90 degrees.
- *CHIL-CLEAR 06 et 07 datasets* were created for the CLEAR evaluation campaign [143]. The video sequences were provided by four synchronized cameras positioned in each corner of a seminar room. Head orientation was provided manually within the 2006 database, while a magnetic sensor was used for the 2007 database.
- *Idiap Head Pose database* [10] is composed of eight sequences of one minute each during a meeting. They were recorded by one camera where two subjects are visible. The annotation of head position and orientation was performed by using a magnetic sensor.

4.7.3 Estimation of Head Pose Based on Global Appearance

We will present the method used to estimate head orientation based on global appearance [74]. This method considers this task as a problem to classify images and convert the received facial image into a feature vector. Feature vectors are produced by images of several persons having the same pose, and is used to learn a classifier for head orientation estimation. These images are coming from a database composed of N poses combined with discrete values of Pan and Tilt angles for M persons. This base is then divided after being pre-processed into two sets: learning and testing. The aim is to determine a discriminative measure to be applied to a feature vector of size n. During the learning process, a classifier is built on a limited number of exclusive poses defining the estimation precision to be reached.

4.7.3.1 Utilized Image Dataset

The Pointing image dataset [43] was used to build and test the head pose model. The dataset is divided into two sets:

- The learning set: it is composed of 20 images per pose for 11 persons (9 persons were captured twice and two persons were captured only once).
- The testing set: it is composed of ten images per pose for six persons (4 persons were captured twice and the two persons who were used only once for the learning phase were catpured once again).

5 poses were selected: bottom-left, bottom-right, full-face, top-right and top-left. These poses correspond to the Pan and Tilt angles respectively, following {(-60, -90), (-60, +90), (0, 0), (+60, -90), (+60, +90)}, as showed in Figure 4.21.

Fig. 4.21 5 Selected poses from Pointing'04 Dataset.

Pre-processing is required for these images in order to extract some characteristics. A rectangle clutched around the head is first localized. The images are then normalized to reach the same dimensions: 64x64. Finally, a histogram equalization is applied to make sure that two facial images taken in different lighting conditions are transformed into two images with similar grey and luminosity scales. Various feature vectors are selected on this basis.

4.7.3.2 Feature Selection

We will present here the extraction of feature vectors on the basis of pre-processed images. This extraction is based on the following hypothesis: various persons having the same pose are more similar than one person having different poses. Two methods were selected in particular:

- Singular Value Decomposition (SVD): it is applied to all images in order to extract a vector;
- Gabor wavelets: allows to extract a vector composed of vectors sampled with different scales and orientations in an image containing a face in a particular pose.

The results for each I image is feature vector F_I of size n (n is chosen depending on the technique utilized to select the features):

$$F_I = (F_{I_1}, F_{I_2}, \ldots, F_{I_n})^t$$

Singular Value Decomposition (SVD)

Singular Value Decomposition [132] of Matrix A is its representation in the product of a diagonal matrix and two orthonormal matrices:

$$A = U * W * V^t$$

W is a diagonal matrix composed of elements represented by a vector with n dimensions. All singular values are positive and listed in descending order. The application of this decomposition on pixel intensities for normalized facial image I (n=64) allows to get the following vector:

$$W_I = (w_{I_1}, w_{I_2}, \ldots, w_{I_{64}})^t$$

2 vectors U_{I_j} and V_{I_j} are combined with each singular value: w_{I_j} avec $j \in \{1, \ldots, 64\}$:

$$U_{I_j} = (u_{I_{j_1}}, u_{I_{j_2}}, \ldots, u_{I_{j_{64}}})^t$$

$$V_{I_j} = (v_{I_{j_1}}^t, v_{I_{j_2}}^t, \ldots, v_{I_{j_{64}}}^t)^t$$

Norm $\|W_I\|$ is then calculated:

$$\|W_I\| = \sqrt{w_{I_1}^2 + w_{I_2}^2 + \ldots + w_{I_{64}}^2}$$

Finally, two types of feature vectors are created for Image i:

- The first one is composed of elements obtained when dividing P primary elements of vector W by its norm $\|W_i\|$:

$$F_{I_j} = \frac{w_{I_j}}{\|W_I\|}, j \in \{1,\ldots,64\}, P \leq 64$$

- The second one is composed of P primary singular values w_{I_j} divided by norm $\|W_I\|$ as well as related vectors U_{I_j} et V_{I_j}:

$$F_{I_j} = (\frac{w_{I_j}}{\|W_I\|}, U_{I_j}, V_{I_j}), j \in \{1,\ldots,P\}, P \leq 64$$

In order to select an appropriate value for P, the input image is rebuilt by using primary singular values P (see Figure 4.22).

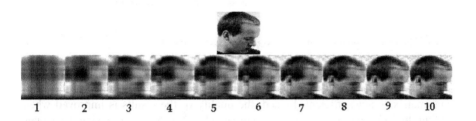

Fig. 4.22 Rebuilding an image depending on the P value

Both feature vectors are used to estimate head orientation. There are three methods for building the classifier: SVM with RBF (Radial Basis Function) kernel, KNN with $K = 10$, and Frobenius distance. Figures 4.23 and 4.24 bring the results obtained to the set of tests by changing the P value when building the two feature vectors.

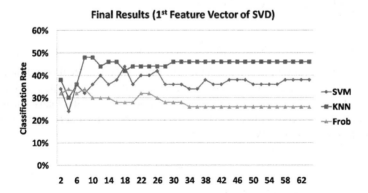

Fig. 4.23 Classification ratio using the first SVD feature vector

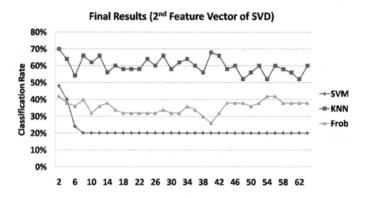

Fig. 4.24 Classification ratio using the second SVD feature vector

The results permit to infer that using the singular values contained in the diagonal matrix is not sufficient. Indeed, the quality of the results is improved when adding the information contained in matrices U and V. Since these singular values are listed, the information contained in the first values are sufficient to perform a good estimation of head orientation.

Utilization of Gabor Wavelets

Gabor wavelets aim at differentiating head orientations from one another. An evaluation of the similarity ratio between the poses is available in [118]. It was performed by varying the orientation of the Gabor filter at a given pose. A Gabor wavelet $\psi_{o,s}(z)$ is defined as follows [157]:

$$\psi_{o,s}(z) = \frac{\|k_{o,s}\|^2}{\sigma^2} e^{-\frac{\|k_{o,s}\|^2\|z\|^2}{2\sigma^2}} \left[e^{ik_{o,s}z} - e^{-\frac{\sigma^2}{2}} \right] \tag{4.1}$$

where point $z = (x, y)$ gets horizontal coordinate x and vertical coordinate y. Parameters o and s define the orientation and scale of the Gabor kernel, while $\| \cdot \|$ is the normal operator. σ is related to the standard deviation of the Gaussian window in the core, and determines the ratio between the width of the Gaussian window and the length of the wavelet. Wavelet vector $k_{o,s}$ is defined as follows:

$$k_{o,s} = k_s e^{i\phi_o}$$

with $k_s = \frac{k_{max}}{f^s}$ and $\phi_o = \frac{\pi o}{O}$. k_{max} is the maximum frequency, f^s is the spatial frequency between the kernels within the frequency domain, and O is the number of selected orientations.

To create the feature vector, eight orientations were selected: { 0, $\frac{\pi}{8}$, $\frac{\pi}{4}$, $\frac{3\pi}{8}$, $\frac{\pi}{2}$, $\frac{5\pi}{8}$, $\frac{3\pi}{4}$, $\frac{7\pi}{8}$ }. They belong to five different scales: { 0, 1, 2, 3, 4 } avec $\sigma = 2\pi$, $k_{max} = \frac{\pi}{2}$, et $f = \sqrt{2}$.

The real part of a Gabor wavelet using the eight orientations is showed in Figure 4.25:

Fig. 4.25 Real response of Gabor wavelets to the eight selected orientations

When using a Gabor wavelet, an image is showed by its convolution with a series of Gabor kernels. Figure 4.26 shows the real response of a posing person's image, using eight orientations and five scales.

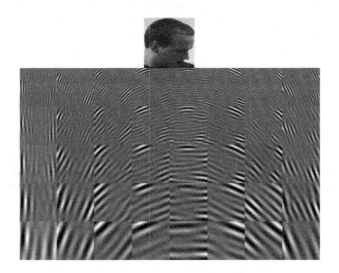

Fig. 4.26 Real response of a head image using eight orientations and five scales

The convolution of image I and Gabor core $\psi_{o,s}(z)$ is defined as follows:

$$Conv_{o,s}(z) = I(z) * \psi_{o,s}(z)$$

Response $Conv_{o,s}(z)$ of each Gabor core is a complex function provided with real part $Re\{Conv_{o,s}(z)\}$ and imaginary part $Im\{Conv_{o,s}(z)\}$ defined as follows:

$$Conv_{o,s}(z) = Re\{Conv_{o,s}(z)\} + i.Im\{Conv_{o,s}(z)\}$$

Magnitude response $\|Conv_{o,s}(z)\|$ is expressed as follows:

$$\|Conv_{o,s}(z)\| = \sqrt{\mathrm{Re}\{Conv_{o,s}(z)\}^2 + \mathrm{Im}\{Conv_{o,s}(z)\}^2}$$

Each image received engenders $O * S$ images recording the real and imaginary responses, as well as the magnitude response to the Gabor filter. The average and diversion with regard to the pixel intensity of the image are then calculated for each response to the Gabor filter. Feature vector F_I related to a specific response of image I is then composed of $2 * O * S$ elements:

$$F_I = (M_1, D_1, M_2, D_2, ..., M_{O*S}, D_{O*S})^t$$

Therefore, three feature vector variations are obtained by using Gabor wavelets according to the selected response (real, imaginary or magnitude).

An evaluation was performed in order to determine the scale influence on the three variations of the feature vector. Three methods were used to build the classifier: SVM with RBF kernel, KNN with $K = 10$, and Frobenius distance. The classification ratios obtained via the three methods for the set of tests are illustrated in Figures 4.27, 4.28 and 4.29 respectively. The eight orientations were used, while the scale varied from 0 to 4.

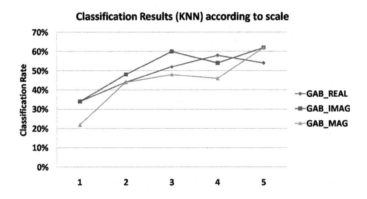

Fig. 4.27 Classification ratio depending on the scale using KNN

The evaluation performed on scale allows to infer that five scales are necessary to extract the feature vector. The second evaluation consists of studying the influence of orientation on head orientation estimation. Figures 4.30 and 4.31 show the classification ratio when using KNN and SVM respectively. The results obtained when using the Frobenius distance were not reported, as the classification rate is very low.

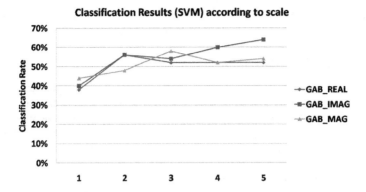

Fig. 4.28 Classification ratio depending on the scale using SVM

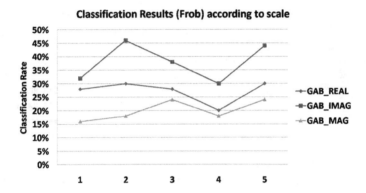

Fig. 4.29 Classification Ratio depending on the scale using Frobenius distance

4.7.3.3 Experimental Results

In order to demonstrate the influence of the number of images during the learning process, 5, 10, 15 and 20 images were randomly selected from the learning set. The classification ratios obtained for the set of tests by using KNN and SVM are showed in Figures 4.32 and 4.33 respectively.

Figures 4.34 and 4.35 present the classification ratios when using the KNN and SVM of five poses. They were labeled from one to 5, corresponding to the following Pan and Tilt angles: {(-60, -90), (-60, +90), (0, 0), (+60, -90), (+60, +90)}.

Based on these figures, the following observations can be expounded:

- The classification precision increases with the number of learning images. This property is typical of supervised learning.

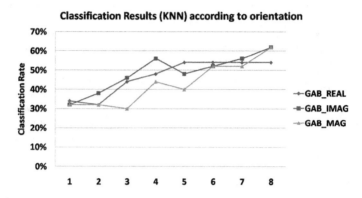

Fig. 4.30 Classification ratio depending on orientation using KNN

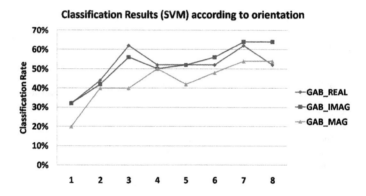

Fig. 4.31 Classification ratio depending on orientation using SVM

- In general, the feature vector obtained with Gabor wavelets leads to better results than with SVD. This is due to the Gabor wavelet's ability to manipulate different orientations and scales with regard to SVD which cannot do that.
- It seems that, in general and among the three Gabor responses, the performances of real and imaginary components are higher than for magnitude response. It is due to the fact that most of information are contained within the phase.

4.7.4 Cylindrical Model for Head Tracking

In order to properly estimate the gaze direction of a user in a personal environment, the information provided by head orientation and eye position shall be taken into consideration. We resorted to the system described in [135] that allows to extract

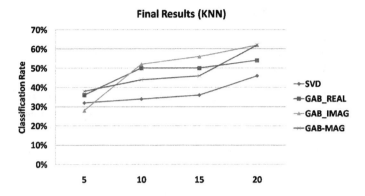

Fig. 4.32 Classification ratio depending on the number of images using KNN

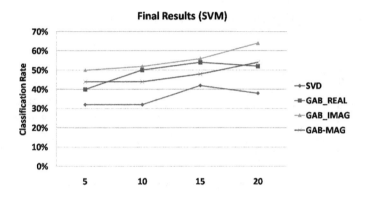

Fig. 4.33 Classification ratio depending on the number of images used during the learning process with SVM

these information with a high precision from a video flow. The cylindrical head model (CHM) for head tracking is used [147], while eye position is determined by resorting to a technique based on isophote properties [134].

The cylindrical model is used to perform head tracking. The perspective position is used to rebuild the focal distance and head height, and projects the image pixels to 3D points and vice versa. The positions of the points on the cylinder are found by resorting to the *ray-tracing* technique. The correct points of the cylinder are then projected backwards on the image plane. Using the optical flow, the new head position and orientation are estimated. Figure 4.36 shows some qualitative examples for head tracking using CHM.

The disadvantage of the first subsystem (head tracking) is that it can wrongly converge to local minimums unable to retrieve the tracking properly, while the second one (eye localization) assumes a semi-frontal head pose to detect the circular tendencies of isophotes, and fails at eye localization when in presence of extreme

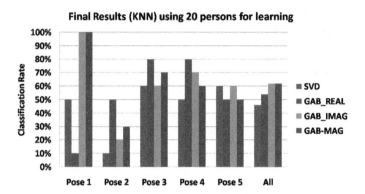

Fig. 4.34 Classification ratio of five poses using KNN

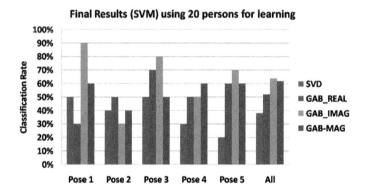

Fig. 4.35 Classification ratio of five poses using SVM

poses. The combination of these two subsystems allows to get better results with regard to a sequential utilization. Indeed, integration permits them to use the transformation matrices obtained by both systems in an interlaced manner. Eye position can then be detected given the head pose, while the head pose is adjusted based on eye position. In the first image, 2D eye coordinates are used as reference markers (red points in Figure 4.36) which are projected to the cylindrical model so they can be used to estimate the successive positions of the eyes. 3D eye position is then used to update the cylindrical model when it becomes unstable.

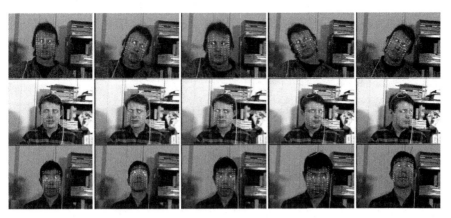

Fig. 4.36 Qualitative examples of head tracking using CHM

4.8 Conclusion

This chapter outlines the various systems used to estimate the visual gaze. These systems have been listed depending on the discomfort caused to the users by data-capturing tools. The applications using information provided by the gaze depending on the domain were presented in particular within the framework of a marketing scenario, to which we have resorted to validate our approaches. The contribution of the two factors that are used to estimate the visual gaze are discussed. We focused on head pose estimation through a complete taxonomy of the different approaches used to estimate the orientation, as well as inherent difficulties. The human ability to perform this task was also described. At last, we have presented two approaches to estimate head orientation (a model based on global appearance and a cylindrical model). To get a robust solution, it is necessary to act within a precise context by resorting to the following general scheme: localization + tracking. However, there is no universal solution but it may occur soon.

Chapter 5
Visual Field Projection and Region of Interest Analysis

Abstract The visual field determines what someone can see. When a person is confronted by a target scene, visual field projection allows to characterize the center of attention by localizing a region of interest. Region-of-interest analysis for various persons throughout time helps to understand the visual behavior of the person observed. It also improves the understanding of the target scene and permits its reorganization when necessary. In this chapter, we will determine the characteristics to estimate the visual field of a person from a video flow. This estimation is first performed when the subject observes a frontal position. When the eyes are visible at a given time in the video flow, the fixation point is corrected by calculating the eye movements with regard to the point of reference. The visual field is then adapted to head orientation via the values of the three degrees of freedom, as calculated previously. When the subject's attention is caught by the target scene, the visual field (or perception volume) related to the subject is projected to that scene. This allows to extract a fixation point as well as a region of interest from the target scene. Various representations can illustrate this information (e.g. fixation point, scanpath followed by the fixation point, shape of the region of interest or *heatmap*). The video flows are collected by a webcam pointing to the subject. An experiment is then performed involving persons watching images and videos in order to analyze how the fixation points are distributed. We resorted to a set of metrics to conduct the analysis.

5.1 Visual Field Estimation

The visual field covers the whole space seen by the eyes. When a person is confronted to a target scene, his/her visual field covers the whole explored scene by a series of fixation points. However, the visual field is empty when the subject has no target to look at. In the following, we will present the method we used for the estimation [73].

C. Djeraba et al., *Multi-Modal User Interactions in Controlled Environments*,
DOI 10.1007/978-1-4419-0316-7_5, © Springer Science+Business Media, LLC 2010

5.1.1 Physiological Data

The visual field usually spreads out with regard to the ocular axis, 60 degrees up, 70 degrees down and 90 degrees laterally, which corresponds to a wide-angle photographic lens of 180 degrees. The visual field is called *monocular* and corresponds to all spatial points (objects, surfaces) that can been seen simultaneously by the eye when fixing a point (fixation point). The central part of the retina - the fovea - enables to have a clear vision (central visual field) whilst the vision is blurred for the rest of the retina (peripheral visual field). Images produced by both eyes are very similar in infinite vision cases, while they are slightly different when the object is closer since the observation point is different for each eye. The brain interprets these images as well as their differences, allowing the object to be seen in three dimensions. The common field for both eyes is called *binocular vision* and covers 120 degrees. Figure 5.1 shows how the human visual field is divided on a horizontal plane, according to Panero and Zelnik [106].

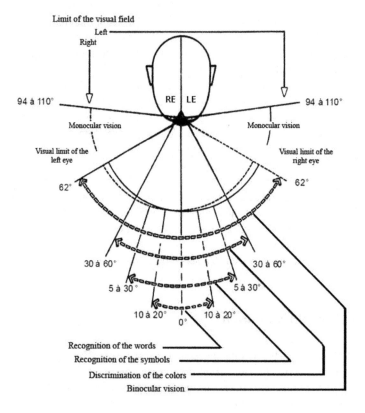

Fig. 5.1 Division of the visual field on a horizontal plane [106].

The limits of the visual field are not strictly circular. The top part is flattened due to the arch formed by the eyebrow's relief, whilst the lower part has a notch corresponding to the nose. The peripheral visual field is measured through stimuli such as finger movements made by the examiner or through a ball stem. The examiner is positioned behind the patient - who is maintaining a static fixation point - and brings the fingers or ball fore-and-aft until the patient says he/she is perceiving the stimuli. Figure 5.2 illustrates the human binocular vision which is common to both monocular fields (right and left) when fixing a point.

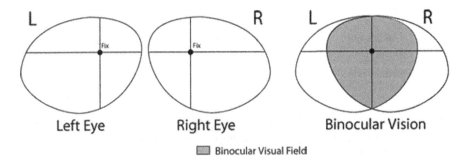

Fig. 5.2 Illustration of binocular vision.

We will resort to binocular vision to represent the visual field of a person. Indeed, the central part of the visual field contains the point fixed by both eyes, allowing a clear vision. Therefore, the values associated with horizontal and vertical beam angles will be equal to 120 and 60 degrees, respectively.

5.1.2 Visual Field Estimation and Fixation Point for Frontal Pose

The aim is to calculate the length and height of the visual field at some distance in order to determine the coordinates of its limits. These calculations are first performed in a frontal pose (i.e. when the degrees of freedom of the head are equal to 0). For modeling reasons, the visual field related to binocular vision is represented by a rectangle defined by four points A, B, C and D. The perception volume of the subject is then represented by pyramid $OABCD$, whose starting point (observation point) is 0 (often related to the eyes). Figure 5.3 shows the visual field in various views.

Fixation point M is positioned at a distance d facing observation point O. Let's consider that both eyes have the same level of vision, and that point M is the center of rectangle $ABCD$. The respective centers of segments $[AD]$ and $[BC]$ are named E and F. Likewise, the respective centers of segments $[AB]$ and $[CD]$ are named G and I. Depending on the frontal view of the visual field, point M is also the center

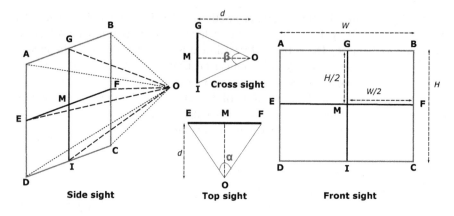

Fig. 5.3 Different views of a same perception volume.

of $[GI]$ and $[EF]$. Angles α and β correspond to the horizontal and vertical beam angles, respectively. From the profile and upper views, it is then possible to infer the following relations:

$$\widehat{MOF} = \widehat{MOE} = \frac{\alpha}{2} \quad \text{and} \quad \widehat{MOG} = \widehat{MOI} = \frac{\beta}{2}$$

Given that $MO = d$, the following trigonometrical relations are infered:

$$\begin{cases} \tan(\frac{\alpha}{2}) = \frac{MF}{MO} = \frac{MF}{d} \Longleftrightarrow MF = d.\tan(\frac{\alpha}{2}) \\ \tan(\frac{\beta}{2}) = \frac{MG}{MO} = \frac{MG}{d} \Longleftrightarrow MG = d.\tan(\frac{\beta}{2}) \end{cases} \qquad (5.1)$$

The length and height of the visual field are marked L and H, respectively. Lengths MF and MG are known according to d, α and β. Equation 5.1 enables to infer that:

$$L = 2MF = 2.d.\tan(\frac{\alpha}{2}) \qquad (5.2)$$

$$H = 2MG = 2.d.\tan(\frac{\beta}{2}) \qquad (5.3)$$

The values of the horizontal and vertical beam angles can be selected according to the required configuration. Figure 5.4 presents the length and height values of the visual field at different distances from the observation point. Values α and β are equal to 120 and 60 degrees respectively (human binocular vision).

Within the marker whose origin is point O, points A, B, C and D have the respective coordinates at distance d_i:

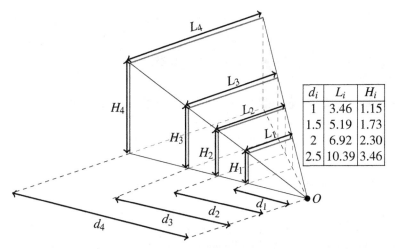

Fig. 5.4 Values of length L_i and height H_i of the visual field at different distances, stated in meters.

$$\begin{cases} A(-\frac{L_i}{2}, \frac{H_i}{2}, d_i) \\ B(\frac{L_i}{2}, \frac{H_i}{2}, d_i) \\ C(\frac{L_i}{2}, -\frac{H_i}{2}, d_i) \\ D(-\frac{L_i}{2}, -\frac{H_i}{2}, d_i) \end{cases} \tag{5.4}$$

When the head observes a frontal pose, the coordinates of these four points can only be defined from distance d, as well as horizontal and vertical beam angles α and β, respectively.

5.1.3 Visual Field Adaptation to Head Orientation

The coordinates of points A, B, C and D - forming with point O the perception volume of a subject standing at a certain distance d - have been defined previously and are correct when the subject observes a frontal pose. However, these coordinates change when the person is moving (translation) and making various head movements (rotations according to the three degrees of freedom). Figure 5.5 presents a person observing various poses in front of the camera.

Adapting the visual field to head orientation can be achieved by resorting to either a matrix or a quaternion approach. Both methods are appropriate for precise application.

Fig. 5.5 Illustrations of the visual field under various poses in front of the camera.

5.1.3.1 Matrix Approach

Coordinates of point P in space can be represented in the form of vector V_P of size 3. The point resulting from the rotation of P around angle φ according to one of the three axes of the marker is P'. The coordinates of point P' are calculated as follows:

$$V_{P'} = R.V_P \tag{5.5}$$

Where V_P and $V_{P'}$ are vectors of size three including the coordinates of P and P' respectively. R is a rotation matrix of size 3×3 (corresponding to the three possible rotation types: Tilt, Pan and Roll). R can take the value of one of the three following matrices (see Figure 5.6):

- $R_{(x,\alpha)}$: matrix of angle rotation α around axis x.
- $R_{(y,\beta)}$: matrix of angle rotation β around axis y.
- $R_{(z,\gamma)}$: matrix of angle rotation γ around axis z.

However, rotations in a 3D-space are not commutative. Indeed, the result obtained with a rotation around axis x followed by another one around axis z, is different from the results obtained when first performing a rotation around axis z, then around axis x. This example is shown in Figure 5.7.

To compensate for this commutativity problem, 12 conventions are possible, listed in two categories:

- **Cardan angle**: six conventions for rotations around three axes: $x-z-y, x-y-z,$ $y-x-z, y-z-x, z-y-x$ and $z-x-y$.
- **Euler angles**: six other conventions for the following rotations: $x-z-x, x-y-$ $x, y-x-y, y-z-y, z-y-z$ and $z-x-z$.

A convention shall be selected to adapt the visual field to head orientation. An orientation matrix is associated to each convention. We used convention "$x-y-z$" (rotation around axis x <u>then</u>, rotation around axis y <u>then</u>, rotation around axis z). The rotation matrix related to this convention is obtained as follows:

$$R_{(\alpha,\beta,\gamma)} = R_{(z,\gamma)}.R_{(y,\beta)}.R_{(x,\alpha)} \tag{5.6}$$

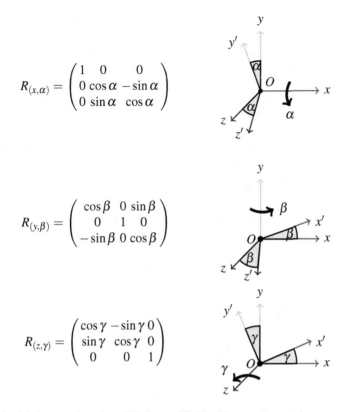

$$R_{(x,\alpha)} = \begin{pmatrix} 1 & 0 & 0 \\ 0 & \cos\alpha & -\sin\alpha \\ 0 & \sin\alpha & \cos\alpha \end{pmatrix}$$

$$R_{(y,\beta)} = \begin{pmatrix} \cos\beta & 0 & \sin\beta \\ 0 & 1 & 0 \\ -\sin\beta & 0 & \cos\beta \end{pmatrix}$$

$$R_{(z,\gamma)} = \begin{pmatrix} \cos\gamma & -\sin\gamma & 0 \\ \sin\gamma & \cos\gamma & 0 \\ 0 & 0 & 1 \end{pmatrix}$$

Fig. 5.6 3 types of rotations (Tilt, Pan and Roll) with respective matrices.

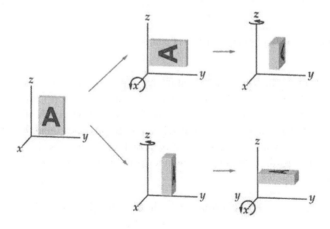

Fig. 5.7 Non-commutativity of rotation compositions in a 3D-space.

$$R_{(\alpha,\beta,\gamma)} = \begin{pmatrix} \cos\beta\cos\gamma & \cos\gamma\sin\alpha\sin\beta - \cos\alpha\sin\gamma & \cos\alpha\cos\gamma\sin\beta + \sin\alpha\sin\gamma \\ \cos\beta\sin\gamma & \cos\alpha\cos\gamma + \sin\alpha\sin\beta\sin\gamma & \cos\alpha\sin\beta\sin\gamma - \cos\gamma\sin\alpha \\ -\sin\beta & \cos\beta\sin\alpha & \cos\alpha\cos\beta \end{pmatrix}$$

$$(5.7)$$

When the subject is moving, he/she performs translation movements with regard to the camera marker, as described by vector $T = (t_x, t_y, t_z)^t$ with: translations t_x, t_y and t_z around axes x, y and z respectively.

Hence, to determine the coordinates of point P'' resulting from the rotation of point P around one or several axes, followed by its translation (see Figure 5.8), the following calculation shall be performed:

$$V_{P''} = R.V_P + T \tag{5.8}$$

With V_P and $V_{P''}$ being two vectors of size three including the coordinates of P and P'' respectively. R is the rotation matrix, and T is the translation vector.

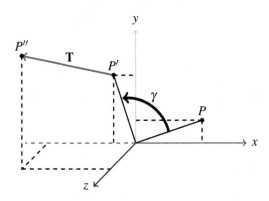

Fig. 5.8 Rotation followed by the translation of point P.

A linear transformation (multiplication by a matrix of size 3×3) followed by translation (addition of a matrix of size 1×3) is a refined application: instead of using two matrices (one for rotation and one for translation), both information can be stored in a matrix of size 4×4. To do this, a fictitious coordinate $w \neq 0$ (usually set to 1) is added. The obtained vector of size four represents the homogeneous coordinates of the point. The inverse change from 3D to homogeneous coordinates is performed as follows:

3D coordinates   homogeneous coordinates
$$(x,y,z) \rightarrow (x,y,z,w)$$
homogeneous coordinates   3D coordinates
$$(x,y,z,w) \rightarrow (x/w, y/w, z/w)$$

Rotation and translation movements are then stated in one matrix R of size 4×4:

$$R = \begin{pmatrix} a_{11} & a_{12} & a_{13} & t_x \\ a_{21} & a_{22} & a_{23} & t_y \\ a_{31} & a_{32} & a_{33} & t_z \\ 0 & 0 & 0 & 1 \end{pmatrix} \tag{5.9}$$

where coefficients a_{ij} are calculated according to the various rotations performed (see equation 5.7). The values of translation vector T are: t_x, t_y and t_z.

5.1.3.2 Quaternion Approach

Quaternions [41] belong to hypercomplex numbers and represent an extension of complex numbers. A quaternion Q can be noted as follows:

$$Q = a.1 + b.i + c.j + d.k \quad \text{with} \quad (a,b,c,d) \in \mathbb{R}^4 \quad \text{and} \quad i^2 = j^2 = k^2 = i.j.k = -1$$

Numbers a, b, c and d are the characteristics of Q, while i, j and k are imaginary coefficients. There are various ways to note Q in this form, and any quaternion with the same characteristics is necessarily equal to Q (the reverse is also true). There is only one way to divide quaternion Q into a pair composed of real number a and vector $\mathbf{V} \in \mathbb{R}^3$ whose coordinates are (b,c,d). Notation $Q = (a,\mathbf{V})$ allows to define:

- the conjugate of Q by: $Q^* = (a,-\mathbf{V})$
- the norm of Q by: $\|Q\| = \sqrt{a + \|\mathbf{V}\|}$

The product of the two respective quaternions $Q_1 = (a_1,\mathbf{V}_1)$ and $Q_2 = (a_2,\mathbf{V}_2)$, is calculated as follows:

$$Q_1.Q_2 = (a_1.a_2 - \mathbf{V}_1 \bullet \mathbf{V}_2, a_1.\mathbf{V}_2 + a_2.\mathbf{V}_1 + \mathbf{V}1 \wedge \mathbf{V}_2) \tag{5.10}$$

where $\mathbf{V}_1 \bullet \mathbf{V}_2$ and $\mathbf{V}1 \wedge \mathbf{V}_2$ represent the scalar and vectorial products of $\mathbf{V}_1$ and $\mathbf{V}_2$ respectively. R^3. It is marked $(0,\mathbf{V})$. The coordinates of $\mathbf{V}$ are $(b,c,d)^t$.

The use of quaternions can be mapped with the vectorial rotation composition. Indeed, vectorial rotation is performed around vector $\mathbf{N}$ originating from marker $(0,x,y,z)$. Angle rotation α which is performed around an axis oriented according to vector $\mathbf{N}$ of coordinates $(N_x,N_y,N_z)^t$ (as shown in Figure 5.9), is associated with normalized quaternion Q represented by:

$$Q = \cos\frac{\alpha}{2} + \sin\frac{\alpha}{2}[i.N_x + j.N_y + k.N_z] \tag{5.11}$$

The image of vector $\mathbf{V}$ is obtained via angle rotation α around vector $\mathbf{N}$, and is marked $\mathbf{V}'$. Therefore, expression of $\mathbf{V}$ is obtained via the following quaternion equality:

$$(0, Rot_{[\alpha,\mathbf{N}]}(\mathbf{V})) = Q.V.Q^* = (\cos\frac{\alpha}{2}, \sin\frac{\alpha}{2}.\mathbf{N}).(0,\mathbf{V}).(\cos\frac{\alpha}{2}, -\sin\frac{\alpha}{2}.\mathbf{N}) \tag{5.12}$$

with Q the quaternion associated to angle rotation α around vector $\mathbf{N}$.

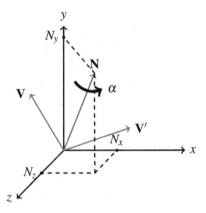

Fig. 5.9 Angle rotation α of vector **V** around vector **N**

The image of a vector resulting from the vectorial rotation composition led by vectors $\mathbf{N_1}, \mathbf{N_2} \ldots \mathbf{N_n}$ for angles $\alpha_1, \alpha_2, \ldots \alpha_n$ respectively, is obtained as follows:

$$(0, Rot_{[\alpha_n, \mathbf{N_n}]}(Rot_{[\alpha_{n-1}, \mathbf{N_{n-1}}]}(\ldots (Rot_{[\alpha_1, \mathbf{N_1}]}(\mathbf{V}))))) = (\prod_{i=1}^{n} Q_{n-i+1}).(0, \mathbf{V}).(\prod_{i=1}^{n} Q_i^*)$$

$$(5.13)$$

with $Q_i = (\cos \frac{\alpha_i}{2}, \sin \frac{\alpha_i}{2}.\mathbf{N_i})$ and $Q_i^* = (\cos \frac{\alpha_i}{2}, -\sin \frac{\alpha_i}{2}.\mathbf{N_i})$.

When performing rotations around the three degrees of freedom of the head, the image of vector **V** - which results from rotation angle α (Tilt) led by vector **X** <u>then</u>, from angle rotation β (Pan) led by vector **Y** <u>then</u>, and from rotation angle γ (Roll) led by vector **Z** - is determined as follows:

$$(0, Rot_{[\gamma, \mathbf{Z}]}(Rot_{[\beta, \mathbf{Y}]}(Rot_{[\alpha, \mathbf{X}]}(\mathbf{V})))) = Q_3.Q_2.Q_1.(0, \mathbf{V}).Q_1^*.Q_2^*.Q_3^*$$

with : $Q_1 = (\cos \frac{\alpha}{2}, \sin \frac{\alpha}{2}.\mathbf{X})$, $Q_1^* = (\cos \frac{\alpha}{2}, -\sin \frac{\alpha}{2}.\mathbf{X})$,
$Q_2 = (\cos \frac{\beta}{2}, \sin \frac{\beta}{2}.\mathbf{Y})$, $Q_2^* = (\cos \frac{\beta}{2}, -\sin \frac{\beta}{2}.\mathbf{Y})$,
$Q_3 = (\cos \frac{\gamma}{2}, \sin \frac{\gamma}{2}.\mathbf{Z})$, $Q_3^* = (\cos \frac{\gamma}{2}, -\sin \frac{\gamma}{2}.\mathbf{Z})$

Figure 5.10 illustrates visual field rotation with radian angle π around axis (Oy).

In this section, we presented two approaches to determine the coordinates of points A, B, C and D of the visual field after the subject had moved and depending on head orientation. We selected the quaternion approach, as quaternions can be composed more easily and prevent the cardan from being blocked. They are also more digitally stable and can be more effective since they are used in graphic, robotic and space satellite applications.

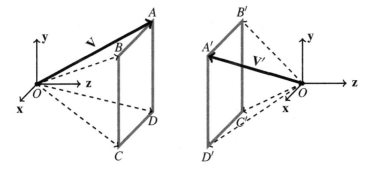

Fig. 5.10 Rotation of radian π for vector **V** around axis Y.

5.2 Visual Field Projection

The purpose of visual field projection [72] consists of determining what someone can see on a target scene (e.g. shelves or shop windows). The target scene is defined by plane $\mathcal{P}$. The layout with regard to the camera will determine the coordinates of points A', B', C' and D' representing the projection of points A, B, C and D respectively, on the target scene. Figure 5.11 illustrates the projection of points A, B, C and D on two different planes.

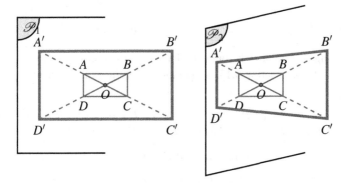

Fig. 5.11 Projection of points A, B, C and D on two different planes $\mathcal{P}_1$ and $\mathcal{P}_2$.

5.2.1 Point Projection

Projection matrices enable to calculate projection P' of point P on plane $\mathcal{P}$ for equation $ax + by + cz + d = 0$ from observation point L. To perform the projection, point L is considered a punctual light source (see 5.12). The following relation can then be inferred:

$$P \in [LP'] \Rightarrow \overrightarrow{PP'} = \lambda \overrightarrow{LP} \qquad (\lambda \in \mathbb{R}) \qquad (5.14)$$

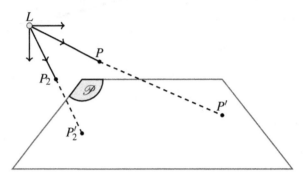

Fig. 5.12 Point projection on plane $\mathscr{P}$ via punctual light source L.

The coordinates of points P, P' and L are x, y and z respectively. They are marked P_x, P_y and P_z for point P (same thing for the coordinates of points P' and L). According to the following equation 5.14:

$$\begin{cases} P'_x - P_x = \lambda(P_x - L_x) \\ P'_y - P_y = \lambda(P_y - L_y) \\ P'_z - P_z = \lambda(P_z - L_z) \end{cases} \quad \Longleftrightarrow \quad \begin{cases} P'_x = \lambda(P_x - L_x) + P_x \\ P'_y = \lambda(P_y - L_y) + P_y \\ P'_z = \lambda(P_z - L_z) + P_z \end{cases} \qquad (5.15)$$

Considering that point P' belongs to plane $\mathscr{P}$ for equation $ax + by + cz + d = 0$, it is possible - from equation 5.15 - to get the following expression λ:

$$\begin{aligned} (5.15) \Rightarrow & \; a(\lambda(P_x - L_x) + P_x) + b(\lambda(P_y - L_y) + P_y) + c(\lambda(P_z - L_z) + P_z) + d = 0 \\ \Rightarrow & \; a\lambda(P_x - L_x) + aP_x + b\lambda(P_y - L_y) + bP_y + c\lambda(P_z - L_z) + cP_z + d = 0 \\ \Rightarrow & \; \lambda(a(P_x - L_x) + b(P_y - L_y) + c(P_z - L_z)) + aP_x + bP_y + cP_z + d = 0 \\ \Rightarrow & \; \lambda(a(P_x - L_x) + b(P_y - L_y) + c(P_z - L_z)) = -(aP_x + bP_y + cP_z + d) \\ \Rightarrow & \; \lambda = \frac{-(aP_x + bP_y + cP_z + d)}{a(P_x - L_x) + b(P_y - L_y) + c(P_z - L_z)} \\ \Rightarrow & \; \lambda = \frac{aP_x + bP_y + cP_z + d}{a(P_x - L_x) + b(P_y - L_y) + c(P_z - L_z)} \end{aligned}$$

$$(5.16)$$

The λ values are reinjected in equation 5.15 in order to get projection matrix M_{Proj}:

$$M_{Proj} = \begin{pmatrix} b.L_y + c.L_z + d & -b.L_x & -c.L_x & -d.Lx \\ -a.L_y & a.L_x + c.L_z + d & -c.L_y & -d.L_y \\ -a.L_z & -b.L_z & a.L_x + b.L_y + d & -d.L_z \\ -a & -b & -c & a.Lx + b.L_y + c.L_z \end{pmatrix}$$
$$\tag{5.17}$$

Multiplying this projection matrix with a vector that includes the homogeneous coordinates of point P leads to a vector, gathering the coordinates of point P' as follows:

$$V_{P'} = M_{Proj}.V_P \tag{5.18}$$

Therefore, the coordinates of points A', B', C' and D', representing the projection of points A, B, C and D on the target scene from observation point O, are calculated.

5.2.2 Perception Volume Projection

When using observation point O as a punctual light source, the quadrilateral bounded by points A', B', C' and D' does not necessarily represent the region of interest for the user on the target scene. Indeed, a discrepancy occurs in the region of interest extracted from projection points A, B, C and D on the target scene when at least one projection of these four points is *incorrect*. Projection P' of point P on plane $\mathscr{P}$ is *incorrect* when $P \notin [OP']$. In order to have a better understanding, Figure 5.13 shows the rear and profile views for the projection of points A, B, C and D of the visual field on plane $\mathscr{P}$, whose surface is in black.

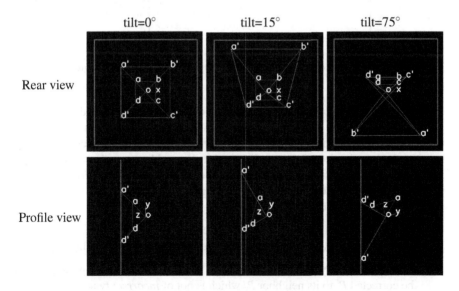

Fig. 5.13 Projection of points A, B, C and D on plane $\mathscr{P}$ according to different Tilt angle values.

- Tilt=0 degree: the extracted region of interest is correct as $A' \in \mathscr{P}$ and $A \in [OA']$.
- Tilt=15 degrees: the extracted region of interest is correct as $A' \in \mathscr{P}$ and $A \in [OA']$.
- Tilt=75 degrees: the extracted region of interest is incorrect since condition $A \in [OA']$ is not observed. This is due to the fact that point A is located behind the light source.

The required conditions for P' - which is the projection of P on plane $\mathscr{P}$ - not to be *incorrect* are the following: $P' \in \mathscr{P}$, $P' \in (OP)$ and $P \in [OP']$. Figure 5.14 shows the projection of segment $[AD]$ under two different orientations. The red segment represents the theoretical projection of $[AD]$, while the green one represents the segment linking both points A' and D'. In the left part of the figure, points A' and D' are the limits of the theoretical projection space corresponding to a correct projection. However, in the right part, point A' has not been correctly projected. It is necessary to correct point A' for the visual field projection to be correctly displayed on plane $\mathscr{P}$.

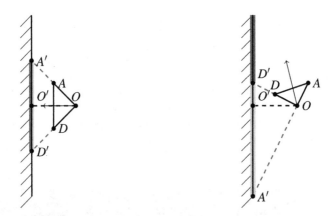

Fig. 5.14 Plane projection of visual field segment $[AD]$ with different rotation angles.

The visual field projection is no longer closed and can be extended endlessly when the projection of one of the following points (A, B, C and D) is *incorrect* (as the user sees part of the target scene extending ad infinitum). Projection opening requires the introduction of intermediary points located between the segments connecting the limits of the visual field. These points allow to correct *incorrect*-type points, as point-alignment is maintained during the projection.

The correction of *incorrect*-type point P' is performed as follows:

1. Check if the neighbors are of *incorrect* type.
2. For each neighbor P_v which is not of *incorrect* type, perform the following steps:

   - Find intermediary point P_t belonging to the segment connecting the point to be corrected P' to its neighbor P_v which is not of *incorrect* type.
   - Draw half line $[P_v P_t)$.

This algorithm is used for each *incorrect* point (A', B', C' and D'). Three is the maximum number of *incorrect* points (since four means the subject is not fixing the target scene anymore).

Figure 5.15 shows a case where it is necessary to correct the visual field projection. Figure 5.15(a) shows an incoherent projection, when points B' and C' are *incorrect*. In Figure 5.15(b), intermediary points are used to correct the projection (the new points are blue). In Figure 5.15(c), the region of interest obtained is correct (resulting from the extension of intermediary points).

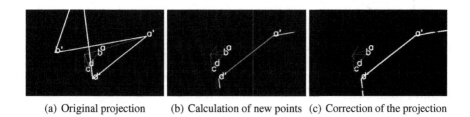

   (a) Original projection   (b) Calculation of new points (c) Correction of the projection

Fig. 5.15 Correction of visual field projection when points B and C are *incorrect*.

5.3 Visual Field Display and Projection on an Image

Once the visual field and the projection have been determined, it is necessary to display them on an image in order to visualize the visual field of the subject, as well as the related projection on an image of the target scene.

The *pin-hole* model [14] is one of the simplest models to describe the imaging process. This model consists of a linear representation of the perspective projection allowing the calculations to be simplified considerably. However, it is just an approximation. This model will be adapted to visual field display. It resorts to three markers (see Figure 5.16):

- Universe marker $(R_u, \overrightarrow{x_u}, \overrightarrow{y_u}, \overrightarrow{z_u})$ in which a point has the following coordinates (x,y,z).
- Camera marker $(R_c, \overrightarrow{x_c}, \mathbf{y_c}, \overrightarrow{z_c})$ with R_c as the optical center of the camera.
- Marker related to the visualized image $(R, \overrightarrow{u}, \overrightarrow{v})$ in which a point has the following coordinates (u,v).

For the sake of simplicity, the optical axis of the camera (axis $\overrightarrow{z_c}$ for marker R_c) is considered orthogonal to the projection plane. The aim is to calculate coordinates u and v (in pixels) resulting from the spatial projection of a point on the image (in marker R). To do this, two types of model parameters shall be defined: extrinsic and intrinsic ones.

Image   Camera   Universe

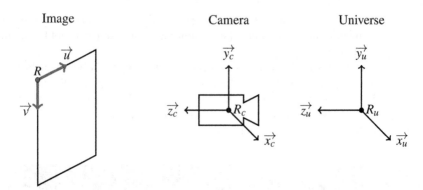

Fig. 5.16 Pinhole model markers.

Extrinsic parameters:

These are related to the spatial position of a point in the camera marker. These parameters were determined in the rotation and translation parts from Section 5.1.3.

Intrinsic parameters:

Instrinsic parameters are as follows:

- Focal distance f: distance (in millimeters) between the image and the camera.
- Scale ratio (in pixels/mm): equivalence of the distance between two points in the image (in pixels) and the real-world distance between these two points (in millimeters). The width (p_x) and height (p_y) of this distance are measured.
- Coordinates (u_0, v_0) in pixels: projection of the optical center of the camera on the image plane.

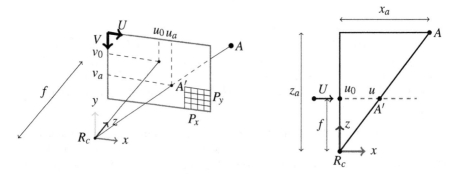

Fig. 5.17 Lateral (left) and bottom (right) views of a perspective projection using the pinhole model.

The perspective projection of a point on an image plane (see Figure 5.17) is given by the following canonical form:

$$u = u_0 + f \cdot \frac{y_a}{p_x \cdot z_a} \tag{5.19}$$

$$v = v_0 + f \cdot \frac{y_a}{p_y \cdot z_a} \tag{5.20}$$

Both forms were obtained using the similar triangle property as follows:

$$\frac{z_a}{f} = \frac{x_a}{p_x \cdot (u - u_0)} \Rightarrow p_x \cdot z_a \cdot (u - u_0) = f \cdot x_a \Rightarrow u - u_0 = \frac{f \cdot x_a}{p_x \cdot z_a} \Rightarrow u = u_0 + \frac{f \cdot x_a}{p_x \cdot z_a}. \tag{5.21}$$

$$\frac{z_a}{f} = \frac{y_a}{p_y \cdot (v - v_0)} \Rightarrow p_y \cdot z_a \cdot (v - v_0) = f \cdot y_a \Rightarrow v - v_0 = \frac{f \cdot y_a}{p_y \cdot z_a} \Rightarrow v = v_0 + \frac{f \cdot y_a}{p_y \cdot z_a}. \tag{5.22}$$

5.4 Region-of-Interest Extraction

The aim here is to extract the regions of interest for one or several users in the target scene [72].

5.4.1 Representation of Gaze Information

There are various ways of representing the information produced by the gaze (see Figure 5.18).

The Boston University dataset [24] was used to validate the proposed approach. We used the following representations, as illustrated in Figure 5.18.

- Visual field of a person looking at a store shelf.
- Path followed by the region of interest's center (i.e. fixation point) over time.
- Region of interest extracted during visual field projection.
- Regions of interest combined for a same person throughout time, with priority given to the central part of the region.

Fig. 5.18 Representation of gaze information.

5.4.2 Gaze Point Correction

Gaze point M' (blue dot in Figure 5.19) is the projection of central point M on the target scene. When the eyes can be located via the method proposed in [134], the gaze point position is impaired (depending on the distance from the marker referring to eye position). This change results in a new gaze point M_{disp} representing a certain displacement percentage of point M within the visual field. The projection of point M_{disp} marked M'_{disp} (represented by the red dot in Figure 5.19) is obtained via the intersection between plane $\mathscr{P}$ and straight line (OM_{disp}) with $M_{disp}(M_x + L * disp_x, M_y + H * disp_y)$.

Considering that eye movements are supposed to compensate for head movements, the standard deviation between the gaze points obtained and the combination of head pose and eye position should be lower than the deviation found with head pose only. To demonstrate this, we analyzed the standard deviation [135] for a subgroup of Boston University's database. The experiment allowed us to reduce the standard deviations of 61.06 percent for X, and 52.23 percent for Y up to standard deviations of 20.48 percent and 19.05 percent respectively. Figure 5.20 shows an example (of subject *jam8*) in which eye movements (blue dots) contribute significantly to reduce the standard deviations of the gaze points produced by head pose

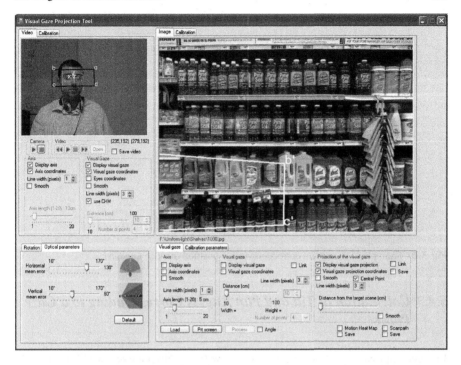

Fig. 5.19 Screen capture of a system performed in real time using a simple webcam. The yellow rectangle shows the user's region of interest (defined by head orientation only) and the red dot represents the gaze point projecion (defined by head orientation and eye position).

only (red crosses). However, the gaze point is localized around the same position by resorting to information from the eyes.

When analyzing the results, we can see that in some videos, head orientation estimation is shifted with regard to the eye position. Indeed, a slight displacement between the current eye position and respective markers leads the system to believe that the user is looking in the same direction as the movement. This problem is inherent in tracking and can be solved by applying a Kalman filter. However, a misguided supposition of the next head position leads to improper head orientation estimation.

In order to evaluate the influence of eye movement on the gaze point, a weighting factor of 0.2 was found in an empirical way. It is to be noted that a weighting factor of 0.1 has little effect on the final estimation, while a higher factor of 0.3 generates a lot of aberrant values, resulting to a large standard deviation.

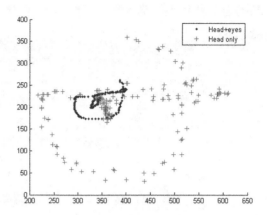

Fig. 5.20 Example of gaze point correction via eye position in video *jam8.avi*.

5.4.3 Calculation of Tilt and Pan Angles Corresponding to a Gaze Point

In some applications, it is necessary to know the rotation angles used for a person standing at distance d from the target scene and looking at a point in it. The Roll angle can be estimated by resorting to this method. The aim is to determine the values of Tilt (α) and Pan (β) angles to move from point O_p (orthogonal projection of point O belonging to the perception volume of the subject on the image) to any point P (see Figure 5.21).

Let A be a point in the image with coordinates $(O_p.x, P.y)$ and $d_2 = |A.x - O_p.x|$ and $d_3 = |A.y - O_p.y|$ of lengths stated in pixels. Length d_1 represents the distance between the subject and the target in meters. In order to use the same unit of measurement, it is necessary to convert values d_2 and d_3 in meters by multiplying them by p_x and p_y respectively (intrinsic parameters of the pinhole model). Tilt angle (α) is then calculated as follows:

$$tan(\alpha) = \frac{d_3 * p_y}{d_1} \iff \alpha = atan\left(\frac{d_3}{d_1}\right) \iff \alpha = atan\left(\frac{|A.y - O_p.y| * p_y}{d_1}\right) \quad (5.23)$$

Angle α permits movement from point O_p to point A. It is then necessary to determine angle β to move from A to P. To do this, length $d4 = \sqrt{d_1^2 + d_3^2}$ is used, and Pan angle (β) is calculated as follows:

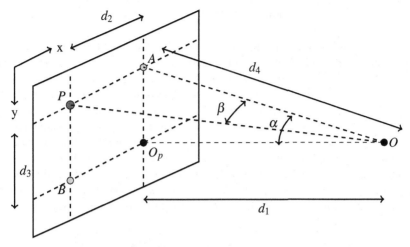

Fig. 5.21 Calculation of Tilt and Pan angles from point O_p to point P. In this case, Tilt is α and Pan β

$$tan(\beta) = \frac{d_4}{d_2 * p_x} \iff \beta = atan\left(\frac{d_4}{d_2 * p_x}\right)$$

$$\iff \beta = atan\left(\frac{\sqrt{d_1^2 + (|A.y - O_p.y| * p_y)^2}}{|A.x - O_p.x| * px}\right) \qquad (5.24)$$

5.5 Metrics for Gaze Analysis

We propose to analyze the fixation points obtained in order to improve our understanding of visual behavior. To validate our approach, we decided to build a system to measure the relevance (or quality) of a visual media [94]. This analysis is based on various metrics [77].

5.5.1 Construction of a System Measuring Media Relevance

For instance, we propose in the following sections a system which measures the quality of a visual media. This system allows us to determine the ability to convey the original idea of the designer (e.g. a commercial message) in order to make recommendations on its creation. Qualitative metrics helping to evaluate media perception are obtained by analyzing the data provided by the gaze directions of the users.

5.5.1.1 Raw Data Collection

The gaze points are determined based on visual field estimation. This allows us to collect the horizontal and vertical output coordinates of the gaze points with regard to the target scene (e.g. screen, store shelf, etc.). Each point P_i is represented by triplet (x_i, y_i, t_i). The point sequence (see example in Figure 5.22), combined with the gaze points of a user, draw the *scanpath* of the gaze. The ocular path is composed of a sequence of fixation points separated by ocular saccades. Saccades are rapid eye movements enabling the gaze to move from one region of interest to another. The fixation points belonging to these regions of interest enable the brain to analyze the information perceived. The fixation point durations can vary depending on the authors from 70ms to 100ms [111, 108]. All the fixation points P_u of a user taking part in the experiment are listed in two categories: fixation points or saccades.

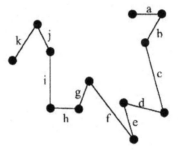

Fig. 5.22 User scanpath.

5.5.1.2 Identification of Fixations

In order to analyze the treatments on the *scanpaths*, it is necessary to identify the fixations and the saccades. Indeed, various metrics interpreting eye movements (e.g. number of fixations and saccades, duration of the first fixation, average amplitude of the saccades, etc.) resort to fixation and ocular saccades as major information. The most common technique is based on velocity calculation for each point. The velocity of a point is the angular speed of the eye (in degrees per second) and corresponds to the distance from its predecessor or successor. Identifying the category of a point depends on a threshold. Two consecutive points separated by a distance which is lower than the threshold is considered as a fixation. Another threshold that correspond to the minimum fixation duration allows insignificant groups to be removed.

5.5.2 Metrics Related to Fixation Distribution

All the fixations of the users are gathered in set F. The gathering process allows the spatial fixation characteristics to be reduced to a limited set of categories K_i. The gathering is performed using a non-supervised classification technique such as *K-means*. These categories define the spatial regions where most of the users focused their attention. Based on the set of categories K_i, the following metrics can be defined:

- **The average number of fixations** $\bar{n}$ for all participants is defined by:

$$\bar{n} = \frac{1}{\|U\|} \sum_u \|F_u\|$$

U represents the whole group of participants, and related cardinal $\|U\|$ represents their number. $\|F_u\|$ is the number of fixation points of a participant u.
- **The average duration of fixations** $\bar{\Delta}$ is obtained using the following formula:

$$\bar{\Delta} = \frac{1}{\|F\|} \sum_{f \in F} \Delta(f)$$

$\Delta(f)$ is the fixation duration f obtained by subtracting the first fixation point instant from the last fixation point instant. $\|F\|$ is the total number of fixation points.
- **The maximum duration of fixation** Δ_{max} is defined by:

$$\Delta_{max} = Max_{f \in F}(\Delta(f))$$

- **The average duration of the first fixation** $\bar{\Delta}_1$ is defined by:

$$\bar{\Delta}_1 = \frac{1}{\|U\|} \sum_u \Delta(f_u^1)$$

f_u^1 corresponds to the first fixation of participant u.
- **The average duration of a path (in images)** $\bar{D}$ represents the average time spent with a participant to explore the target scene. It is defined as follows:

$$\bar{D} = \frac{1}{\|U\|} \sum_u D_u$$

- **The average length of a path** $\bar{L}$ is defined as follows:

$$\bar{L} = \frac{1}{\|U\|} \sum_u L_u$$

L_u corresponds to the path length of participant u and is calculated via the sum of the lengths of the segments connecting the fixation points:

$$L_u = \sum_{i=1}^{\|F_u\|-1} Dist(f_i, f_{i+1})$$

- **The average number of visits** $\bar{H}^r$ within specific region r of the image or video is defined as follows:

$$\bar{H}^r = \frac{1}{\|U\|} \sum_u H_u^r$$

H_u^r is the number of visits within specific region r for participant u. It is defined as follows:

$$H_u^r = \|\{f_i | f_i \in r\}\|$$

- **The convex average zone corresponding to path** $\bar{S}$ is defined as follows:

$$\bar{S} = \frac{1}{\|U\|} \sum_u S_u$$

S_u corresponds to the surface of the convex envelope encompassing the fixations of participant u. It is defined as follows:

$$S_u = convexHullSurface(F_u)$$

- **The average number of regressions** $\bar{R}$ is defined as follows:

$$\bar{R} = \frac{1}{\|U\|} \sum_u R_u$$

R_u corresponds to the number of regressions produced for participant u. It is defined as follows:

$$R_u = \|\{f_i | \widehat{f_{i-1} f_i f_{i+1}} < 90\}\|$$

- **Gini coefficient** G is a measure of statistical dispersion used in economics to estimate the inequality of income or wealth. The following Gini definition is used on the target scene which has been partitioned into rectangles:

$$G = \sum_{i,j} (\frac{\phi_{i,j}}{\|F\|})^2$$

$\phi_{i,j}$ is the number of fixation points in block (i, j). The Gini coefficient value belongs to interval $[0, 1]$. It quantifies the degree of concentration (or dispersion) for the whole fixation points of an image. A value which is close to one shows that the points are highly dispersed, while when close to 0 means that the points are highly concentrated in some parts of the image.

5.5.3 Experiment

The experiment allows the recording of information provided by the gaze of ten persons. The participants are invited to look carefully at various successive images and video sequences. Every gaze information is recorded and processed. Below are the results obtained for images and videos:

5.5.3.1 Images

Figure 5.23 represents two posters (relating to social and scientific events respectively). The first poster is displayed through the superimposition of the path onto the image. It is composed of various points (each one is connected to the previous one in order to represent the access path). The second one is displayed through the superimposition of a heatmap to the image. This results in the gathering of fixation points defined by hot and cold regions, depending on the number of times the zone was looked at. This gives some indications of how to determine whether the main information is noticed or not. These pieces of information are mapped with the requirements of the author of the media (e.g. to check if the list of sponsors was properly highlighted).

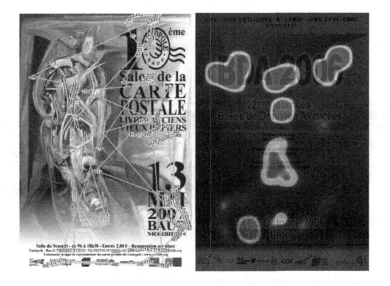

Fig. 5.23 Examples of images representing commercial posters for social or scientific events.

Figure 5.24 shows how this approach enables commercial designers to evaluate the impact of their advertisements during a sporting event so that to find the most appropriate location. In this particular application, it is possible to just focus on the image zones containing the advertisement. A fixation counter can then be installed on the model within the zones containing the advertisement.

Fig. 5.24 Illustration of the approach to evaluate a commercial campaign during a sporting event.

5.5.3.2 Videos

The approach is validated using a video from a beverage commercial campaign. It is displayed on a 25-inch screen. Figure 5.25 shows image samples from the video sequence containing the fixation points - superimposed to the video - for ten participants.

Fig. 5.25 Illustration of the approach to evaluate a commercial video for a beverage.

Based on the metrics defined above, it is necessary to estimate the dispersion value for each video image indicating the dispersion of the fixation points for all participants. A high dispersion value reveals a lack of information within the attention zone, while a low dispersion value allows the attention zone to be estimated precisely. Figure 5.26 presents the evolution of the dispersion value throughout time applying to the video. Time intervals are highlighted under the graph. Some key-images corresponding to the moments captured from the videos are also illustrated.

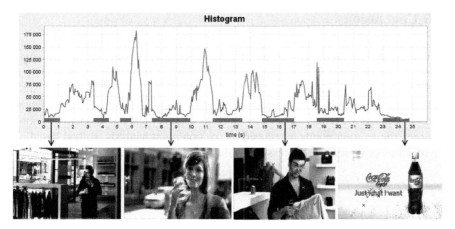

Fig. 5.26 Evolution of the dispersion throughout time applying to a commercial video for a beverage.

The dispersion value reveals the structure of the video. It is composed of rapid and short sequences, including other shots of longer durations in which the faces of the actors can be seen clearly. Intervals of low dispersion (i.e. concentration moments) correspond to long shots, and intervals of high dispersion (i.e. uncertain concentration) correspond to several short shots with strong disconnections during the transitions. In such situations, the center of attention moves from the last relevant position in a shot to the first position in the next shot. Due to individual physiological variations, the duration used to change the gaze direction is not the same for all participants, explaining the high dispersion values. We notice that, in the last shot corresponding to a static display of a red product on a white background, the dispersion value is very low.

5.5.4 Discussions

Analyzing the results of the video sequence allows us to reveal its structure and make the following recommendation to the authors of commercial videos: to enhance the preservation of the center of attention, the prominent locations between two consecutive shots should coincide. Indeed, when the locations are different, the gaze moves naturally with different durations.

Although it is still difficult to evaluate the quality of a visual support based on the fixation points, the satisfaction of media authors who used this approach is a first validation in term of quality [3]. Comparing a relevance map with the fusion of all fixation points for all participants may then be a solution.

5.6 Conclusion

In this chapter, we presented the approach to extract the gaze direction from a target scene. It is mainly based on physiological data relating to human vision as well as projective geometry. To extract the region of interest for a user within the target scene, we resort to the data provided by head pose estimation. When eye position is precise, the fixation point can be determined more easily and the standard deviation between the fixation points is reduced. A fixation point analysis method based on metrics was proposed and successfully validated for collective gaze data.

Chapter 6
Conclusion

Abstract In this section, we conclude the book by summarizing the key points, the challenges we met and the perspectives for future research. The societal issues are presented in the annex, where we will ask the fundamental questions about the societal recommendations for using these technologies in real applications.

6.1 Challenge

In this book, we analyzed several complex modalities of user interactions (abnormal event, flow and gaze), extracted from video streams. We presented methods and prototypes that detect and track these user interactions. Our methods contributed to the scientific research at several levels.

- Firstly, we studied very complex and important aspects of human interaction, and presented operational prototypes, namely abnormal event, flow estimation and gaze.
- Secondly, we considered a challenging form of user interaction with his environment (abnormal event detection), where the computer is pervasive. For example, as soon as a potentially dangerous event happens, the alert is triggered and the security personnel is alerted, allowing the people in need to receive help immediately.
- Thirdly, we sketched the impact of profiling and contextual dimensions on the performance of the systems. These aspects have not been very much considered in the area as it currently stands.
- Fourthly, we synchronized, in the annex, the technical developments with societal (legal, social, ethic) dimensions, mainly motivated by the desire to make the related technical developments socially acceptable. We also talked about satisfying human dignity.
- Fifthly, we developed several applications to validate the results, related to security and marketing. More precisely, the study has been validated in application

domains of detecting collapsed situations in escalator exits of an airport, estimating the people flow in front of a shop or the hot areas inside a shop. Furthermore, several results (e.g. abnormal event detection method) are currently under investigation for use in the relevant industries.

- Finally, considering all these issues, we allowed for a coherent and complete investigation of the multimodal interaction problem in which the knowledge coming from different fields of research was integrated seamlessly.

The technical and societal achievements of the book presented several challenges:

- The first challenge revolves around data. The technical investigations of the book rely on data (videos and processed data). Much more effort than expected had to be made to obtain this data. See, for example, the situation within the security scenario in an airport. Video data captured from the video surveillance system of an airport is for internal use exclusively. It is impossible to share them with the scientific community. These videos are the exclusive property of the airport, and we used this data under drastic restrictions. However, other data may be shared with the community. Among these we include the benchmark for gaze estimation, complementary to the Pointing-2004 database, the benchmark for abnormal event detection for context and profiling discovery, and the benchmark for eye gaze in a personal environment.
- The second challenge involves the gaze in a non-constrained environment, despite the important efforts made in this direction. So far, we consider the user to be facing the camera and not far away from it. Important results have been obtained by considering pose and eye location and their interrelation. Several publications have been published on this subject.
- The third challenge involves context and profiling in a non-personal environment. Important achievements have been reported in personal environments. However, much more effort has to be made to deal with the problematic situation when there are several contextual parameters, and the evaluation of all the dimensions of interest is time-consuming.

6.2 Perspectives

The perspectives of the work develop in two main directions. The first one focuses on the different modalities of interaction in separate manners. Each modality could be studied separately. The second direction would involve synchronizing different modalities to deal with specific application tasks. In the first direction we include:

- The estimation of the gaze in an unconstrained environment. We have to estimate the gaze using both eye location and pose, considering different camera positions and whether a person is moving or not.
- The capture of context and profiling parameters in a non-personal environment. Up to now, we can use machine learning approaches to estimate the importance of specific parameters (e.g. abnormal event detection method). However, we have

to ask what happens if the context changes and the problem of dealing with large numbers of context parameters is still interesting. The system has to know when the context changes and needs to integrate those changes into its previously existing knowledge.

- The third subset within this direction concerns the generalization methodology for detecting abnormal events (e.g. urgency in metros, train stations, etc.), based on the methodology developed in the book that deals with specific events (collapsing, panic, crowd splitting, crowd merging).

The second direction would involve fusing together several modalities to deal with application tasks. For example, estimating the flow of people passing by a shop or looking inside and determining what they are looking at are both interesting, unresolved problems. In this example, we have three modalities of user interaction, body detection and counting, gaze estimation, and attention discovery.

References

1. A. Albiol, I. Mora, and V. Naranjo. Real-time high density people counter using morphological tools. *IEEE Conference on Intelligent Transportation Systems, Spain*, 2001.
2. S. Ali and M. Shah. A lagrangian particle dynamics approach for crowd flow segmentation and stability analysis. *18th International Conference on Computer Vision and Pattern Recognition (CVPR)*, pages 1–6, 17–22, 2001.
3. Projet ANAFIX. http://www.ouestaudio.com/anafix.
4. E. L. Andrade, S. Blunsden, and R. B. Fisher. Hidden markov models for optical flow analysis in crowds. *International Conference on Pattern Recognition (ICPR)*, 1:460–463, 2006.
5. L. Angell, J. Auflick, P.A. Austria, D. Kochhar, L. Tijerina, W. Biever, T. Diptiman, J. Hogsett, and S. Kiger. Driver workload metrics task 2 final report. *Nat. Highway Traffic Safety Admin., U.S. Dept. Transp.*, November 2006.
6. J. Anliker. *Eye movement : On-line measurement, analysis and control.* Eye mouvement and Psychological Processes, 1976.
7. Hirotaka Aoki, John Paulin Hansen, and Kenji Itoh. Learning to interact with a computer by gaze. *Behaviour & Information Technology*, 27(4):339–344, 2008.
8. Michael Argyle and Janet Dean. Eye-contact, distance and affiliation. *Sociometry*, 28(3):289–304, 1965.
9. Tamar Avraham and Michael Lindenbaum. Esaliency (extended saliency): Meaningful attention using stochastic image modeling. *IEEE Transactions on Pattern Analysis and Machine Intelligence (TPAMI)*, 99(1), 2009.
10. Sileye O. Ba and Jean-Marc Odobez. A probabilistic framework for joint head tracking and pose estimation. In *17th International Conference on Pattern Recognition (ICPR)*, volume 4, pages 264–267, 2004.
11. Kevin Bailly and Maurice Milgram. Head pan angle estimation by a nonlinear regression on selected features. In *International Conference on Image Processing (ICIP)*, pages 3589–3592, Cairo - Egypt, 2009.
12. J. Barandiaran, B. Murguia, and Fe. Boto. Real-time people counting using multiple lines. *IEEE Ninth International Workshop on Image Analysis for Multimedia Interactive Services, Klagenfurt, Austria*, 2008.
13. Mikhail Belkin and Partha Niyogi. Laplacian eigenmaps for dimensionality reduction and data representation. *Neural Computation*, 15(6):1373–1396, June 2003.
14. Mohamed Bénallal. *Système de calibration de Camera: Localisation de forme polyedrique par vision monoculaire.* PhD thesis, Ecole des Mines de Paris, 2002.
15. D. Beymer. Person counting using stereo. *Workshop on Human Motion, Washington, USA*, pages 127–133, 2000.
16. David Beymer. Person counting using stereo. In *Proceedings of the Workshop on Human Motion (HUMO)*, Austin, TX - USA, December 2000.

17. B. Boghossian and S. Velastin. Motion-based machine vision techniques for the management of large crowds. *6th International Conference on Electronics, Circuits and Systems.*, 2:961–964, 1999.

18. O. Boiman and M. Irani. Detecting irregularities in images and in video. *International Journal of Computer Vision (IJCV)*, pages 17–31, 2007.

19. M. Bozzoli and L. Cinque. A statistical method for people counting in crowded environments. *The 14th International Conference on Image Analysis and Processing (ICIAP), IEEE Computer Society, Italy*, pages 506–511, 2007.

20. Neil D. B. Bruce and John K. Tsotsos. Saliency, attention, and visual search: An information theoretic approach. *Journal of Vision*, 9(3):1–24, March 2009.

21. Vicki Bruce, Patrick R. Green, and Mark A. Georgeson. *Visual Perception: Physiology, psychology and ecology*. Psychology Press, 1996.

22. G. T. Buswell. *How People Look at Pictures: A Study of The Psychology of Perception in Art*. University of Chicago Press, 1935.

23. J Canny. A computational approach to edge detection. *IEEE Trans. Pattern Anal. Mach. Intell.*, 8(6):679–698, 1986.

24. M. La Cascia, S. Sclaroff, and V. Athitsos. Fast, reliable head tracking under varying illumination: An approach based on registration of texture-mapped 3D models. *IEEE Transactions on Pattern Analysis and Machine Intelligence (TPAMI)*, 22(4):322–336, 2000.

25. Sen-Ching S. Cheung and Chandrika Kamath. Robust techniques for background subtraction in urban traffic video. *Visual Communications and Image Processing 2004*, 5308(1):881–892, 2004.

26. T. F. Cootes, C. J. Taylor, D. H. Cooper, and J. Graham. Active shape models—their training and application. *Comput. Vis. Image Underst.*, 61(1):38–59, 1995.

27. Timothy F. Cootes, Gareth J. Edwards, and Christopher J. Taylor. Active appearance models. *IEEE Transactions on Pattern Analysis and Machine Intelligence (TPAMI)*, 23(6):681–685, 2001.

28. Timothy F. Cootes, Christopher J. Taylor, David H. Cooper, and Jim Graham. Active shape models-their training and application. *Computer Vision and Image Understanding*, 61(1):38–59, 1995.

29. F. Cupillard, A. Avanzi, F. Bremond, and M. Thonnat. Video understanding for metro surveillance. *IEEE International Conference Networking, Sensing and Control*, 1:186–191, 2004.

30. A. Davies, J. H. Yin, , and S. Velastin. Crowd monitoring using image processing. *Electronics & Communication Engineering Journal*, 7:37–47, 1995.

31. J. W. Davis and A. F. Bobick. The representation and recognition of action using temporal templates. m.i.t media laboratory perceptual computing section technical report no. 402. *Internation Conference on Computer Vision and Pattern Recognition (CVPR)*, 1997.

32. Doug DeCarlo and Anthony Santella. Stylization and abstraction of photographs. In *29th annual conference on Computer graphics and interactive techniques (SIGGRAPH)*, pages 769–776, San Antonio, Texas, 2002.

33. R. Dodge and T.S. Cline. *The angle velocity of eye movements*. Psychological Review, 1901.

34. Anup Doshi and Mohan M. Trivedi. On the roles of eye gaze and head pose in predicting driver's intent to change lanes. *IEEE Transactions on Intelligent Transportation Systems*, 10(3):453–462, September 2009.

35. Krista Ehinger, Barbara Hidalgo-Sotelo, Antonio Torralba, and Aude Oliva. Modeling search for people in 900 scenes: A combined source model of eye guidance. *Visual Cognition*, 17(6-7):945–978, August 2009.

36. P.M. Fitts, R.E. Jones, and J.L. Milton. *Eye movements of aircraft pilots during instrument-landing approaches*. Aeronautical Engineering Review, 1950.

37. Y. Fu and T.S. Huang. Graph embedded analysis for head pose estimation. In *International Conference Automatic Face and Gesture Recognition (AFGR)*, pages 3–8, 2006.

38. A. Gardel, I. Bravo, P. Jimenez, J.L. Lazaro, and A.Torquemada. Real time head detection for embedded vision modules. *IEEE International Symposium on Intelligent Signal Processing (WISP 2007), IEEE Computer Society, India*, pages 1–6, 2007.

39. G.García-Bunster and M. Torres-Torriti. Effective pedestrian detection and counting at bus stops. *IEEE Latin American Robotic Symposium, Brazil*, pages 158–163, 2008.
40. A.R. Gilliland. *Photographic methods for studying reading*. Visual Education, 1921.
41. P.K. Girard. *Quaternions, algèbre de Clifford et physique relativiste*. PPUR, 2004.
42. Arne John Glenstrup and Theo Engell-Nielsen. Eye controlled media: Present and future state. Technical report, Laboratory of Psychology, 1995.
43. N. Gourier, D. Hall, and J. L. Crowley. Estimating face orientation from robust detection of salient facial features. In *Pointing 2004, ICPR Workshop on Visual Observation of Deictic Gestures*, 2004.
44. Nicolas Gourier. *Machine Observation of the Direction of Human Visual Focus of Attention*. PhD thesis, Iinstitut National Polytechnique de Grenoble, 2006.
45. P. Hallett. *Eye movements*. Handbook of perception and human performance, 1986.
46. Dan Witzner Hansen and Qiang Ji. In the eye of the beholder: A survey of models for eyes and gaze. *IEEE Transactions on Pattern Analysis and Machine Intelligence*, 2010.
47. Ismail Haritaoglu, David Beymer, and Myron Flickner. Ghost3d: Detecting body posture and parts using stereo. In *Proceedings of the Workshop on Motion and Video Computing (MOTION)*, 2002.
48. Ismail Haritaoglu and Myron Flickner. Attentive billboards: Towards to video based customer behavior. In *Proceedings of the Sixth IEEE Workshop on Applications of Computer Vision (WACV)*, 2002.
49. C. Harris and M.J. Stephens. A combined corner and edge detector. *Alvey Vision Conference*, pages 147–152, 1988.
50. Sébastien Hillaire, Anatole Lécuyer, Rémi Cozot, and Géry Casiez. Using an eye-tracking system to improve camera motions and depth-of-field blur effects in virtual environments. *IEEE Virtual Reality Conference*, pages 47–55, 2008.
51. Xiaodi Hou and Liqing Zhang. Saliency detection: A spectral residual approach. In *IEEE Conference on Computer Vision and Pattern Recognition (CVPR)*, pages 1–8, 2007.
52. Nan Hu, Weimin Huang, and Surendra Ranganath. Head pose estimation by non-linear embedding and mapping. In *International Conference on Image Processing (ICIP)*, volume 2, pages 342–345, Genoa - Italy, 2005.
53. Y. Hu, L. Chen, Y. Zhou, and H. Zhang. Estimating face pose by facial asymmetry and geometry. In *6th IEEE International Conference on Automatic Face and Gesture Recognition (AFGR)*, Seoul - Korea, May 2004.
54. J. Huang, X. Shao, and H. Wechsler. Face pose discrimination using support vector machines (svm). In *International Conference on Pattern Recognition (ICPR)*, volume 1, pages 154–156, Brisbane - Australia, 1998.
55. K.S. Huang and M.M. Trivedi. Robust real-time detection, tracking, and pose estimation of faces in video streams. In *17th International Conference on Pattern Recognition (ICPR)*, volume 3, pages 965–968, 2004.
56. E.B. Huey. On the psychology and physiology of reading. *The American Journal of Psychology*, 11(3), 1900.
57. T.E. Hutchinson, K.P. White Jr, W.N. Martin, K.C. Reichert, and L.A. Frey. Human-computer interaction using eye-gaze input. *IEEE Transactions on Systems, Man and Cybernetics (SMC)*, 19(6):1527–1534, 1989.
58. Laurent Itti and Christof Koch. A saliency-based search mechanism for overt and covert shifts of visual attention. *Vision Research*, 40:1489–1506, 2000.
59. A. B. Y. Ivanov, C. Stauffer, and W. E. L. Grimson. Video surveillance of interactions. *In CVPR Workshop on Visual Surveillance*, 1999.
60. Emile Javal. *Essai sur la physiologie de la lecture*. Annales d'Oculistique, 1878.
61. Natasa Jovanovic and Rieks op den Akker. Towards automatic addressee identification in multi-party dialogues. In *5th SIGdial Workshop on Discourse and Dialogue*, page 89Ŭ92, Cambridge, MA -USA, 2004.
62. C.H. Judd, C.N. McAllister, and W.M. Steel. *General introduction to a series of studies of eye movements by means of kinetoscopic photographss*. Psychological Review, 1905.

63. Yvonne Kammerer, Katharina Scheiter, and Wolfgang Beinhauer. Looking my way through the menu: the impact of menu design and multimodal input on gaze-based menu selection. In *Eye Tracking Research & Application Symposium (ETRA)*, pages 213–220, Savannah, Georgia - USA, 2008.

64. L. Kaufman and P.J. Rousseeuw. Finding groups in data an introduction to cluster analysis. 1990.

65. D. Kersten, N.F. Troje, and H.H. Bülthoff. *Phenomenal competition for poses of the human head*, volume 25. Perception, 1996.

66. Wolf Kienzle, Felix Wichmann, Bernhard Schölkopf, and Matthias Franz. A nonparametric approach to bottom-up visual saliency. In *Conference on Neural Information Processing Systems (NIPS)*, page 689Ű696, 2006.

67. Kurt Koffka. *Principles of Gestalt psychology*. NewYork: Harcourt, Brace and World, 1935.

68. N. Krahnstoever, J. Rittscher, P. Tu, K. Chean, and T. Tomlinson. Activity recognition using visual tracking and rfid. In *Proceedings of the Seventh IEEE Workshops on Application of Computer Vision (WACV/MOTION)*, volume 1, pages 494–500, 2005.

69. Norbert Krüger, Michael Pötzsch, and Christoph von der Malsburg. Determination of face position and pose with a learned representation based on labelled graphs. *Image Vision Computing*, 15(8):665–673, 1997.

70. Harold W. Kuhn. The hungarian method for the assignment problem. *Naval Research Logistic Quarterly*, 83-97:1995, 2.

71. Adel Lablack. Head pose estimation for visual field projection. In *16th ACM International Conference on Multimedia (MM '08)*, Vancouver, BC - Canada, October 2008.

72. Adel Lablack, Frédéric Maquet, Nacim Ihaddadene, and Chabane Djeraba. Visual gaze projection in front of a target scene. In *2009 IEEE International Conference on Multimedia and Expo (ICME)*, New York City, NY - USA, 2009.

73. Adel Lablack, Frédéric Maquet, and Chabane Djeraba. Determination of the visual field of persons in a scene. In *3rd International Conference on Computer Vision Theory and Applications*, Funchal, Portugal, January 2008.

74. Adel Lablack, Zhongfei (Mark) Zhang, and Chabane Djeraba. Supervised learning for head pose estimation using svd and gabor wavelets. In *1st International Workshop on Multimedia Analysis of User Behaviour and Interactions (MAUBI) in conjunction with the 10th IEEE International Symposium on Multimedia (ISM)*, pages 592–596, Berkeley, California - USA, December 2008.

75. S.R.H. Langton, R.J. Watt, and V. Bruce. Do the eyes have it? cues to the direction of social attention. *Trends in Cognitive Sciences*, 4(2):50–59, February 2000.

76. Stephen R.H. Langton, Helen Honeyman, and Emma Tessler. The influence of head contour and nose angle on the perception of eye-gaze direction. *Perception & psychophysics*, 66(5):752–771, 2004.

77. Stanislas Lew. Extraction de connaissances à partir du suivi des positions du regard. Master's thesis, Laboratoire d'Informatique Fondamentale de Lille, 2006.

78. Y.M. Li, S.G. Gong, J. Sherrah, and H. Liddell. Support vector machine based multi-view face detection and recognition. *Image and Vision Computing (IVC)*, 22(5):413–427, May 2004.

79. Sheng-Fuu Lin, Jaw-Yeh Chen, and Hung-Xin Chao. Estimation of number of people in crowded scenes using perspective transformation. *IEEE Transactions on Systems, Man and Cybernetics, Part A, no.6*, 31:645–654, 2001.

80. D. Little, S. Krishna, J. Black, and S. Panchanathan. A methodology for evaluating robustness of face recognition algorithms with respect to variations in pose angle and illumination angle. In *IEEE International Conference on Acoustics, Speech, and Signal Processing (ICASSP)*, volume 2, pages 89–92, 2005.

81. X. Liu, N. Krahnstoever, T. Yu, and P. Tu. What are customers looking at? In *IEEE Conference on Advanced Video and Signal Based Surveillance (AVSS)*, London, 2007.

82. X. Liu, P. H. Tu, J. Rittscher, A. Perera, and N. Krahnstoever. Detecting and counting people in surveillance applications. *IEEE Int. Conf. on Advanced Video and Signal Based Surveillance, NY, USA*, pages 306–311, 2005.

83. Chen Change Loy, Tao Xiang, and Shaogang Gong. Learning to predict where humans look. In *International Conference on Computer Vision (ICCV)*, Kyoto - Japan, 2009.
84. B. Lucas and T. Kanade. An iterative image registration technique with an application to stereo vision. *roceedings of the International Joint Conference on Artificial Intelligence*, 674-679, 1981.
85. B D. Lucas and T. Kanade. An iterative image registration technique with an application to stereo vision. *maging understanding workshop*, pages 121–130, 1981.
86. R. Ma, L. Li, W. Huang, and Q. Tian. On pixel count based crowd density estimation for visual surveillance. *IEEE Conference on Cybernetics and Intelligent Systems*, 1:170–173, 2004.
87. Yong Ma, Yoshinori Konishi, Koichi Kinoshita, Shihong Lao, and Masato Kawade. Sparse bayesian regression for head pose estimation. In *18th International Conference on Pattern Recognition (ICPR)*, pages 507–510, 2006.
88. J.F. Mackworth and N.H. Mackworth. Eye fixations recorded on changing visual scenes by the television eye-marker. *Journal of the Optical Society of America*, page 439Ũ445, 1958.
89. J.B. Macqueen. Some methods for classification and analysis of multivariate observations. In *Procedings of the Fifth Berkeley Symposium on Math, Statistics, and Probability*, volume 1, pages 281–297. University of California Press, 1967.
90. A. N. Marana, L. Da Fontoura Costa, R. A. Lotufo, and S. A. Velastin. Estimating crowd density with minkowski fractal dimension. *International Conference on Acoustics, Speech, and Signal Processing*, 6:15–19, 1999.
91. A.N. Marana, M.A. Cavenaghi, R.S. Ulson, and F.L. Drumond. Real-time crowd density estimation using images. *First International Symposium, ISVC, Lake Tahoe, NV, USA*, 2005.
92. A.N. Marana, S.A. Velastin, L.F. Costa, and R.A.Lotufo. Estimation of crowd density using image processing. *IEEE Colloquium on Image Processing for Security Applications (Digest No.: 1997/074)*, pages 11/1–11/8, 1997.
93. Jean Martinet, Adel Lablack, Nacim Ihaddadene, and Chabane Djeraba. *Gaze tracking applied to image indexing*. Springer, 2008.
94. Jean Martinet, Adel Lablack, Stanislas Lew, and Chabane Djeraba. Gaze based quality assessment of visual media understanding. In *1st International Workshop on Computer Vision and Its Application to Image Media Processing (WCVIM) in conjunction with the 3rd Pacific-Rim Symposium on Image and Video Technology (PSIVT)*, Tokyo - Japan, January 2009.
95. Joseph E. McGrath. *Groups: Interaction and Performance*. Prentice Hall College Div, 1984.
96. Stephen J. McKenna, Sumer Jabri, Zoran Duric, Azriel Rosenfeld, and Harry Wechsler. Tracking groups of people. *Computer Vision and Image Understanding*, 80(1):42–56, 2000.
97. R.A. Monty and J.W. Senders. Eye movements and psychological processes. *Journal of Experimental Psychology : Human Perception and Performance*, 1976.
98. H. Moravec. Obstacle avoidance and navigation in the real world by a seeing robot rover. *Technical Report CMU-RI-TR-3, Carnegie-Mellon University, Robotics Institute*, 1980.
99. Louis-Philippe Morency, Ali Rahimi, and Trevor Darrell. Adaptive view-based appearance models. *IEEE Conference on Computer Vision and Pattern Recognition (CVPR)*, 1:803–810, 2003.
100. A. Mustafa and I. Sethi. Detecting retail events using moving edges. In *Advanced Video and Signal Based Surveillance (AVSS)*, pages 626–631, 2005.
101. S. Niyogi and W.T. Freeman. Example-based head tracking. In *2nd International Conference on Automatic Face and Gesture Recognition (AFGR)*, pages 374–378, 1996.
102. David G. Novick, Brian Hansen, and Karen Ward. Coordinating turn-taking with gaze. In *International Conference on Spoken Language Processing (ICSLP)*, pages 1888–1891, 1996.
103. Masoud O. and Papanikolopoulos N. P. A camera-based system for tracking people in real time. *IEEE Proc. of Int. Conf. Pattern Recognition (CVPR)*, 3:63–67, 1996.
104. Margarita Osadchy, Yann Le Cun, and Matthew L. Miller. Synergistic face detection and pose estimation with energy-based models. *Journal Machine Learning Research*, 8:1197–1215, 2007.
105. Y. Pan, H. Zhu, and R. Ji. *3-D Head Pose Estimation for Monocular Image*. Fuzzy Systems and Knowledge Discovery. Springer, 2005.

106. Julius Panero and Martin Zelnik. *Human Dimension and Interior Space: A Source Book of Design Reference Standards.* Watson-Guptill, 1979.

107. Thies Pfeiffer, Marc E. Latoschik, and Ipke Wachsmuth. Evaluation of binocular eye trackers and algorithms for 3d gaze interaction in virtual reality environments. *Journal of Virtual Reality and Broadcasting*, 5(16), December 2008.

108. Alex Poole, Linden J. Ball, and Peter Phillips. In search of salience: A response-time and eye-movement analysis of bookmark recognition. In *BCS HCI*, pages 363–378, Leeds Ű UK, 2004.

109. Hermes Project. http://www.cvmt.dk/projects/Hermes/head-data.html.

110. H. Rahmalan, M. S. Nixon, and J. N. Carter. On crowd density estimation for surveillance. *In International Conference on Crime Detection and Prevention*, 2006.

111. K. Rayner. Eye movements in reading and information processing: 20 years of research. *Psychol Bull*, 124(3):372–422, November 1998.

112. Bisser Raytchev, Ikushi Yoda, and Katsuhiko Sakaue. Head pose estimation by nonlinear manifold learning. In *17th International Conference on Pattern Recognition (ICPR)*, volume 4, pages 462–466, 2004.

113. David A. Robinson. A method of measuring eye movement using a scleral search coil in a magnetic field. *IEEE Transactions on Bio-Medical Electronics*, page 137Ű145, 1963.

114. Sam T. Roweis and Lawrence K. Saul. Nonlinear dimensionality reduction by locally linear embedding. *Science*, 290(5500):2323–2326, December 2000.

115. Anthony Santella, Maneesh Agrawala, Doug DeCarlo, David Salesin, and Michael Cohen. Gaze-based interaction for semi-automatic photo cropping. In *CHI '06: Proceedings of the SIGCHI conference on Human Factors in computing systems*, pages 771–780. ACM, 2006.

116. T. Schlögl, B. Wachmann, W.G. Kropatsch, and H. Bischof. Evaluation of people counting systems. *25th Wksh of the Austrian Assoc. for Pattern Recognition*, 2001.

117. C. Schmid, R. Mohr, and C. Bauckhage. Evaluation of interest point detectors. *International Journal of Computer Vision (IJCV) Nr. 37*, 2:151–172, 2000.

118. J. Sherrah, S. Gong, and E. J. Ong. Face distributions in similarity space under varying head pose. *Image and Vision Computing*, 19(12):807–819, October 2001.

119. Jianbo Shi and Carlo Tomasi. Good features to track. In *IEEE Conference on Computer Vision and Pattern Recognition (CVPR)*, pages 593–600, 1994.

120. O. Sidla, Y. Lypetskyy, N. Brandle, and S. Seer. Pedestrian detection and tracking for counting applications in crowded situations. *EEE International Conference on Video and Signal Based Surveillance (AVSS 2006), IEEE Computer Society , Washington, DC, USA*, pages 70–75, 2006.

121. Terence Sim, Simon Baker, and Maan Bsat. The cmu pose, illumination, and expression database. *IEEE Transactions on Pattern Analysis and Machine Intelligence (TPAMI)*, 25:1615–1618, 2003.

122. S. Srinivasan and K. Boyer. Head-pose estimation using view based eigenspaces. In *16th International Conference on Pattern Recognition (ICPR)*, Quebec City - Canada, 2002.

123. C. Stauffer and W. E. L. Grimson. Learning patterns of activity using real-time tracking. *IEEE Transactions on Pattern Analysis and Machine Intelligence*, 22(8):747–757, 2000.

124. William Steptoe, Oyewole Oyekoya, Alessio Murgia, Robin Wolff, John Rae, Estefania Guimaraes, David Roberts, and Anthony Steed. Eye tracking for avatar eye gaze control during object-focused multiparty interaction in immersive collaborative virtual environments. In *2009 IEEE Virtual Reality Conference (VR)*, pages 83–90, 2009.

125. R. Stiefelhagen and J. Zhu. Head orientation and gaze direction in meetings. In *Conference on Human Factors in Computing Systems*, Minneapolis, Minnesota, 2002.

126. Rainer Stiefelhagen. *Tracking and Modeling Focus of Attention in Meetings.* PhD thesis, Université de Karlsruhe, 2002.

127. Rainer Stiefelhagen, Jie Yang, and Alex Waibel. Modeling focus of attention for meeting indexing. In *7th ACM International Conference on Multimedia*, volume 1, pages 3–10, 1999.

128. Rainer Stiefelhagen, Jie Yang, and Alex Waibel. Modeling focus of attention for meeting indexing based on multiple cues. *IEEE Transactions on Neural Networks*, 13:928–938, 2002.

129. Vildan Tanriverdi and Robert J.K. Jacob. Interacting with eye movements in virtual environments. In *SIGCHI conference on Human factors in computing systems*, pages 265–272, 2000.
130. K. Terada, D. Yoshida, S. Oe, and J. Yamagushi. A counting method of the number of passing people using a stereo camera. *IEEE 25th Annual Conference of Industrial Electronics Society, San Jose, California, USA*, pages 338–342, 1999.
131. M.M. Trivedi, T. Gandhi, and J.C. McCall. Looking-in and looking-out of a vehicle: Computer-vision-based enhanced vehicle safety. *IEEE Transactions on Intelligent Transportation Systems*, 8(1):108–120, March 2007.
132. Richard J. Vaccaro. *SVD and Signal Processing II: Algorithms, Analysis and Applications*. Elsevier Science Inc., New York, NY, USA, 1991.
133. R. Valenti, N. Sebe, and T. Gevers. Simple and efficient visual gaze estimation. In *Workshop on Multimodal Interactions Analysis of Users in a Controlled Environment*, 2008.
134. Roberto Valenti and Theo Gevers. Accurate eye center location and tracking using isophote curvature. In *IEEE Conference on Computer Vision and Pattern Recognition (CVPR)*, 2008.
135. Roberto Valenti, Adel Lablack, Chabane Djeraba, and Nicu Sebe. Towards multimodal visual gaze estimation. In *20th International Conference on Pattern Recognition (ICPR)*, Istanbul - Turkey (under preparation), August 2010.
136. Roel Vertegaal, Robert Slagter, Gerrit van der Veer, and Anton Nijholt. Eye gaze patterns in conversations: there is more to conversational agents than meets the eyes. In *Proceedings of the SIGCHI conference on Human factors in computing systems*, pages 301–308, 2001.
137. Roel Vertegaal, Harro Vons, and Robert Slagter. Look who's talking: the gaze groupware system. In *CHI '98: CHI 98 conference summary on Human factors in computing systems*, pages 293–294, 1998.
138. Paul Viola and Michael Jones. Rapid object detection using a boosted cascade of simple features. In *IEEE Conference on Computer Vision and Pattern Recognition (CVPR)*, pages I: 511–518, Lihue, Hawaii, USA, 2001.
139. R. R. Wang and T. Huang. A framework of human motion tracking and event detection for video indexing and mining. *DIMACS Workshop on Video Mining*, 2002.
140. Y. Wang. A new approach to fitting linear models in high dimensional spaces. *PhD thesis, Department of Computer Science, University of Waikato, New Zealand*, 2000.
141. Zhou Wang, Ligang Lu, and Alan C. Bovik. Foveation scalable video coding with automatic fixation selection. *IEEE Trans. Image Processing*, 12:243–254, 2003.
142. W.H. Wollaston. *On the apparent direction of eyes in a portrait*, volume 114. Philosophical Transactions of the Royal Society of London, 1824.
143. CLEAR Workshop. http://www.clear-evaluation.org.
144. C. R. Wren, A. Azarbayejani, T. Darrell, and A. P. Pentland. Pfinder: real-time tracking of the human body. *IEEE Transactions on Pattern Analysis and Machine Intelligence*, 19(7):780–785, 1997.
145. Junwen Wu and Mohan M. Trivedi. A two-stage head pose estimation framework and evaluation. *Pattern Recognition*, 41(3):1138–1158, 2008.
146. T. Xiang and S. Gong. Incremental and adaptive abnormal behavior detection. *In IEEE International Workshop on Visual Surveillance*, pages 65–72, 2006.
147. J. Xiao, T. Kanade, and J. Cohn. Robust full motion recovery of head by dynamic templates and re-registration techniques. In *Fifth IEEE International Conference on Automatic Face and Gesture Recognition*, pages 156–162, Washington, DC - USA, May 2002.
148. T. T. D. Xie, W. Hu, and J. Peng. Semantic-based tracffic video retrieval using activity pattern analysis. *International Conference on Image Processing*, 1:693–696, 2004.
149. XiaoWei. Xu, ZhiYan Wang, YingHong Liang, and YanQing Zhang. A rapid method for passing people counting in monocular video sequences. *The Sixth International Conference on Machine Learning and Cybernetics, Hong Kong*, pages 1657–1662, 2007.
150. T. Yahiaoui and L. Khoudour. A people counting system based on dense and close stereovision. *IEEE International Conference on Image and Signal processing (ICISP 2008), Springer,Cherbourg France*, pages 59–66, 2008.

151. Y.Jeon and P. Rybski. Analysis of a spatio-temporal clustering algorithm for counting people in a meeting. *tech. report CMU-RI-TR-06-04, Robotics Institute, Carnegie Mellon University*, 2006.

152. Shengsheng Yu, Xiaoping Chen, Weiping Sun, and Deping Xie. A robust method for detecting and counting people. *International Conference on Audio, Language and Image Processing (ICALIP 2008), Iceland*, pages 1545–1549, 2008.

153. E. Zhang and F. Chen. A fast and robust people counting method in video surveillance. *Int. Conf. on Computational Intelligence and Security, China*, pages 339–343, 2007.

154. Yanqing Zhang, Zhiyan Wang, and Bin Wang. A camera calibration method based on nonlinear model and improved planar pattern. *JCIS/CVPRIP*, 3:707–7012, 2005.

155. Tao Zhao and Ram Nevatia. Bayesian human segmentation in crowded situations. *IEEE Computer Society Conference on Computer Vision and Pattern Recognition (CVPR)*, 2:459, 2003.

156. Tao Zhao and Ram Nevatia. Tracking multiple humans in complex situations. *IEEE Trans. Pattern Analysis and Machine Intelligence (PAMI)*, 26(9):1208–1221, 2004.

157. Mian Zhou and Hong Wei. Face verification using gaborwavelets and adaboost. In *18th International Conference on Pattern Recognition (ICPR)*, volume 1, pages 404–407, Hong Kong, August 2006.

158. Jie Zhu and Jie Yang. Subpixel eye gaze tracking. In *5th IEEE International Conference on Automatic Face and Gesture Recognition (AFGR)*, pages 124–129, 2002.

159. Y.D. Zhu and K. Fujimura. Head pose estimation for driver monitoring. In *IEEE Intelligent Vehicles Symposium (IVS)*, pages 501–506, 2004.

160. Md. Haidar Sharif, Chabane Djeraba: A Simple Method for Eccentric Event Espial Using Mahalanobis Metric. CIARP 2009: 417-424

161. Md. Haidar Sharif, Chabane Djeraba: PedVed: Pseudo Euclidian Distances for Video Events Detection. ISVC (2) 2009: 674-685

162. Samira Ait Kaci Azzou, Slimane Larabi, Chabane Djeraba: Angles Estimation of Rotating Camera. VISSAPP (1) 2009: 575-578

163. Nacim Ihaddadene, Md. Haidar Sharif, Chabane Djeraba: Crowd behaviour monitoring. ACM Multimedia 2008: 1013-1014

164. Adel Lablack, Chabane Djeraba: Analysis of human behaviour in front of a target scene. ICPR 2008: 1-4

165. Anthony Martinet, Jean Martinet, Nacim Ihaddadene, Stanislas Lew, Chabane Djeraba: Analyzing eye fixations and gaze orientations on films and pictures. ACM Multimedia 2008: 1111-1112

166. Nacim Ihaddadene, Chabane Djeraba: Real-time crowd motion analysis. ICPR 2008: 1-4

167. Adel Lablack, Zhongfei (Mark) Zhang, Chabane Djeraba: Supervised Learning for Head Pose Estimation Using SVD and Gabor Wavelets. ISM 2008: 592-596

168. Md. Haidar Sharif, Nacim Ihaddadene, Chabane Djeraba: Covariance Matrices for Crowd Behaviour Monitoring on the Escalator Exits. ISVC (2) 2008: 470-481

169. Thierry Urruty, Chabane Djeraba, Joemon M. Jose: An efficient indexing structure for multimedia data. Multimedia Information Retrieval 2008: 313-320

170. Sylvain Mongy, Chabane Djeraba, Dan A. Simovici: On Clustering Users' Behaviors in Video Sessions. DMIN 2007: 99-103

171. Thierry Urruty, Fatima Belkouch, Chabane Djeraba, Dan A. Simovici: RPyR: Nouvelle Structure d'Indexation avec Classification par Projections Aléatoires. INFORSID 2007: 242-257

172. Thierry Urruty, Chabane Djeraba, Dan A. Simovici: Clustering by Random Projections. Industrial Conference on Data Mining 2007: 107-119

173. Rokia Missaoui, Petko Valtchev, Chabane Djeraba, Mehdi Adda: Toward Recommendation Based on Ontology-Powered Web-Usage Mining. IEEE Internet Computing 11(4): 45-52 (2007)

174. Chabane Djeraba: Data mining from multimedia. IJPEDS 22(6): 405-406 (2007)

175. Gilbert Ritschard, Chabane Djeraba: Extraction et gestion des connaissances (EGC'2006), Actes des sixièmes journées Extraction et Gestion des Connaissances, Lille, France, 17-20 janvier 2006, 2 Volumes Cépaduès-Éditions 2006

176. Chabane Djeraba, Stanislas Lew, Dan A. Simovici, Sylvain Mongy, Nacim Ihaddadene: Eye/gaze tracking in web, image and video documents. ACM Multimedia 2006: 481-482

177. CiteSeerX Google scholar BibTeX bibliographical record in XML Thierry Urruty, Fatima Belkouch, Chabane Djeraba: Indexation Multidimensionnelle : KpyrRec, une amélioration de Kpyr. INFORSID 2006: 831-846

178. Gregory Piatetsky-Shapiro, Robert Grossman, Chabane Djeraba, Ronen Feldman, Lise Getoor, Mohammed Javeed Zaki: Is there a grand challenge or X-prize for data mining? KDD 2006: 954-956

179. Thierry Urruty, Fatima Belkouch, Chabane Djeraba, Bruno Bachimont, Edouard Gérard, Jean de Bissy, Olivier Lombard, Patrick Alleaume: Optimization of Video Content Descriptions for Retrieval. Encyclopedia of Multimedia 2006

180. Sylvain Mongy, Fatma Bouali, Chabane Djeraba: Video Usage Mining. Encyclopedia of Multimedia 2006

181. Chabane Djeraba, Moncef Gabbouj, Patrick Bouthemy: Multimedia indexing and retrieval: ever great challenges. Multimedia Tools Appl. 30(3): 221-228 (2006)

182. Gregory Piatetsky-Shapiro, Chabane Djeraba, Lise Getoor, Robert Grossman, Ronen Feldman, Mohammed Javeed Zaki: What are the grand challenges for data mining?: KDD-2006 panel report. SIGKDD Explorations 8(2): 70-77 (2006)

183. Michael S. Lew, Nicu Sebe, Chabane Djeraba, Ramesh Jain: Content-based multimedia information retrieval: State of the art and challenges. TOMCCAP 2(1): 1-19 (2006)

184. Thierry Urruty, Fatima Belkouch, Chabane Djeraba: KPYR: An Efficient Indexing Method. ICME 2005: 1448-1451

185. Thierry Urruty, Fatima Belkouch, Chabane Djeraba: Kpyr, une structure efficace d'indexation de documents vidéo. INFORSID 2005: 403-418

186. Chabane Djeraba, Nicu Sebe, Michael S. Lew: Systems and architectures for multimedia information retrieval. Multimedia Syst. 10(6): 457-463 (2005)

187. Michael S. Lew, Nicu Sebe, Chabane Djeraba: Proceedings of the 6th ACM SIGMM International Workshop on Multimedia Information Retrieval, MIR 2004, October 15-16, 2004, New York, NY, USA ACM 2004

188. Younes Hafri, Chabane Djeraba: High performance crawling system. Multimedia Information Retrieval 2004: 299-306

189. Nicu Sebe, Michael S. Lew, Chabane Djeraba: Proceedings of the 5th ACM SIGMM International Workshop on Multimedia Information Retrieval, MIR 2003, November 7, 2003, Berkeley, CA, USA ACM 2003

190. Osmar R. Zaïane, Simeon J. Simoff, Chabane Djeraba: Mining Multimedia and Complex Data, KDD Workshop MDM/KDD 2002, PAKDD Workshop KDMCD 2002, Revised Papers Springer 2003

191. Younes Hafri, Chabane Djeraba, Peter L. Stanchev, Bruno Bachimont: A Web User Profiling Approach. APWeb 2003: 227-238

192. Abdelghani Ghomari, Chabane Djeraba: Towards a Timed-Petri Net Based Approach for Multimedia Scenario Synchronization. ICEIS (1) 2003: 267-272

193. Younes Hafri, Chabane Djeraba, Peter L. Stanchev, Bruno Bachimont: A Markovian Approach for Web User Profiling and Clustering. PAKDD 2003: 191-202

194. Chabane Djeraba: Association and Content-Based Retrieval. IEEE Trans. Knowl. Data Eng. 15(1): 118-135 (2003)

195. Chabane Djeraba, Osmar R. Zaïane: International Workshop on Knowledge Discovery in Multimedia and Complex Data (KDMCD 2002), in conjunction with the Sixth Pacific-Asia Conference on Knowledge Discovery and Data Mining (PAKDD-02), Taipei, Taiwan, May 6-8 KDMCD 2002

196. Chabane Djeraba: Multimedia Mining: A Highway to Intelligent Multimedia Documents Kluwer 2002

197. Akmal B. Chaudhri, Rainer Unland, Chabane Djeraba, Wolfgang Lindner: XML-Based Data Management and Multimedia Engineering - EDBT 2002 Workshops, EDBT 2002 Workshops XMLDM, MDDE, and YRWS, Prague, Czech Republic, March 24-28, 2002, Revised Papers Springer 2002

198. Simeon J. Simoff, Chabane Djeraba, Osmar R. Zaïane: Proceedings of the Third International Workshop on Multimedia Data Mining, MDM/KDD'2002, July 23rd, 2002, Edmonton, Alberta, Canada University of Alberta 2002

199. Gregory Fernandez, Abdelouahab Mekaouche, Philippe Peter, Chabane Djeraba: Intelligent Image Clustering. EDBT Workshops 2002: 406-419

200. Gregory Fernandez, Philippe Peter, Abdelouahab Mekaouche, Chabane Djeraba: K-automatic discovery in large image databases. INFORSID 2002: 365-379

201. Gregory Fernandez, Chabane Djeraba: Cluster Analysis in Image Repositories. KDMCD 2002: 29-37

202. Gregory Fernandez, Chabane Djeraba: Partition Cardinality Estimation in Image Repositories. Revised Papers from MDM/KDD and PAKDD/KDMCD 2002: 232-247

203. Chabane Djeraba: Guest Editor's Introduction. IEEE MultiMedia 9(2): 18-22 (2002)

204. Simeon J. Simoff, Chabane Djeraba, Osmar R. Zaïane: MDM/KDD 2002: Multimedia Data Mining between Promises and Problems. SIGKDD Explorations 4(2): 118-121 (2002)

205. Chabane Djeraba: Rule and Visual Content-Based Indexing. MDM/KDD 2001: 44-49

206. Chabane Djeraba: Guest Editorial: Content-Based Multimedia Indexing and Retrieval. Multimedia Tools Appl. 14(2): 107-111 (2001)

207. Chabane Djeraba, Cherif El Asri Mohamed: Intelligent content-based retrieval. ICTAI 2000: 262-

208. Chabane Djeraba: When image indexing meets knowledge discovery. MDM/KDD 2000: 73-81

209. Chabane Djeraba: Image Access and Data Mining: An Approach. PKDD 2000: 375-380

210. Chabane Djeraba, Marinette Bouet, Henri Briand, Ali Khenchaf: Visual and Textual Content Based Indexing and Retrieval. Int. J. on Digital Libraries 2(4): 269-287 (2000)

211. Marinette Bouet, Chabane Djeraba, Ali Khenchaf, Henri Briand: Shape Processing and Image retrieval. L'OBJET 6(2): (2000)

212. Marinette Bouet, Chabane Djeraba: Powerful Image Organization in Visual Retrieval Systems. ACM Multimedia 1998: 315-322

213. Chabane Djeraba, Marinette Bouet, Henri Briand: Concept-Based Query in Visual Information Systems. ADL 1998: 299-308

214. Chabane Djeraba, Marinette Bouet: Introduction of high level descriptions in a visual information system. BDA 1998

215. Marinette Bouet, Chabane Djeraba: Visual Content Based Retrieval in an Image Database with Relevant Feedback. IW-MMDBMS 1998: 98-105

216. Chabane Djeraba, Karima Hadouda, Henri Briand: Scènes multimédias dans une base de données à objets. BDA 1997

217. Chabane Djeraba, Marinette Bouet: Digital Information Retrieval. CIKM 1997: 185-192

218. Karima Hadouda, Chabane Djeraba, Henri Briand: Objects and Interactive Application in Term of Scenario in a Multimedia Database. DEXA Workshop 1997: 246-251

219. Chabane Djeraba, Patrick Fargeaud, Henri Briand: A Search System based on Image Features. DEXA Workshop 1997: 80-85

220. Chabane Djeraba, Henri Briand: Temporal and Interactive Relations in a Multimedia Database System. ECMAST 1997: 457-473

221. Chabane Djeraba, Patrick Fargeaud, Henri Briand: Retrieval and extraction by content of images in an object oriented database. INFORSID 1997: 507-525

222. Chabane Djeraba, Karima Hadouda, Henri Briand: Management of Multimedia Scenarios in an Object-Oriented Database System. Multimedia Tools Appl. 4(2): 97-114 (1997)

223. Chabane Djeraba, Karima Hadouda: Multimedia Scenes in a Database System. DEXA 1996: 177-186

224. Chabane Djeraba, Karima Hadouda: Gestion des scénarios multi-média. INFORSID 1996: 391-405

225. Chabane Djeraba, Karima Hadouda, Henri Briand: Management Of Multimedia Scenarios In An Object-Oriented Database System. IW-MMDBMS 1996: 64-71

226. Laurent Fleury, Chabane Djeraba, Henri Briand, Jacques Philippe: Some Aspect of Rule Discovery in Data Bases. CISMOD 1995: 192-205

227. Laurent Fleury, Chabane Djeraba, Henri Briand, Jacques Philippe: Rule Evaluations in a KDD System DEXA 1995: 405-414

228. Chabane Djeraba: Objets composites dans un modele a objets. BDA 1994

229. Chabane Djeraba, A. Ait Hssain, B. Descotes-Genon: Composition and Dependency Relationships in Production Information System Design. DEXA 1993: 605-610

230. Dominique Rieu, Gia Toan Nguyen, A. Culet, J. Escamilla, Chabane Djeraba: Instanciation multiple et classification d'objets. BDA 1991: 51-

231. Dan A. Simovici and Chabane Djeraba Mathematical Tools for Data Mining: Set Theory, Partial Orders, Combinatorics. Springer Publishing Company, Incorporated. 2008.

Appendix A
Societal Recommendations

No technology diffusion without societal acceptability

In this appendix, we address the major recommendations which came about as a result of the European project MIAUCE, and which were compiled by the University of Namur, namely by a team composed of Yves Poulet, Claire Lobet, Philippe Darquene, Antoinette Rouvroy, Denis Darquennes and Philippe Gougeon. Those recommendations came about in different ways: some of them are the result of our scientific investigation and societal exploration of the technologies presented in the book; others are based on legal stipulations that regulate other related technologies - such as RFID - but that could be successfully adapted to address the legal issues raised by Observation Technologies; lastly, several recommendations were put forward by the public, as recorded in focus group exercises. While some of the latter might sound a bit naïve to experts used to EU programs, projects and policies, they have to be taken seriously since they attest to a disparity of mutual comprehension between the academic and non-academic spheres. The recommendations are divided into two main parts. The first one addresses societal recommendations and the second one envisages new legal considerations to be considered. First of all, the societal recommendations take into account public awareness regarding, not only the technologies discussed here, but also the ethical and societal issues that they raise. It also addresses the widespread ignorance regarding the legal framework which regulates those technologies. The second set of societal recommendations concerns R&D policy and management. It addresses the imperative need to both broaden the ex-ante and ex-post discussion regarding the final decisions by the R&D policy and to assess the projects that receive its support. The third set of societal recommendations regards the democratic requirements to sustain and spread the use of Observatory System Technologies (OST) in our society. The legal recommendations address firstly the critical issue of data protection and, in a further step, the issue of civil liberties. Secondly, it raises the question of profiling systems embedded in those OSTs and considers different recommendations to shape their design and to moderate their individual and democratic impacts. The third set of legal recommendations considers the problem from the point of view of consumers' rights and suggests different recommendations to reinforce their protection.

A.1 Societal Recommendations

A fundamental though obvious lesson to be learnt from our research, and especially from our consultation of the public, is the imperative need for more widely available information for the general population, and for intensified discussions about research agendas for publicly funded R&D in the field, as well as about the deployment of such observation systems in public and semi-public spaces. Ex-post legitimation will not be enough in this regard. We are of the opinion that the public must be involved in discussions from the very early stages of technological agendas. The trends drawn by public consultation provide empirical evidence when consulting experts through the online survey. Both groups point out the need to better inform people about the issues of OST systems and to organize public and democratic discussion which includes the public, and not only the usual industrial and technological stakeholders. Both of them also make very clear that this discussion has to precede both the significant orientations of research and development agenda setting, and the application of the resulting technologies to society. The following recommendations take into account the results of our online survey, the conclusions formulated by the FG participants, and our own conclusions, developed from previous years of research.

A.1.1 Public Awareness

The *public awareness* recommendations are addressed to the EU authorities in charge of R&D policies and to academics and scholars since they bear a clear responsibility with regard to keeping the public informed.

A.1.1.1 Observation and Surveillance Technology Awareness

Our results identify a general lack of awareness regarding OSTs and the ethical, legal and societal issues that they raise. Our surveys (online survey and focus groups) showed a very low percentage of respondents considered themselves sufficiently informed about OST. In addition, we also observed that standpoints are sometimes based on myth and preconception. The online survey emphasized to what extent myths about video-surveillance persist in public opinion. Two major myths should be mentioned: the first is that video-surveillance decreases the feeling of insecurity; the second, that it is a useful way to combat terrorism and an efficient system for protecting children and securing public spaces.

All the respondents from the online survey and the focus groups referred to the two myths, whilst expressing criticism of the relevance and legitimacy of observation and surveillance systems. This paradoxical standpoint denotes a lack of elaborated knowledge about OST systems. We can indicate here a real need for wider public awareness about the existence and actual functioning of OST systems. This concerns both the general intelligibility of socio-technical systems and the societal issues that they raise. Improving communication and information on this point is crucial. As mentioned before, we suggest communicating more effectively with the public on the subject of OSTs.

A.1.1.2 Legal Awareness

This lack of awareness also applies to the legal framework in place which covers the right to privacy and data protection, and thus regulate the use of OST systems. To some extent, this framework remains largely unknown to the general public and, even more worryingly, to groups of experts and/or activists. That situation demands a wide-ranging educational effort to explain and distribute information on the relevant legal issues. Clear explanation, and assimilation by the public, is critical for public awareness and therefore for the development of a democratic society based on mature and democratic decision-making.

A.1.1.3 Recommendation 1

We must encourge a large-scale diffusion of general information, as well as specialized information concerning the issues raised by OST systems. This information must explain the ethical, social, and political issues, and the relevant legal framework. In regard to disseminating this information, the media seem the most active. This means that the media offer an ideal opportunity for awareness campaigns initiated by public authorities, civil liberties or consumers' associations, and academics.

A.1.2 Public Policy of Research and Development

A.1.2.1 EU R&D Awareness

Our study provides evidence of a general ignorance and lack of public understanding of the EU R&D programs and policies. Actually, the results of the online survey conducted amongst the experts and the activists, as well as the results of the Focus Groups, have shown a lack of information concerning the contents of current scientific and technological research and development agendas and programs. They also show a wide ignorance of the political goals and industrial objectives that frame the EU R&D policy and programs. Improving the situation in this regard would only increase the legitimacy of European and national research policies, while empowering European and national citizens with means to influence their own future to a greater degree than they do today. For example, several participants of the Focus Groups question the relevance of public funding of programs such as the Miauce *Marketing* and *Web-TV*, considering that these programs would benefit the private sector primarily, with little or no significant benefit for the public sector. Why do European scientific policies support such projects? This seems to have shocked a large number of participants, as these programs do not aim at improving the *common good*. This example shows the importance of making the intentions, issues and ambitions of a project fully transparent.

A.1.2.2 Recommendation 2

In order to bridge in the divide between European scientific policy decision-makers and European citizens, the EU must take the appropriate steps to ensure the public's general awareness of scientific and technological research programs, either actual or those planned for the future, by promoting a wider popularization, diffusion and communication, using relevant media such as TV programs, popular journals, Internet, etc.

A.1.2.3 Democratic Discussion

The results emerging from the studies undertaken during the last year of the project confirm the need for intensified democratic debate and deliberation about the design orientations and deployments of emerging observation and surveillance systems. Increased involvement of the general public in decision-making in the field, given the societal issues involved, is absolutely necessary from a democratic point-of-view. Moreover, such deliberation processes would not merely guarantee the legitimacy of such technological deployment in our society, but would also contribute to creating a sort of *collective intelligence* with regard to the domains and issues that those technologies could support. Rethinking the role of all the actors involved in the definition and the funding of the research programs is very crucial. It means that, parallel to what exists as regards the environmental regulatory framework, where it is the duty of the States to support financially the participation of citizens' representatives in the discussion, the same solution must provide that financial support to help civil liberties' and consumers' association to full participate in the public policy discussion about the Information Society development.

In this regard, a precondition to the public funding of research projects must be their capacity to drastically reevaluate their compatibility with and contribution to the full implementation of fundamental individual rights and liberties, and with their sustaining values: respect and enhancement of individual self-reflective autonomy, and of collective deliberative democracy.

Besides, even for research and development initiatives developed on private industrial funding, implementation of their resulting applications, in so far as they impact on individual fundamental rights and liberties, and/or affect the modalities of enjoyment of such rights and liberties in whatever manner, and/or affect the structures and specificities of either physical or virtual public spaces (including, to a certain extent, the Internet), must sustain a prior privacy (in the broadest sense, this means not only Data Protection) and democracy impact assessment.

A.1.2.4 Recommendation 3

We advise opening the processes of choice of scientific projects to civil society, including stakeholders from NGO, civil associations, interest groups, etc. concerned by the relevant issues. A democratic discussion between all interested stakeholders - e.g. scientists, OST producers or designers, OST users , civil liberties associations, consumer associations, Data Protection authorities lobbyists, etc - should be the target to attain.

A.1.2.5 R&D Program Evaluation

The same problem arises at the *results evaluation* stage of industrial techno-scientific programs. It is necessary to innovate in giving accounts of the results of scientific projects. We propose to enlarge the reviewers' panels so as to include scientists, industry representatives and civil society associations. A scientific project should respond to three requirements: firstly, scientific excellence requirements: *Does the project amount to scientific progress?* Secondly, industrial requirements: *Does the project render the European Union more competitive?* Lastly, ethical and social requirements: *Does the project render the European Union more ethical and social, by fully respecting human dignity and the liberty of its citizens?* The attributions of the European Technology Assessment Group (ETAG) should be enforced and enlarged in this direction.

Additionally, we advocate the implementation of a kind of *social audit* which could be conducted ex-post, followed by a wide publication and diffusion of the project's results, through media such as the Internet and popular TV programs.

A.1.2.6 Recommendation 4

Evaluation of the research supported by public funds needs to be conducted a priori and a posteriori, and be based on criteria that overtake economic or scientific excellence requirements. The scope of the assessment should also be enlarged to include discussion and critical evaluation of research agendas, which should have a demonstrable social-added value, assessed by reviewers from all relevant fields and backgrounds.

A.1.2.7 Management and Human Science Researchers' Role

In the case of projects like MIAUCE, the position of human science researchers is very delicate because they are expected both to take responsibility for the social acceptability of the project (external control) and to actively participate to the project (internal involvement). This paradoxical role is very difficult, with the ever-present risk of SHS researchers being somewhat relegated to mere *producers* or *guarantors* of social acceptability. This difficulty has been considered at length and a guide has been drawn up in order to institute rules of governance.

A.1.2.8 Recommendation 5

We propose, firstly, to strengthen, enrich and fine-tune the guide, detailing other *best practices*, so as to provide a robust and operational methodology for the internal and external governance of industry-driven technological projects contributing to the future of information society. EU funding for such SHS guide for the technological development of the information society would ensure its feasibility and its publicity across European borders. Secondly, we encourage the EU to launch research programs and calls to submit research projects lead by, and mainly composed of, SHS teams about the specific theme of ethical, legal and societal governance of technological development and deployment in the information society. Ensuring the SHS leadership would allow for more independent and more specific inquiries, which would benefit the entire community of decision makers, industry representatives, scientists, and citizens.

A.1.3 Democratic Requirement for OST Regulation

A.1.3.1 Reinforcement of Public Authorities' Assets with Regard to the Protection of Privacy and Data Protection

The European and national public authorities in charge of privacy and data protection issues occupy a strategic position for the regulation of OST systems. However, such institutions, deployed in most of the European countries, suffer from severe shortages. Their lack of human means and authority to sustain the qualitative and quantitative importance of these institutions' missions and to meet expectation must be addressed. This appears critical when considering, as shown by the online survey and FG results, the large expectations regarding the protective and democratic roles of those authorities. Moreover, most of these institutions would benefit from improvements as regards their compositions, structures and methods. They would then be able to play their role and effectively protect the individual rights of the citizens while keeping an eye on prospective developments of information society and anticipate future ethical, legal and social challenges. In order to address that necessity,

European Data Protection Authorities must (see in that sense the existing Article 29 W.P.) jointly accept an increasingly watchdog-like role, raising debate and calling to the table all the stakeholders. It means that they must take the risk not only to be at the service of their legislation, but also to open the debates towards societal and ethical impact and to enter in the technology experts and users' circles in order to ensure that the technology will take ethical values into account from its earliest development.

A.1.3.2 Recommendation 6

The European Union should promote a wider presence and efficiency in public independant authorities in charge of privacy protection and encourage them to play a significant and active role in prospective assessment and evaluation of future challenges of information society.

A.1.3.3 Intelligibility of the OST Systems

As raised by the results of our surveys, if informed consent is a basic precondition for socially acceptable OST systems, the system of notification in use to advise people of the presence of CCTVs and other observation systems appears insufficient to reassure and inform the population about the purposes, management and the functionalities of OST systems. These systems must be rendered more readable or transparent in their finalities, their processes and the identities of the data controllers and managers/owners. Transparency is, for our respondents, one of the most critical conditions to making OST systems socially acceptable. This requirement for transparency must be read as a political demand to balance the powers between the system operators and the general population.

A.1.3.4 Accessibility to the OST Systems

The accessibility of the systems and, more precisely, the right for people to have access to data collected on and processed about themselves, and also the right to correct these data in case of mistake, is also a critical factor in making these OST systems socially acceptable. This claim has considerable social meaning, considering the very low level of trust our respondents have in profiles and preferences inferred by these systems. Here again, this requirement must be read as a political demand for a fair balance of powers between citizens and systems.

A.1.3.5   Recommendation 7

In order to fairly empower the citizens vis-à-vis OST systems, OST systems must be more readable or transparent regarding their finalities, their processes and their managers/owners; OST systems must allow individuals to access the collected and processed data concerning themselves.

A.1.3.6   Legitimacy of the OST's Finalities

Setting up OST systems with legitimate finalities is a major condition for making these systems socially acceptable. This is well attested by our respondents. However, these legitimate finalities appear difficult to identify. This is well addressed by our survey respondents when suggesting to them some commonly programmed finalities (such as child protection, fight against terrorism, etc.). This is also demonstrated when considering the very pessimistic assessment of the scenarios. This raises a major question regarding the social usefulness or added value of these technologies, seen by our respondents as reassuring the population but not impacting the security positively, or assisting the staff in their surveillance activities but simultaneously diminishing their sense of responsibility.

A.1.3.7   Recommendation 8

The question of the legitimacy of OST's finalities requires both more innovative attitudes with regard to the social directions that these technologies could take, and collective and democratic discussion to assess the legitimacy of those finalities. The EU should encourage democratic discussion on the topic, and propagate greater awareness about their consequences, notably those concerning social usefulness.

More than social usefulness, insuring the protection of fundamental rights and liberties should be enshrined as a final outcome of OSTs. A related problem is the fact that, to take law enforcement as an example, the authorities give excessive or privileged *truth value* to the information gathered and processed by this technological *interface*, while neglecting other information which could be more favorable to the suspects. The ease of the technological production of evidence should never absolve law enforcement officials from fairly evaluating the risks of false positives, nor take precedence over the presumption of innocence and the necessity of allowing other traditional reports of events, such as testimony, and all kinds of oral and written statements.

A.1.3.8   Recommendation 9

Whenever OST systems provide the information relevant for law enforcement purposes or counter-terrorism, or for any other purpose impacting on an individual's liberties and/or opportunities, information thus produced should never be considered sufficient in itself to overcome the presumption of innocence, nor the right to equal access to opportunities.

A.1.3.9 Privatization of Public Issues

Private industries' activities in the field of private and public security have increased dramatically over the last years. Their technical expertise in the sector has made them unavoidable interlocutors of public authorities who contract increasing shares of security activities and responsibilities. This renders the public sector increasingly dependent on what the private sector proposes in terms of equipment and methods, as well as for maintenance and operation of this equipment and methods. In such circumstances, there is a real risk that some typically public prerogatives become somewhat or totally privatized. An additional risk is technological escalation, and the development of increasingly liberty-invasive systems ensuing from the harsh competition among industrial parties submitting public invitations to tender, favoring technological innovation over the fundamental principles of data minimization, proportionality, etc. A current example is that of the electronic bracelet: industrial parties submitting a proposal in which a GPS or a RFID system is included get a better chance than those submitting less innovating - but perhaps less invasive - systems, even though the latter would be more protective of fundamental rights and liberties.

A.1.3.10 Recommendation 10

A fundamental challenge is preventing excessive privatization of tasks which lie typically in the public authorities' remit. The risk of increasing dependency on industrial entities for maintenance and operation of multimodal observation systems must be acknowledged and addressed at the European level, and through European legislation if necessary.

A.2 Legal Recommendations

A.2.1 Data Protection and Privacy Issues

A.2.1.1 Recommendation 11

The data protection regimes would benefit from a clarification of definitions and possibly an extension in scope of the fundamental concept of *personal data*. The question is whether the notion of personal data should be extended to include data

which, intrinsically, does not refer, either directly or indirectly, to societal codes
of identity, and, as such, do not relate to identified or identifiable individuals, when,
however, certain uses and processing of these data, especially for profiling purposes,
may impact on individuals.

A.2.1.2 Recommendation 12

As regards the concept of sensitive data, the question arises whether the list of sensitive data of article 8 of the Data Protection Directive, should be extended as to
include *identifiers*, allowing the cross-matching of several data bases (see cookies,
RFID tags numbers, etc.) Moreover, these *identifiers* may render perceptible certain
sensitive individual attributes (such as religious beliefs, political opinions, sexual
preferences, ethnicity, etc.), as they reveal consumption and cultural habits and cat-
egorize individuals accordingly. If the purpose of the special regime set to protect
sensitive data is to protect against potential discrimination, it may be legitimate to
consider extending the list of sensitive data to certain types of *identifiers* to protect
them more stringently.

A.2.1.3 Recommendation 13

As regards the status of various actors, it is difficult to qualify either as data controllers or as data processors the companies dedicated to providing functionalities
and services, such as data warehousing or data mining. That difficulty must be
solved by an improvement of the criteria set out in the definition of data controllers.
In particular, the implications of having multiple data controllers for the same processing, as rendered possible by the Directive, should be identified in terms of joint
and multiple liability. Besides, the status of each actor participating within an Information system involved and combining several techniques of multimodal observation must be defined contextually in each case and made transparent to the data
subjects. Advanced model contracts addressing all relevant issues and the respective
responsibilities and liabilities, should be elaborated between all involved actors, in
cooperation with the EU article 29 W.Party.

A.2.1.4 Recommendation 14

As regards the purposes of information systems supporting applications like MI-
AUCE, a continuous monitoring is needed due to the fact that the scenarios initially
chosen might evolve rapidly and transform radically, displacing and/or intensifying
the risks they carry for the data subjects. So for instance, a safety application like the
one implemented in the *escalator scenario* might rapidly be changed into a security
application detecting *abnormal* individual and/or collective behaviors. Furthermore,
specific attention must be paid to the fact that a single technique might be used in

very different contexts and with various purposes. So facial recognition techniques might be used for scientific research reasons, marketing purposes or job candidate selection. Therefore, our recommendation is to impose rules of strict compliance with the compatibility principle, as well as demanding from the data controller(s) very precise description of the purpose(s) for which the data will be used.

A.2.1.5 Recommendation 15

Regarding the legitimacy of the processing, the principle of proportionality must be enforced, despite the banalization and intensification of data capture and storage (which allows even the most trivial and fleeting moments of an individual's existence to be committed to memory), despite the tremendous growth and sophistication of data processing capacities. Efficiency and security, in economic or other terms, which benefits governments, private enterprises, consumers or even citizens, is often presented as the ultimate justification of any type of data capture and processing (see the e-government efficiency myth). The temptation to allow efficiency and security goals take precedence over fundamental rights (such as the right to privacy) and the protection of data subjects must be resisted, even though the ease and relative cost-effectiveness (compared to employing human monitoring) of multimodal observation and profiling systems may appear promising in terms of profit maximization, spending optimization, comfort and convenience, safety, security, monitoring of public services and infrastructures, and law enforcement. Despite these significant advantages, they do not provide by themselves sufficient justification for the data processing they involve, absent careful scrutiny of the legal criteria of legitimacy provided in the Directive, including the often overlooked principle of proportionality. Societal control measuring the impact of ICT applications on both individuals' autonomy and collective deliberative democracy is therefore crucially needed. As a consequence, the balance between increased efficiency and other goals of public interest has to follow extensive and continuous monitoring relying on multidisciplinary (ethical, legal, psychological, political) evaluations of these systems' societal impacts.

A.2.1.6 Recommendation 16

Whenever the data subject's consent may constitute a legitimate justification for the processing of personal data, that consent must be, according to the EU directive requirement, free and fully informed about the specificities of the sensors, terminals, and algorithms used for the capture and processing of data including the use or not of profiling methods. Additionally, the consent must be specific and in certain cases must be withdrawable. Finally, there are cases where the consent is insufficient justification for the processing envisioned.

A.2.1.7 Recommendation 17

As regards both proportionality and legitimacy of the processing created in the context of these applications, two main principles have to be complied with. The first principle is avoidance of the risks of *decontextualisation*. This means that if personal data is captured or disclosed in a given context for a given purpose (in a shopping mall, for marketing purposes, for example), it must never be used for other purposes and/or in other contexts (such as determining the suitability of a job candidate in an employment context). The second principle requires the strict *minimization* of the amount of data processed: that amount must be restricted to the minimum necessary to achieve the legitimate purpose(s) contemplated.

A.2.1.8 Recommendation 18

As regards the right to be informed, we advocate an extension scope of this right in the context of applications involving multimodal observation technologies. So information must be provided not merely about the purposes of the processing, the data controller and the existence of subjective rights (access, rectification, consent withdrawal) that such data processing involves, but also about the specific risks carried by the use of and reliance on these technologies. The right to information implies the possibility to get detailed information about the trajectories of data flows, the actors involved in the operation of the information systems and [see after recommendation]. The imperative of transparency requires, among other things, a clear identification and publicity of the nature and trajectories of the data collected and processed, and of the identity of the controllers: Who has access? For which purposes?. Furthermore, whenever they are in operation, the data subject must be aware of the profiling methods used, of their right not to be submitted to profiling activities, and of the means of exercising this right.

A.2.1.9 Recommendation 19

[See also Recommendation on profiling] As regards the right to access, when data is captured through interactive media [see the interactive web TV scenario], the data subject must have the opportunity to use this same channel in order to have access to the data relating to him or herself.

A.2.1.10 Recommendation 20

As regards the obligation to security, due to the peculiar risk linked with observation society applications functioning in public spaces, collecting huge amounts of data and using profiling methods, high-level security measures must be taken in order to avoid any risk of illicit access during the capture and transmission of data, but also as regards the possibility of misuse of the profiles. When the data controller uses the services of a third party (a data processor) the requirements of Article 16 of the data processor activities must be entirely respected.

A.2.1.11 Recommendation 21

In general, as clearly demonstrated by the enquiry, a serious effort must be made in order to improve awareness by both data subjects and data controllers. From that point of view, integrating specific courses on data protection into the curriculum of computer scientists would be useful.

A.2.2 Beyond Data Protection

Reports by the University of Namur clearly indicate that more is at stake than data protection issues in the emerging field of multimodal observation. So it must be clear for the policy makers that (a) data protection issues do not exhaust privacy and other societal concerns, and that (b) we need specific provisions about terminals and infrastructures. Furthermore, we highly recommend adopting regulatory provisions about profiling activities.

A.2.2.1 Data Protection and Fundamental Liberties

Contrary to understanding privacy as a matter of intimacy, confidentiality and data protection, the right to privacy is not a purely defensive or negative right, but has positive dimensions to the extent that it constitutes a precondition to individual self-development and, as a consequence, to the vitality of deliberative democracy.

A.2.2.2 Recommendation 22

In an *observed society*, serious concerns arise with regard to fundamental liberties such as freedom of expression, freedom of association and freedom of movement. Therefore, the development and deployment of technologies of the kind of those which are specifically developed must be evaluated and monitored, not only according to their compliance with requirements set by Data Protection legislations, but also according to their compatibility with the full and uninhibited enjoyment and implementation of fundamental rights and liberties. The deployment and presence of observation systems must not be perceived as a disincentive to make use of any of the fundamental human right or liberty, including economic and social rights.

A.2.2.3 Recommendation 23

Profiling methods developed in the context of applications may lead to discrimination between individuals (adaptive and dynamic pricing, or selection of goods and services to be offered on the basis of an individual's *profile*) and may infringe on fundamental principles of social justice. Specific research has to be done on that point in order to evaluate present and future practices. It is the role of the State to prevent such risks from spreading in our information societies and we recommend interdisciplinary studies on that issue, involving sociologists, computer scientists, philosophers and lawyers.

A.2.2.4 Recommendation 24

Equal attention and initiative must be devoted to the risk of anticipative conformism of individual behaviors in an observed society functioning in a non-transparent way and increasingly characterized by informational power imbalances between the *information haves* and the *information have-nots*. We strongly emphasize the long-term negative impact, and even the incompatibility of conformism with democracy.

A.2.2.5 Specific Provisions about Terminals and Infrastructures

From regulation confined to data controllers and data subjects' rights and duties to governance of information systems (infrastructure and terminals), data protection legislation is not enough to address the new challenges of the multimodal observed society. Taking inspiration from recent EU regulatory initiatives on RFID, one should consider how technology and technological design might help to protect privacy more efficiently.

A.2.2.6 Recommendation 25

The terminals must be configured in accordance with privacy requirements. The *privacy design* of terminals must implement the various data protection requirements such as data minimization, security of terminals, and transmissions. Pursuant to the EC Recommendation on PETS, the design of the information systems must enhance the data subjects' rights (e.g. it must be possible to use the technology in place for accessing his or her personal data). Finally, the terminals must be configured in such way that they enable the data subject to avoid identification and/or profiling. This presupposes the possibility of deactivating the terminal to prevent any recording of data. As the design of the equipment influences many processing operations, certain security responsibilities should be imposed on them to prevent operations being carried out in an unfair or illicit manner by third parties. They should be required to ensure transparency since the user of the equipment must be able to exercise a certain degree of control over the data flows generated by their use.

A.2.2.7 Recommendation 26

In order to ensure the effectiveness of this *privacy by design* principle, it is the duty of the EU Commission through research projects to encourage the development of appropriate technologies or according to article 14.2 of the e-Privacy directive and to appeal to standardization bodies (ISO, CEN, ETSI) in order to define adequate standards. The introduction of *privacy labels* applying to certain terminals and even to certain information systems must be envisaged. Once again, the EU Commission should encourage the building up and the public acknowledgement of independent labeling authorities like Euro-Prise (private or public), able to analyze the information systems from a privacy point of view. These labeling authorities, as trusted third parties, must be regulated with regard to the quality of their creation (independence, professional quality). Exchanges on best privacy practices must be encouraged.

A.2.2.8 Recommendation 27

As regards information systems which have a major impact on privacy, their operators must be submitted to a *Privacy Impact Assessment*. This PIA must be conducted in an interdisciplinary way. It must be transparent and accessible to data subjects, associations and DPA. Once again, we might imagine the best possible practices or models elaborated in the context of research projects of the EU Commission and made widely available to all relevant stakeholders. We might also imagine a role for consultancy or auditing services specialized in that domain.

A.2.2.9 Recommendation 28

It is quite clear that most of the DPA are suffering of a lack of technological knowledge in order to face the new challenges. The reinforcement of their technological knowledge and the recruitment of computer scientists specialized in security and privacy issues must be a priority.

A.2.2.10 Recommendation 29

As emphasised in article 29 W.P., the developers and operators of the information systems, the producers of terminals and the operators dedicated to infrastructures must be held accountable and liable in case of privacy security breaches. They have to ensure that their products or services function in compliance with all data protection and privacy requirements and, if needed, must inform their customers (e.g. the supermarket) about possible risks in case of defection or breakdown of the systems.

A.2.2.11 Recommendation 30

The European Parliament in the context of STOA must launch debate and hearings on the development of certain technologies which characterize the observed society. In that context, we strongly support the idea of taking MIAUCE applications as a good basis for these debates, since the technologies herein developed raise the relevant issues for the future of our society and liberty. On top of that, a permanent Observatory with regard to *ICT and Liberties* should be created.

A.2.2.12 Towards a Regulation of Profiling Activities

Profiling may be defined as the computerized method involving data mining from data warehouses, which may classify individuals, with a certain degree of probability, and hence with a certain induced error rate, in a particular category in order to take individual decisions relating to them. That activity has to be regulated, provided the risk of *reductionism* (person reduced to his/her profile, which is construed broadly by statistical inferences defined apart from data coming from other individuals), beyond the present regulation proposed by Article 15 of the EU directive on Data Protection and limited only to certain kinds of automated decisions.

A.2.2.13 Recommendation 31

As regards profiling operations, special attention must be paid to ensuring awareness of their existence and information about their functioning, as well as to the possibility of refusing enrolment into profiling applications and blocking certain automated data flows. If the recourse to profiling methods results in products' or services' prices adapting to the individual according to his/her profile, the individual must be previously informed in a explicit manner about the existence of the profile and the incidence of each element of the profile on the determination of the price. In any case, he or she must have the ability to refuse the operation.

A.2.2.14 Recommendation 32

Everyone must have the right to oppose decisions taken only on the basis of a profiling, whether these decisions have legal consequences or not, or exhibit a significant impact on him/her.

A.2.2.15 Recommendation 33

Profiling methods must not be used with regard to the provision of essential goods or services or for services of general interest. In particular, processing must not lead to discriminatory measures or to measures incompatible with human dignity. Any use of profiling that entails depriving specific individuals of access to goods and services must be prohibited, unless appropriate legal safeguards are provided.

A.2.2.16 Recommendation 34

The data controller should preiodically reevaluate the quality of data and statistical inferences used.

A.2.2.17 Recommendation 35

From unsolicited communications to unsolicited adjustments: the main idea is to consider whether the observation technologies used in the MIAUCE project lead to *unsolicited adjustments*, meaning unsolicited behavior or attitudes, since they might be used to influence individuals (choice of programming, specifically targeted advertising based on one-to-one marketing techniques). Starting from that point, we suggest applying the same rules to these unsolicited adjustments as those applied to unsolicited communications (the spam) under Article 13 of the e-privacy directive, particularly with regard to the opt-in system.

A.2.3 Consumer Protection

A.2.3.1 Recommendation 36

In the marketing context, some commercial practices based on multimodal observation technologies may fall into the scope of Article 8 of Directive 2005/29 on unfair commercial practices because of their nature and persistence. For example, if retailers tell customers every time they come to the shop that it would be a great idea to buy this shirt because they bought these trousers last time, this could be seen an aggressive practice. If professionals use someone's hobby - for example, video games - to influence his or her purchases excessively, the practice could also be considered aggressive. It as been suggested that DG SANCO carry out interdisciplinary research on current and potential practices in order to distinguish commercial practice which legitimately affects the consumer's perception of products and influences their behavior without endangering their ability to make informed decisions, from commercial practice which appreciably impairs the consumer's ability to make informed decisions so that he takes a decision he would not have taken otherwise.

A.2.3.2 Recommendation 37

Advertisements based on the use of profiles must be accompanied with a notice indicating clearly that marketing technique.

A.2.3.3 Recommendation 38

Child protection against one-to-one marketing is important due to the easy and pervasiveness of the messages based on these marketing techniques on children. It imposes regulation as regards the prohibition of capturing data from children but also prohibition of the use of certain practices without parental authorization.

A.2.3.4 Recommendation 39

Consumer Privacy policy must be developed with regard to marketing applications since consumer protection and privacy protection are quite complementary. In order to give the greatest effective, different actions must be taken. This involves, firstly, creating greater sensitivity.

Glossary

Capture device: Device used to take pictures, either singly or in sequence.

Classification: Making measurements on the patterns to be recognized.

Computer vision: Study and application of methods which allow computers to interpret image content.

Data mining: Process of extracting patterns from data.

Feature extraction: Transformation of the input data into a reduced representation set of features.

Head pose estimation: Locating a person's head and estimating its three degrees of freedom than can be described by the rotation angles: Tilt, Pan and Roll.

Head pose tracking: Process of locating a person's head and estimating its orientation in space over time.

Hybrid approaches: Two methods or more could be combined to overcome the limitation of each of them.

Intrusive system: Any system that requires the wearing of special equipment by the user or which creates visual or audible interferences.

Monitored area: Place filmed by the capture device, such as a street or shopping mall.

Multi-person tracking: Locating and tracking several persons overtime in the monitored area.

Region of interest: Selected subset of samples within a dataset identified for a particular purpose.

Shape-based geometric approaches: Set of specific features are used to perform the recognition task.

Supervised learning: Predicting the value of a learned function for any valid input object after having seen a number of training examples.

Target scene: Specific scene under analysis, such as an advertizing poster, a shop window or a shelf.

Template matching approaches: Instead of concentrating on the specific features, the appearance of the entire image is modeled and learned from the training data.

Visual field: Total area in which objects can be seen while the eyes are focused on a central point.

Index